C000212348

Best walks in Northumberland

By the same author

Rambling complete (Kaye and Ward, 1978)
Adventure walking for young people (Kaye and Ward, 1980)
The complete rambler (Granada, 1980)
Great walks of North Wales (Ward Lock, 1982, 1986)
Great walks of the Yorkshire Dales (Ward Lock, 1983, 1986)
Best walks in the Lake District (Constable, 1986)
Best walks in the Peak District (Constable, 1988)
Great walks: The Pennine Way (Ward Lock, 1990)

Best walks in Northumberland

Frank Duerden

Constable · London

First published in Great Britain 1990
by Constable and Company Limited
3 The Lanchesters
162 Fulham Palace Road
London W6 9ER
Copyright © 1990 Frank Duerden
ISBN 0 09 469100 2
Set in Linotron Times 9pt
by CentraCet, Cambridge
Printed in Great Britain
by The Bath Press Limited, Avon

A CIP catalogue record for this book
is available from the British Library

To my father, to whom I owe my love of books and of faraway places.

Contents

Contents

Illustrations

Photographs taken by Frank Duerden

Maps and diagrams

(*Maps drawn by Frank Duerden*)

Acknowledgements

Although for some years now I have been very fortunate in being able to spend a great deal of time walking in Britain in areas of beauty, 1989 stands out as an exceptionally good year. A major factor in this was the warm hospitality of the people of Northumberland and the tremendous help that they gave me when I was engaged in the research for this book and in walking the routes described in it. It would not be possible to mention individually all who made a contribution, but I would like to express my gratitude to every one of them.

In particular, I must mention the staff of the Northumberland National Park and Countryside Department who dealt with many queries; the Countryside Commission for information on the North Pennines Area of Outstanding Natural Beauty; Mr Brian Long of the Forestry Commission, Kielder Castle for his help with the routes in Kielder Forest; Mr Peter Bolam of R. G. Bolam & Son and the staff of the Forestry Commission office at Rothbury for help with the Simonside route; Dr D. J. Townshend of the Nature Conservancy Council for information on the Lindisfarne National Nature Reserve; Rennie and Agnes McOwan for information on the Faa gypsies of Kirk Yetholm; Lt-Colonel R. N. R. Cross RHF for information on the Otterburn Training Area; and Iain Liddell of the Long Distance Paths Advisory Service for help with long-distance routes. A word of gratitude should also go to the wardens of the youth hostels at Alston, Bellingham, Byrness, Greenhead, Once Brewed, Wooler and Kirk Yetholm, and to the many people who gave me accommodation in their guest-houses.

Some information was taken from the Landranger maps of Northumberland by permission of the Ordnance Survey; the Countryside Access Charter is included by permission of the Countryside Commission, the Code of Conduct near Mines by permission of the Peak Park Joint Planning Board, and *Seaside Safety on the East Coast* by permission of HM Coastguard.

I walked almost all of the routes on my own and found them all enjoyable, but those that I completed with Tom Lyons in

September were particularly pleasant. Finally, I must thank my wife, Audrey, for her usual valuable contribution with the proof-reading and for her constant encouragement; but, most important of all, for putting up with those long periods of absence when I am away walking.

Introduction

This guide is the fourth in the *Best Walks* series published by
Constable, the three earlier titles covering the Lake District, Peak
District and North Wales. It is on the same general lines as the
earlier guides, the only important difference being that this book is
concerned with walks from a whole county, whereas the earlier
guides were concerned with individual National Parks.

The same policy could, of course, have been followed here and
the guide restricted to the Northumberland National Park. It was
decided, however, after some discussion, to widen its scope.
Firstly, because so many of the best walks in Northumberland lie
outside the National Park. The coastline from Amble-by-the-Sea
to Berwick-upon-Tweed, the sandstone hills of Doddington Moor
and Bewick Moor in the north of the county, and the valleys of the
Allens and the Derwent in the south, are all superb walking areas,
yet none is within the National Park. Secondly, because the
Northumberland National Park is considerably smaller than the
three covered by the earlier guides – in the case of the Lake
District and Snowdonia less than half the size. And finally, thirdly,
because so many of the walkers coming on day or weekend visits
from Tyneside or on holidays from further afield spend a good
proportion of their time outside the Park. To be more precise,
visitors spend fewer days in the Northumberland National Park
than in any of the others; for every day spent by visitors in
Northumberland there are twenty spent in the Lake District,
twenty more in the Peak District, and nine in Snowdonia!

Otherwise the aim has been the same: to select about thirty
walks which are the best that the county can offer. Once again,
this was not an easy task. My final choice was based upon a great
deal of reading, a lot of walking, endless perusal of large-scale
maps and finally discussions and correspondence with others who
know the area well.

The ground rules within which the final choice was made were
the same as before. These were: (1) the routes were to be taken
from all areas of the county – in this way they would reflect the
varied landscape of Northumberland, although naturally the final

coverage was not likely to be even as some parts of it are indisputably more attractive than others; (2) they had to vary in length and in difficulty, from short easy strolls to long tough fell walks – in that way the guide would be useful to as wide a range of walkers as possible; (3) where possible the routes were to be circular – so as to avoid problems with local transport; (4) they had to pass through good viewpoints or near features of interest such as hillforts, castles, old mines, etc. – because those are the kind of things that interest me and I am sure interest other people; (5) the walking had to be of good quality and over firm ground – because that is what the vast majority of walkers prefer; and (6) as far as I could ascertain there were to be no problems of access – so that walkers could follow the routes with full confidence in their right to be there.

For whatever reason, at the end of the day some good walks had to be left out. I would have liked very much to have included a route over Deadwater Fell and Knox Knowe, for instance, but a limit had to be set somewhere. However, as before, I extend an invitation to anyone who feels that my final choice could be improved on in any way to write to me via my publisher and let me know. I would be very pleased to hear from them with a view to making changes in any future edition of the guide.

Over the course of the years – and particularly recently for work on this guide – I have paid many visits to Northumberland. I can only say that I have never gone there without excitement at the prospect ahead, and never come away without regret at leaving it. Although no doubt, the county, like all the others, must have some people who are unhelpful and lacking in courtesy, I can only say that I have never met them. The people that I came across were just the opposite: friendly and helpful and good to be with.

I hope very much that you find these walks as enjoyable as I found them.

Frank Duerden
1990

General Information

Public transport into and within Northumberland

Railways
Two lines serve the area of Northumberland:

(1) The Inter-City line from Newcastle to Berwick-upon-Tweed which runs along the coast, with stations at Cramlington, Morpeth, Pegswood, Widdrington, Acklington, Alnmouth and Chathill. In the main, the intermediate stations between Newcastle and Berwick-upon-Tweed are served only by local trains.

(2) The line from Newcastle to Carlisle (linking with Inter-City lines at these stations) with stations within the county at Wylam, Prudhoe, Stocksfield, Riding Mill, Corbridge, Hexham, Haydon Bridge, Bardon Mill and Haltwhistle.

A Principal Information Office is available at Tyneside (091) 232 6262.

In addition, there are two short privately owned narrow-gauge railways (note that services may be restricted or stop altogether in the winter months):

(1) The Heatherslaw Light Railway. Operated by the Heatherslaw Light Railway Company Ltd, this runs between Heatherslaw Mill and Etal Castle. Information from the company at Ford Forge, Heatherslaw Mill, Etal, Northumberland; telephone: Crookham (089 082) 317.

(2) South Tynedale Railway, operated by the South Tynedale Railway Preservation Society between Alston and Gilderdale. Information from the Society at Alston, Cumbria, CA9 3JB; telephone: Alston (0434) 381696.

Buses
As a result of the 1985 Transport Act (operative from 26 October 1986) considerable changes have taken place in the bus services in this county, although fewer in Northumberland than elsewhere. Nowadays anyone who holds an operator's licence may run a service on any route, to any timetable and at any fare, and may make any changes that he wishes, subject only to the need to give

a period of notice of such arrangements.

At the present time about fifty public transport operators provide services in Northumberland. Although many of these are only local in operation, it would clearly be impracticable to contact each individually to obtain information about their services. Fortunately, however, the County Council has provided a central information service on those within its area.

Telephone enquiries may be made to the Public Transport Team, Northumberland County Council, County Hall, Morpeth, Northumberland, NE61 2EF; telephone: Morpeth (0670) 514343. In addition, the council publishes an excellent *Northumberland Public Transport Guide* available from the above address or at local libraries for a small sum. Small changes, of course, occur all the time, but supplements are not issued. However, up-dated copies may be consulted at the County Hall and at certain main libraries. Also useful, but less informative, is the free *Northumberland Public Transport: Route Map and Town Plans*.

Accommodation

Camp-sites
In principle campers have no right to pitch their tents on any area of private ground without the permission of the landowner concerned. Some will not object to anyone camping on their land, but prior permission should always be obtained.

Information about camp-sites can be obtained from several sources:

(a) The Camping and Caravanning Club publishes a list of camp-sites either owned by them or run in conjunction with local authorities.

(b) *The Kingdom of Northumbria – 1990 Northumbria Holiday Guide*, etc. (see below) includes a list of camp-sites, as do some of the guides produced by local authorities.

(c) Tourist Information Centres will hold lists of local camp-sites.

The county boundary, coastline and the main towns and villages of Northumberland.

FIGURE 1

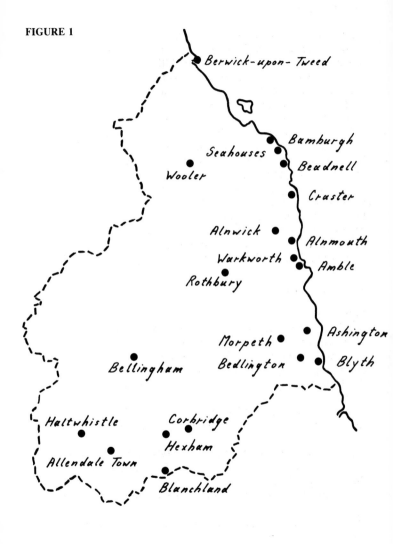

Berwick-upon-Tweed

Bamburgh

Seahouses

Beadnell

Wooler

Craster

Alnwick

Alnmouth

Warkworth

Amble

Rothbury

Ashington

Morpeth

Bellingham

Bedlington

Blyth

Haltwhistle

Corbridge

Hexham

Allendale Town

Blanchland

(d) The Forestry Commission runs camp-sites at Stonehaugh and Kielder; information is obtainable from Forestry Commission, Eals Burn, Bellingham, Hexham, Northumberland; telephone: Hexham (0660) 20242.

Caravans
There are many caravan-sites within Northumberland which provide caravans for hire, temporary sites for touring vans and permanent sites for static vans; trailer tents and motor caravans are accepted on some sites. The majority are open from March to October only, but a few remain open all year. *Northumbria Holiday Guide*, etc. (see below) lists caravan parks. Local Tourist Information Centres should also be able to help.

HF Holidays Guest Houses
HF Holidays Limited, 142/144 Great North Way, London, NW4 1EG; telephone: 081-203 6411, runs one guest house, Nether Grange, at Alnmouth. Guest houses are open to all and provide comfortable accommodation: single or shared bedrooms, full meals and evening entertainment. Normally walking excursions are available, but these are optional and centres may be used simply for accommodation.

Hotels and private guest houses
As this region is a major holiday area, there is an abundance of private accommodation in the villages and in farmhouses and cottages in the country. These will be heavily booked in the main tourist months of July and August and at those times advance booking is advised; there should be no problem at other times.
   The Rambler's Yearbook & Accommodation Guide, published annually by the Ramblers' Association and free to members, lists hundreds of addresses throughout the United Kingdom.
   The Kingdom of Northumbria – 1990 Northumbria Holiday Guide, etc., published annually by the English Tourist Board, is a superb publication giving full information on all types of accommodation. Many local authorities, e.g. Alnwick, Morpeth and Tynedale, also produce their own booklets to local

accommodation, which should be obtainable at local Tourist Information Centres.

Tourist Information Centres offer good advice and information about local accommodation. In addition, all offer a Local Bed-Booking Service and most a Book-A-Bed-Ahead Service to personal callers – the first local to the Centre and the second in an area served by another Centre.

Youth hostels
There are eight hostels within Northumberland, at Acomb (87-934666), Bellingham (80-843834), Byrness (80-764027), Greenhead (86-659655), Rock Hall (75-201203), Ninebanks (86/87-771513), Once Brewed (86/87-752668) and Wooler (75-991278). Four others are just outside – Alston (86/87-717461), Edmundbyers (87-017500), Newcastle upon Tyne (88-257656) and Kirk Yetholm (74-826282). Full information about all these hostels can be obtained from the *YHA Accommodation Guide: England and Wales* given to members. (Kirk Yetholm is a hostel of the Scottish Youth Hostels Association, the others are of the England and Wales Association.)

Maps

The following maps cover the area of the County of Northumberland:
Ordnance Survey *1:25 000 Pathfinder Maps* (40 sheets)
438 NT95/NU05 Berwick-upon-Tweed
451 NT84/94 Norham
452 NU04/14 Holy Island (Northumberland)
462 NT63/73 Kelso
463 NT83/93 Coldstream
464 NU03   Lowick (Northumberland)
465 NU13/23 Belford, Seahouses and Farne Islands
475 NT82/92 Cheviot Hills (North)
476 NU02/12 Chatton and Ellingham
477 NU21/22 Embleton and Alnmouth

486 NT61/71 Chesters and Howman
487 NT81/91 Cheviot Hills (Central)
488 NU01/11 Alnwick and Whittingham
498 NT60/70 Catcleugh
499 NT80/90 Harbottle
500 NU00/10 Rothbury and Felton
501 NU20   Amble
508 NY49/59 Hermitage and Saughtree
509 NY69/79 Kielder
510 NY89/99 Otterburn
511 NZ09/19 Longhorsley and Simonside Hills
512 NZ29   Lynemouth
520 NY48/50 Newcastleton and Copshaw Holm
521 NY68/78 Kielder Water
522 NY88/98 Bellingham and Kirkwhelpington
523 NZ08/18 Morpeth (West)
524 NZ28/38 Ashington and Blyth
533 NY67/77 Wark Forest
534 NY87/97 Wark
535 NZ07/17 Ponteland
536 NZ27/37 Whitley Bay
546 NY66/76 Haltwhistle and Gilsland
547 NY86/96 Hexham and Haydon Bridge
548 NZ06/16 Blaydon and Prudhoe
559 NY65/75 Slaggyford
560 NY85/95 Allendale Town and Blanchland
561 NZ05/15 Consett
569 NY64/74 Alston
570 NY84/94 Allenheads and Rookhope
571 NZ04/14 Lanchester

As each Pathfinder sheet covers a very small area, a complete set
to cover the entire county is expensive; they are, nevertheless,
ideal for the walker as they show all public rights of way in relation
to field boundaries, etc. They are usually more difficult to obtain
locally than Landranger maps.

Ordnance Survey *1:50 000 Landranger Maps* (7 sheets)
74 Kelso
75 Berwick-upon-Tweed
80 Cheviot Hills & Kielder Forest
81 Alnwick & Morpeth
86 Haltwhistle, Bewcastle & Alston
87 Hexham & Haltwhistle
88 Tyneside & Durham
Landranger maps also show all public rights of way, although with
less detail than the Pathfinder maps. They are very widely used
and usually easily obtainable.

Ordnance Survey *1:158 400 Touring and Holiday Maps* (1 sheet)
14 Northumbria
This covers the main holiday features of the region, showing
features of interest, camping- and caravan-sites, and parking
facilities. It is not sufficiently detailed, however, for walking
purposes.

Ordnance Survey *1:250 000 Routemaster Maps* (2 sheets)
RM 4 Central Scotland & Northumberland
RM 5 Northern England
These maps show most roads and are intended to enable motorists
to find the best routes. Most of the area is covered by Sheet No. 4.
Like the Touring and Holiday Maps, they are not sufficiently
detailed for walking purposes.

Ordnance Survey *Historical Map & Guide 'Hadrian's Wall'*
(1:50 000 and 1:25 000)
A series of strips with text, colour illustrations and photographs.

Kielder Water. Northumberland Leisure Map
Scale approx. 5 inches to 1 mile. Published by Hexham Tourist
Information Centre on behalf of Northumbrian Water Authority.
This map shows trails and public paths in the immediate vicinity of
Kielder Water.

Harvey's Mountain Map 'The Cheviot'
Detailed map of the northern Cheviots at a scale of 1:40 000.
Harvey Map Services Limited, 12–16 Main Street, Doune, FK16
6BJ; telephone: Doune (0786) 841202.

Northumberland

The geology of Northumberland

The rocks which form the core of the Northumberland landscape were formed almost entirely in the Devonian and Carboniferous periods between 280 and 400 million years ago. Broadly speaking, but with some important exceptions, those which make up the Cheviot Hills are igneous (i.e. rocks which were molten at some stage in their history), formed during the former period; while those which cover the remainder of the county and the adjacent areas of southern Scotland and the northern Pennines are sedimentary (i.e. produced by the accumulation of sediments derived from the erosion of earlier rocks), formed in the latter.

At the outset of the Devonian period, the area that is now Northumberland was occupied by a large sea sandwiched between extensive mountain masses. Accumulation of debris in this sea, caused by the erosion of these mountains, was later to produce a rock characterized by a deep red/orange colour. This colour – produced by an iron oxide, haematite, which was precipitated under the oxidizing conditions prevalent at those times – gave rise to its name, Old Red Sandstone. Exposures of this can be found over the Border to the north-west of Northumberland, but in the county itself crustal instability with extensive volcanic activity, an aftermath of an earlier mountain-building stage, was a much more important factor. Violent eruptions with falls of hot ash and rock, followed later by extensive lava flow, forming layers thousands of feet thick, built up high cones which rose above the Devonian seas. Andesites, speckled purple or grey rocks, produced from these lava flows, now form most of the Cheviot Hills, a roughly circular area about 20 miles (32 km) in diameter.

Later in the Devonian, after this deposit had solidified, a great mass of molten rock (magma) swelled up from the interior, gradually melting rock as it rose, until it came to rest some distance short of the surface. This was to give rise to an extremely hard, silica-rich granite, which subsequent erosion, stripping off the overlaying andesites, has now exposed in the area of The Cheviot and Hedgehope Hill. Outcrops can be found near Linhope Spout, north of the Breamish, and its limits traced by an aureole of outcropping metamorphic rocks (i.e. andesites changed by the high temperature of the magma) as in The Hen Hole and the Bizzle.

During the Carboniferous period which followed, the seas which surrounded these volcanic peaks were the receiving areas for vast amounts of debris brought down by rivers and mountain streams. Fine particles of sand and mud gradually settled on the sea bed, giving rise later to sandstones and shales and, where clear conditions prevailed, calcareous oozes collected which were to form thin beds of limestone. The earliest rocks of the Carboniferous, therefore, consist of alternating layers of sandstones, shales and limestones known collectively as the Cementstone Group.

For a time during this period the area became the estuary of a large river which flowed into it from the north-west. The extensive sandbanks that formed were responsible for the thick sandstones which overlie the Cementstones, now known as the Fell Sandstone Group. Forming an almost continuous arc around the Cheviot massif from Peel Fell in the south-west to Berwick-upon-Tweed at the northernmost point of the county, they are seen at their best in the Simonside and Harbottle Hills.

Later in the Carboniferous period further sequences similar to the Cementstone Group were formed, this time, however, accompanied by the formation of relatively thin coal seams. Rocks of this period – the Scremerston Coal Group – outcrop only in the south-east corner of the county.

Finally, towards the end of the period, came deposition of Limestone Groups which now form a wide band across the southern part of the county and up the western coast, and Coal Measures upon which the important Northumberland and Durham coalfield was founded.

The Carboniferous came to an end with a further period of mountain building, known as the Hercynian or Armorican Orogeny. The Cheviot igneous rocks were raised, causing a dipping of peripheral sedimentary strata with the development of fractures and fault lines. These faults were later to produce the long, straight valleys of the Harthope Burn and the College. The fractures also offered an easy line for the intrusion of magma which pushed itself up into the Carboniferous rocks. The Whin Sill, a hard grey quartz-dolerite on which the central section of Hadrian's Wall was built, as well as the great castles of Bamburgh and Dunstanburgh, was the product of this intrusion.

The White Lands

The Cheviot Hills – as defined approximately by the extent of the igneous andesites and granite – lie between Redesdale and the valley of the Glen, a total length of about 25 miles (40 km). At no point do they attain any real height – the highest point is The Cheviot itself at 2,674 ft (815 m). Nor are there great cliffs and scree slopes that are so much a feature of Snowdonia, the Lake District or the Scottish Highlands. As a walking area, however, they are second to none. Tom Stephenson, the first full-time secretary of the Ramblers' Association and the creator of the Pennine Way, declared them his favourite ground and there are many others who would echo his sentiments.

Apart from the higher reaches of the granite core, the predominant feature of the Cheviots is grassland: sheep's fescue and the bents on the well-drained lower slopes giving way to moor mat-grass and to purple moor-grass where wetter and more acid conditions prevail on higher and flatter ground. It is this predominance of grass which has given the Cheviot Hills one of their most attractive names – 'The White Lands'.

On the tops of the higher hills and in dips in the ridges, where the ground is flat or gently sloping and high rainfall combines with slow run-off, anaerobic blanket bogs have produced thick layers of peat. In the usual way these have become eroded with the formation of groughs and hags. In drier areas of peat, on the very acid and heavily leached soils of the granite, heather flourishes. Lower down on the slopes the hill soils are sufficiently deep to

allow the development of bracken which is seen at its best in the autumn when its colour changes. Wet hollows or sikes are often revealed by the presence of rushes and the bright green of sphagnum mosses.

Although the central ridge of the Cheviot Hills forms a main watershed, all the rivers which rise there flow eventually into the North Sea. The northern and western slopes are drained by the Tweed, and the eastern and southern areas by the Aln, Coquet and North Tyne. As the andesites are weak and easily eroded, the valleys are deep and steep-sided. Some of them contain scraps of relict woodlands – mainly of oak, alder and birch – with an accompanying rich variety of ferns, mosses and flowering plants; while the valley haughs of rich soil, glacial or alluvial in origin, have usually been improved for hay and for grazing.

The Ice Age, which began about two million years ago and covered the region in a thick sheet of ice, has left its mark upon much of the Cheviot Hills. The long straight valleys of the Harthope Burn and of the College are the result of glacial action along the line of a fault, and it is likely that glaciers were also responsible for The Hen Hole and the Bizzle which cut into the edge of the granite core of The Cheviot. The curious dry V-shaped valleys, which can be seen, for example, near Humbleton Hill in the north-eastern corner of the Cheviot Hills, were probably formed by the action of meltwater flowing under enormous pressure at the base of the ice sheet.

The Black Country

The Fell Sandstone, which was laid down in the estuary of a great river system during the Carboniferous period, now forms a wide arc of hills around the Cheviots from Berwick-upon-Tweed in the north to the Border at Carter Fell. Massive earth movements which took place towards the end of the period have tilted the

The White Lands. The valley of the Usway Burn near Batailshiel Haugh (Route 27).

strata, so that these hills are now characterized by a steep and often craggy inward-facing scarp and an outer, gently falling slope towards the south and east. This characteristic configuration can be easily discerned on Doddington Moor to the north of Wooler, at Bewick Moor further south towards Alnwick, in the Simonside range overlooking Rothbury, and in the Harbottle Hills near Alwinton on the edge of the National Park.

The thin and stony soils of the sandstone uplands, relatively dry but very acid and heavily leached, suit few plants, but heather and bilberry are able to flourish. It is these which have given the sandstone moors their dark appearance and their local name of 'The Black Country'. Sheep-grazing and grouse-shooting are the traditional uses made of them, although more recently large areas have received much attention from the Forestry Commission. Where grouse shooting is practised, it is the custom to burn the heather at frequent intervals, usually every seven to fifteen years, to encourage the formation of young shoots, although with disastrous consequences for other plant species.

For the walker the Black Country is attractive at any time, offering good walking with the prospect of magnificent views from the scarp crest, but the best time is undoubtedly those few glorious weeks of late summer when the moors are ablaze with the deep purple of the flowering heather.

The Northumberland coast

Undoubtedly one of the finest features of Northumberland is the magnificent coast which stretches from St Mary's Island in the south to Berwick-upon-Tweed on the Border. Still largely unspoilt, it is a wonderful region of wide sandy beaches, dunes and rock outcrops with lovely estuaries, fishing villages and great castles, such as Bamburgh and Dunstanburgh. It is a birdwatcher's paradise, for there are major sea-bird colonies on the mainland cliffs and on the Farne Islands, while the area around Budle Bay

A typical Northumbrian stell.

and Holy Island is a National Nature Reserve. All this was
recognized in 1958 by the designation of 50 square miles (130 sq
km) of it as an Area of Outstanding Natural Beauty. The Area is
43 miles (69 km) long from the mouth of the Coquet to Berwick,
and includes Holy Island and the Farne Group.

The North Pennines

The North Pennines were confirmed as an Area of Outstanding
Natural Beauty (AONB) in June 1988, bringing the number of
such areas up to thirty-eight. With a total area of 772 square miles
(1998 sq km), it is by far the largest yet designated. It extends
from Stainmore Forest in the south almost to the valley of the
South Tyne in the north, and from the Eden valley in the west to
the vicinity of Consett, Tow Law and Barnard Castle in the east. It
is largely an area of wild, lonely and windswept moorlands, but it
also holds some valleys of considerable charm, of which Allendale,
Weardale, Teesdale and that of the South Tyne are outstanding.
As yet it is for the connoisseurs of walking, for unlike the three
National Parks which surround it – the Lake District,
Northumberland and the Yorkshire Dales – relatively few have
discovered its attractions.

Hadrian's Wall

The battle of Mons Graupius in AD 84 – on a site that has not as
yet been identified with certainty – marked the northern limit of
the Roman conquest of Britain. Although work began on a
legionary fortress at Inchtuthil, which would serve as the focus of a
series of forts to control movement in and out of the Highlands
and might have been the base for further advance, the victory was
not pursued. In any event, reverses on the Danube, which
necessitated the recall of the Legion II Adiutrix from Britain,

Doddington Moor, one of the sandstone ridges of The Black Country
(Route 4).

made even the holding of the Southern Uplands difficult, and a general retreat began which had by the end of the century led to the abandonment of all Britain north of the Tyne and Solway and to the acceptance of a permanent frontier along that line.

The structure of the first system of frontier control – the Stanegate System – which was established under the Emperor Trajan (see page 168) is still obscure. It appears, however, that it was not particularly effective for there is evidence of trouble in Britain about AD 117 in which large numbers of soldiers were killed, and we have the statement that 'the Britons could not be kept under Roman control'. It was against this background that the Emperor Hadrian, on his visit to Britain in 122, considered the security of the northern border.

As originally planned, Hadrian's Wall was to consist of a continuous barrier from the Tyne to the Solway, a mile or so to the north of the line of forts in the Tyne valley. The eastern part was to be a stone wall, whilst that to the west was to be of turves, in each case with a facing ditch. During construction, however, the design was considerably and significantly altered. The forts were brought into the line of the Wall itself; the turf wall was replaced by one of stone; the stone wall throughout was reduced in thickness; and finally, a second ditch, the Vallum, was dug to the south.

In its final form, therefore, the Wall was a continuous stone barrier, 73 miles (117 km) – 80 Roman miles – long and 15 ft (4.5 m) high, from Wallsend on the Tyne estuary to Bowness on the Solway. At intervals of one Roman mile (1620 yards, 1481 m) milecastles were constructed – in reality fortified gatehouses – with double gates to north and south and with accommodation for a maximum of thirty-two men. In between each pair of milecastles were two turrets which served as watchtowers. Approach to the front of the Wall was made more difficult by a V-shaped ditch about 10 ft (3 m) deep, while a second ditch with mounds on each side (the Vallum), a short distance to the south, clearly defined the

Bamburgh Castle in the Northumberland Coast AONB, viewed from the north-west around Harkess Rocks (Route 8).

limits of the military zone. Forts were placed at intervals along the Wall, on average about 7 miles (11 km) apart; those at Stanwix and Benwell on the flanks were probably cavalry forts; Housesteads, Greatchesters and Birdoswald in the centre were for infantry; the rest probably held both. Three forts were built to the north of the Wall on the western flank, probably to guard part of the territory of the Brigantes which would otherwise have been isolated. From the western end of the Wall a chain of milecastles and turrets extended down the Cumbrian coast, whilst the eastern flank was secured by the harbour defences on the Tyne. Before the end of Hadrian's reign in AD 138, the Wall was probably complete.

The Wall was built almost entirely by the three legions then stationed in Britain: II Augusta, XX Valeria Victrix and VI Victrix, but was eventually manned by auxiliary troops. These were not, in general, citizens of Rome, but volunteers recruited from other areas of the Empire. They would receive less pay, but were subject to lower discipline and to less intensive training.

It cannot be emphasized enough that the Wall did not serve as a fighting platform in the way that the ramparts of a medieval castle did. It was instead a frontier barrier through which passage could be closely controlled, so that potentially troublesome tribes to the north would be separated from those to the south. If necessary, the numerous gateways to the north enabled fighting men to be speedily deployed in front of the Wall where the superior fighting qualities of the Roman army would usually bring about a favourable result.

The Wall was abandoned on two occasions when the frontier was moved further north to the Forth-Clyde line where another wall, the Antonine, was built. It was also overrun and badly damaged on at least two other occasions, after its garrison had been withdrawn or so weakened that it could not function as intended. Finally, towards the end of Roman rule in 367, it was probably bypassed altogether as the barbarian hordes came in from a number of directions. But for nearly three centuries, when it was maintained and garrisoned as intended, it was a highly effective military installation.

The beacon on Emmanuel Head, the north-eastern tip of Holy Island (Route 3).

Kielder Forest

The potential of Kielder and the North Tyne valley for large scale
afforestation was recognized as early as 1910 in a report by R. L.
Robinson to the Board of Agriculture. Apart from an early
unsuccessful attempt at Newcastleton, however, the first plantings
– at Smales Farm near Falstone – did not take place until 1926.
The establishment of a large commercial coniferous forest in the
harsh uplands of the Border region was a new venture, and
considerable technical problems had to be overcome in the early
days; nevertheless, progress was sufficiently advanced by 1930 to
justify the purchase of Kielder Castle and a large block of land
from the Duke of Northumberland. Further purchases on both
sides of the Border continued up to 1969. Nowadays the planting
of new areas is virtually complete and a continuous cycle of
maintenance, felling and replanting is established.

Direct planting into the thin, poorly drained and impoverished
topsoil of the high moors is not a viable method. As an alternative
the ground is first prepared by cutting shallow furrows
approximately 6–7 ft (1.8–2.1 m) apart, to give a turf strip which is
folded back on to the adjacent surface. The young trees, two-to-
three-year-old seedlings raised in a nursery, are then planted into
the strip. The rooting vegetation of the turf provides some
nourishment for the young tree, while the immediate area is kept
free of competitive weed growth until it is established. Limited
surface drainage is also provided by the shallow cut from which the
turf was taken. About 70 per cent of the plantings were of Sitka
spruce, a variety from British Columbia with a great tolerance for
poor soil and exposure, but Norway spruce was planted on lower
more fertile ground, Scots and Lodgepole pines in areas of deep
heather, and deciduous Japanese larch where drainage was
particularly good.

Thinning of the crop is carried out after twenty to thirty years in

The Knag Burn gateway on Hadrian's Wall, built towards the end of
Roman rule in the fourth century to allow civilian access across the Wall
(Routes 11, 13 and 23).

forest areas below 750 ft (230 m), and the trees are finally felled when sixty to eighty years old. Above that altitude, however, shallow rooting and increased exposure lead to excessive damage due to 'windblow'; some 85 per cent of the total area, therefore, is not thinned, and felling occurs after forty to fifty years. When clearing has been completed the area is surrounded by a high wire-mesh fence to keep out roe-deer, which have proliferated to a remarkable extent in the forest, and replanting is carried out when the 'brash' of earlier planting has rotted sufficiently to provide nourishment and before weeds can establish too firm a hold. At the moment, as most of the trees are still immature, the forest-yield is increasing, but eventually in the late 1990s a constant output will be achieved.

Altogether there are nine forests in the Border region: Falstone, Kielder, Kershope, Redesdale, Spadeadam and Wark in England (collectively referred to as Kielder Forest), and Leithope, Newcastleton and Wauchope in Scotland. These nine are to form a new Border Forest Park to be launched in 1991. Together they form one of the largest man-made forests in Europe. About 85 per cent of the land purchased has now been planted. Of the remainder, a large area of open fell to the north is managed by the Forestry Commission and the Nature Conservancy Council as a nature reserve. Three new villages were built to house the forest workers at Byrness, Kielder and Stonehaugh, and smaller developments took place at existing communities such as Falstone.

With the increasing maturity of the forest and the construction of Kielder Water, plus a greater interest in the environment on the part of the Forestry Commission, the forest areas have become much more attractive. Free access for walkers is allowed to all areas of the forest apart from an area around Kielder Dam, although this access may be restricted when essential forestry operations are being carried out or in periods of extreme fire risk. There is a Visitor Centre at Kielder Castle open from Easter to the end of October; there are car-parks and picnic places; camping-

New plantings in Kielder Forest near the shoreline of Kielder Water (Route 15).

and caravan-sites at Stonehaugh, Kielder, Leaplish and Byrness; a 12-mile (19 km) Forest Drive for cars; and a number of forest walks and trails.

Kielder Water

Work on the Kielder Water Scheme, which was intended to meet an increasing demand for water from the north-east, began in February 1975 with the construction of a new road up the valley of the North Tyne as far as Kielder. The building of the main dam, Kielder Dam, about 1 mile (1.6 km) to the west of Falstone, was begun the following year. By the time the scheme was completed one of the largest man-made lakes in northern Europe had been created, with a total area of 2,684 acres (1086 ha), a length of 7½ miles (12 km) and a shoreline 27½ miles (44 km) long. Another – but much smaller – dam was built further up the valley (forming Bakethin Reservoir) to avoid the formation of unsightly mud-flats if the draw-down of water from the main reservoir was excessive. Water is taken from the reservoir through a valve tower near the dam and fed into the North Tyne a short distance below. Lower down the river at Riding Mill, water is extracted to feed the rivers Wear and Tees, and at the Horsley Treatment Works for Newcastle. From beginning to end the beautifully managed project was the result of public enterprise in which private finance played no part.

In addition to its main purpose for water supply, Kielder Water has been developed for recreational pursuits. A Visitor Centre has been established at Tower Knowe, an Activity Centre for the disabled at Low Cranecleugh, and a Scout Adventure Centre at Hawk Hirst. There are facilities for sailing, canoeing, windsurfing and waterskiing at the Leaplish Waterside Park. Bakethin Reservoir, with the forest immediately around it, has been designated as a nature reserve. Of particular interest to walkers is the regular ferry service which calls at several jetties around the Water.

The Northumberland National Park

Probably the best description of a National Park – at least, as we know them in this country – was given by John Dower in 1945: '. . . an extensive area of beautiful and relatively wild country in which, for the nation's benefit and by appropriate national decision and action: (a) the characteristic landscape beauty is strictly preserved, (b) access and facilities for public open-air enjoyment are amply provided, (c) wildlife and buildings and places of architectural and historic interest are suitably protected, while (d) established farming use is effectively maintained.' Broadly speaking, it still describes the work of the National Park Authorities.

The main groundwork for the establishment of the National Parks in England and Wales – there are none in Scotland or Northern Ireland at the present time – was done by two committees, either during the Second World War or immediately afterwards. These are usually referred to by the names of their chairpersons and are therefore known as the Dower and Hobhouse Committees. Their work culminated in the National Parks and Access to the Countryside Act of 1949 under which a National Parks Commission (now the Countryside Commission) was established which was charged with the creation of National Parks.

Ten Parks were created between 1951 (Peak District) and 1957 (Brecon Beacons). The Northumberland National Park, designated on 5 June 1956, was the ninth of these. Since then there have been no further additions, although the Norfolk and Suffolk Broads – under a new statutory body, the Broads Authority, established in 1989 – may be considered to be one in all but name. Each Park has its own distinctive symbol; that for Northumberland is the curlew.

The Northumberland National Park is one of the smallest of the Parks (only Exmoor and the Pembrokeshire Coast are smaller) with a total area of 398 sq miles (1031 sq km). Its southern boundary is the general area of the Military Road (B6318), south of Hadrian's Wall, and its northernmost boundary the valley of the

River Glen to the north-west of Wooler, a maximum distance of about 45 miles (72 km). In width it is very irregular, at its greatest between Rothbury and Byrness, and at its minimum around Bellingham. As the low-lying, intensively farmed country towards the coast was excluded, the Park consists almost entirely of rough pasture, moorland and high fell.

It is important to avoid confusion between the National Park and the Border Forest Park, which are quite separate. The Border Forest Park was established by the Forestry Commission (see page 40) and lies outside the western boundary of the National Park.

Astonishingly few people live within the area of the Park; with only about 2,000 residents it is, in fact, the least densely populated of all. A corollary to this, of course, is the absence of any towns and all but a few very small villages. One unusual feature is the large military training area which occupies about one-fifth of the total area of the Park (see page 49).

Under the Local Government Act of 1972 each National Park must have a separate Authority which is responsible for its administration. In the case of the Northumberland National Park this is the National Park and Countryside Committee of the County Council, although unlike all other Authorities this has additional responsibility for countryside properties and the rights of way network outside the Park. Most of the money (75 per cent) for the National Park work comes from the government in a National Park Supplementary Grant, with the remainder coming from the County Council. The committee acts as the planning authority for the area (but only in matters related to the countryside, not for such things as education, housing and highways), although in view of the low level of population this part of their work is light compared to other Parks. In addition, it has the power to promote various schemes for the benefit of the environment and for visitors. As a policy, the Authority endeavours to proceed by negotiation and by agreement, rather than by using any legal powers that it may have. One outstanding

The location of the National Park and the two Areas of Outstanding Natural Beauty within Northumberland.

FIGURE 2

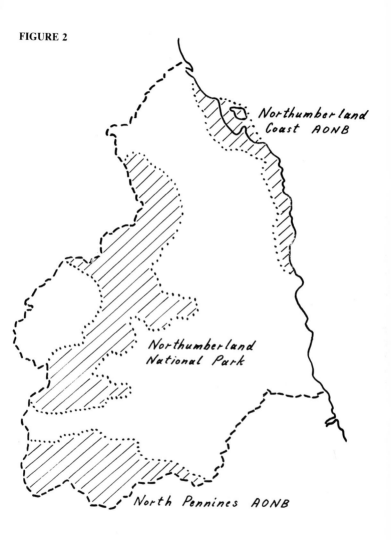

Northumberland
Coast AONB

Northumberland
National Park

North Pennines AONB

feature of the Authority's work is the publication of guides and booklets on the Park; in general these are of the highest quality. Among other activities a very large number of guided walks are organized by the Authority throughout the year.

It should be emphasized that the title 'National Park' does not mean that the land area of the Park is owned by the nation. About one-fifth is owned by the Forestry Commission, about the same amount by the Ministry of Defence, and small amounts by the National Trust and the County Council, but the remainder is in private hands. In general, therefore, the public's right to cross land is the same as it is anywhere else. However, in some cases the Authority has negotiated concessionary paths and access agreements for areas which can then be used by the public in addition to public rights of way. At present there are access agreements in three main areas: on riverside land in the Harthope Valley, east and west of Ingram in the Breamish Valley, and adjoining Hadrian's Wall at Housesteads.

The chief officer of the Authority is the National Park Officer who heads a team of full-time, part-time and voluntary staff. Of these, the ones that the public are most likely to meet are those at the Information Centres and the wardens out in the field.

Visitor Centres are situated at:

Church House, Rothbury. Telephone: Rothbury (0669) 20887

Housesteads, Military Road, Bardon Mill. Telephone: Bardon Mill (0434) 344525 (With National Trust)

Once Brewed, Military Road, Bardon Mill. Telephone: Bardon Mill (0434) 344396

The Old School House, Ingram. Telephone: Powburn (066 578) 248

Tower Knowe Centre. Telephone: Bellingham (0434) 240398. In addition, there is a seasonal van at Cawfields on Hadrian's Wall.

The Border

Although Kenneth Mac Alpin's claim in the ninth century to all the lands between the Forth and the Tweed identified the latter river as the natural boundary between England and Scotland, the matter was not finally settled for some three hundred years. From the twelfth century onward, however, Northumberland was accepted as the northernmost county of England, and the border with Scotland was established in substance along its present-day line. Even so, detailed surveys of the Border were still thought necessary in 1542 and 1550, and areas such as around the Halter Burn near the Yetholms and around Deadwater north-west of Kielder were considered 'Disputed Ground' as late as the end of the eighteenth century.

By 1292 when Edward I decided the succession to the Scottish throne in the Great Hall of the castle at Berwick (see page 77), the Border had enjoyed over a century of peace and comparative prosperity. Strong ties – religious, social and economic – had been established across the Border, and the overlordship of the English king was recognized, although not in any way that would permit strong interference in Scottish affairs. It was this, rather than Edward's decision in favour of John Balliol, which led to conflict and ushered in some three centuries of intermittent strife which only ended with the Union of the Crowns in 1603. As would be expected, friendships and arrangements of mutual advantage which had been built up over many years did not long survive the clamour of outright war.

The great battles, such as Dunbar (1296), Stirling Bridge (1297), Falkirk (1298), Bannockburn (1314) and Flodden (1513) are the ones best documented, but more limited frontier raids by lords on both sides of the Border were openly encouraged. The Battle of Otterburn in 1388 was fought after an English army under Henry Percy, Constable of Berwick Castle, caught up with a Scottish pillaging force under Lord Douglas, and is said to have involved great slaughter. Homildon Hill in 1402 occurred in similar circumstances.

The effect on the Border regions was catastrophic. However

much popular history may glorify the affairs of kings, and the Border Ballads sing of the deeds of men, the sordid reality of the Border conflict was homelessness, impoverishment, fear and violent death. As wealth usually resided only in cattle and sheep, the stealing of them – and of anything else worth having – became for ordinary people a way of life. The quiet passage of armed bands – mosstroopers or reivers – through the Border Hills was only an inevitable extension of the greater conflict, with the added justification that for many of them it was done in the name of survival.

Some attempt was made to curb the lawlessness. The Border region was divided into three Marches: the East March extended from Berwick to the Hanging Stone on The Cheviot, the Middle March from there to Kershopefoot in Liddesdale, and the West March was over the county border in Cumberland. Each was the responsibility of two Wardens – a leading Border Lord authorized by royal appointment on the English side and by family connection on the Scottish – who met together on days of truce at selected points on the Border to air grievances and attempt to right wrongs. Border Laws were designed to reduce tension and to provide a formula by which justice could be dispensed. All this, however, depended for success upon co-operation, which was not always forthcoming, and upon trust, which was sometimes abused.

In the circumstances most people looked to their own safety and Northumberland is noteworthy for the very high number of fortified structures which can still be found there. Large tower-houses (such as at Thirlwall and Featherstone), smaller pele-towers(as at Alnham, Great Tosson and Elsdon), and fortified farmhouses or bastles (such as Black Middens) were erected in considerable numbers between the fourteenth and sixteenth centuries by those who could afford them.

With the Union of the Crowns in 1603 and the succession of James VI of Scotland to the English throne, the need for a border disappeared. Lawlessness was, however, at a height and needed special attention. It is to James's credit that this was given. The destruction of fortified dwellings, abolition of the Border Laws, the establishment of a commission to administer the common law, and a determined drive against the reivers themselves, which resulted in many being hanged or transported, were some of the measures used. By about the middle of the century the once violent lands had become quiet.

The Otterburn Training Area

The history of the Training Area goes back to 1911 when the Secretary of State for War purchased about 20,000 acres (8094 ha) of land in Redesdale. A tented camp was established there which was replaced by a permanent hutted camp during the 1940s. Since then the range has been extended, so that nowadays it occupies an area of 58,000 acres (23 500 ha), all of which is within the Northumberland National Park.

Some 30,000 regular and volunteer servicemen from within the NATO forces train there each year for periods of between two days and two weeks. The Royal Air Force also make use of it for aircrew survival training and as a range for ground attack. All the weapons systems used by the British Army can be fired there with the exception of main battle tanks and certain missiles.

The live-firing ranges are south of the River Coquet. Firing takes place on them on about 300 days each year (this excludes the lambing period from 15 April to 15 May, and Bank Holidays) and at such times red flags or lamps are hoisted, barriers are closed, and the public is not permitted within the area. When no firing takes place the public is permitted to use public footpaths, public bridleways and MOD roads. The dates and times of firing are sent to Northumberland National Park Visitor Centres, local post offices and some shops and inns. North of the Coquet there is a Dry Training Area where exercises are carried out without the use of live ammunition: the public rights of way there are open at all times. However, about 8000 acres (3250 ha) of this area were used for firing in the past and it is possible that some unexploded ammunition may still be there. All the public ways have been cleared, but there are notices warning the public not to pick up any strange objects.

The Northumbrian small pipes

Bagpipes have been played in England since at least the fourteenth
century for Geoffrey Chaucer mentions in The Prologue of *The
Canterbury Tales* that the Miller – that 'great stout fellow big in
brawn and bone' – used them to play the pilgrims out of town.
Although widely played to all groups of society at dances, on
pilgrimage and by wandering minstrels, the earliest instruments
were fairly simple, consisting of nothing more than a bag, one or
two chanters and a mouthpiece, and their music was rather crude.
By Tudor times, therefore, the preference of fashionable society
had turned to instruments such as the lute, which was softer and
capable of much greater expression, and the bagpipe was
increasingly left as the instrument of the rougher country classes.
Regional varieties developed during this period, such as in
Lancashire, Lincolnshire, Worcestershire and Northumberland,
but little is known about most of them.

By the beginning of the nineteenth century only those of
Northumberland survived in general use, and even interest in
those had waned and continued to wane further as the century
progressed. Surprisingly, it was during this period of decline that
the main technical developments were made to the Northumbrian
pipes. The closing of the chanter produced clearer notes, the
addition of keys increased their range and the addition of drones
widened the background harmony. Music composed specifically
for the bagpipes also appeared in this period.

Fortunately, interest revived at the end of the nineteenth
century. The Northumbrian Small Pipes Society was established in
1893 and the Northumbrian Pipers' Society in 1928. Today, the
playing of the small pipes – on their own, in duets or accompanied
by other instruments – is very much a part of the northern scene.

Stick dressing

The craft or art of producing finely finished decorated sticks for
show is widely practised in the north of England and in Scotland,

but nowhere is interest greater than in Northumberland and the Borders. The Border Union Show, held at Kelso each year on the last Friday and Saturday of July, has some fourteen classes for 'Shepherds' Crooks, etc.', but every local show will include some competitions, and evening classes are held at several institutions. Apart from the show aspect, the stick is an indispensable tool to many a countryman and quantities of walking sticks and shepherds' leg cleeks and neck crooks are made for use or sale.

Knob sticks and thumb sticks are the easiest and quickest to make, the former from a straight shank with an attached branch or root and the latter either all wood or capped with deer horn – although even these are capable of some decoration. Sticks and crooks with wood heads, whether one piece or two, are more difficult to make, but have considerably more scope for originality. Sticks and crooks with horn heads are considered the greatest challenge of all.

Many woods have been used in stick-making, but the favourites are hazel, holly, ash and blackthorn, best gathered in autumn or early winter. After cutting, at least one year's drying is necessary before use, and this is usually done in bundles of a dozen or so. Ram horns, preferably from older animals, are best, most of them coming from mountain and moorland breeds. After maturing, the horn is heated to make it pliable so that it can be flattened, squeezed solid and shaped before being fitted to the shank. Final shaping is done with files and with progressively finer sandpapers.

At the present time the financial rewards of stick competitions are not high, but standards are, and the top awards are fiercely contested. The overall balance of the stick and its soundness of construction are taken into consideration as well as the finish, beauty and accuracy of its decoration.

The Border Ballads

Nothing evokes more vividly the turbulent history of Northumberland and the Border, and the lives, hopes, fears and fate of the people who made it, than the Border Ballads. 'Made for singing an' no for reading', they formed the main oral record in medieval times when other means were not available. It says much for their quality that they are still read and sung to this day.

Much of the credit for their endurance goes to Sir Walter Scott, whose roots were in the Border country and who lived there for most of his life. His collection of Border songs, *The Ministrelsy of the Scottish Border*, published in 1802, was influential not only in preserving a tradition that was in danger of being lost, but in bringing them to wider notice. In this he was assisted by several remarkable men who deserve to be remembered in their own right: by James Hogg, the self-educated 'Ettrick Shepherd', who had no schooling beyond his seventh year, but who eventually became a writer of considerable merit; by William Laidlaw, a friend and later his steward; and by John Leyden, the son of a Border shepherd who was later to become an authority on eastern languages. He was also indebted to earlier compilations such as Bishop Percy's *Reliques of Ancient English Poetry* and James Wilson's *Collection of Scottish Poems 1706–11*.

The most famous of the Border Ballads is an English one, 'Chevy Chase', which describes an incident arising from a long-standing feud between the Percy and the Douglas families. Most likely the ballad did not relate to a particular encounter, but drew upon several, in particular those of Otterburn (1388), Homildon Hill (1402) and Piperdean (1436). The Scottish 'The Battle of Otterbourne', which has some similarities, relates more directly to the first of these.

Other famous encounters such as Flodden; the lives of leading Border characters such as Parcy Reed, Jamie Telfer, Jock o' the Side and Dick a' the Cow; the Faa gypsies of Yetholm; love and treachery; triumph and disaster; honour and chivalry; witchcraft and superstition – all these form the fabric of the Border Ballads. Probably no more fitting tribute has ever been paid to them than the words of Sir Philip Sydney in *The Apologie for Poetrie* (1580): 'I never heard the old song of Piercy and Douglas that found not my heart more moved than by a trumpet; and yet it is sung by some blind crowder with no regular voice than rude style.'

Safety

The thirty routes described in this book vary considerably in length and in difficulty. Some of the easiest routes should be safe for most people at any time of the year and under almost all weather conditions, provided that the walkers behave in a reasonable and sensible way; some of the more difficult walks, however, cross very wild country and are only suitable, even on good summer days, for fit walkers who have the correct clothing and equipment and know what they are doing. At all times walkers should take their safety and the safety of others into consideration. In all situations particular care should be taken of children who can wander off very easily and quickly become lost or get into dangerous situations.

(a) *In mountain, hill and moorland areas*:

It must be emphasized that conditions can change very rapidly in mountain and hill areas, not only during the day but from one part of a mountain to another or as you climb to higher ground. You must bear this in mind when choosing your clothing and equipment before a walk. The challenge of a walk will also generally be greater (perhaps very much greater) in winter, when snow and ice are lying on the mountains, than it will be in the summer months.

Therefore, for your own safety in mountain and moorland areas: DO:

Carry suitable clothing and equipment, which should be in good condition.

Carry sufficient food for the day, plus more for emergencies.

Carry a map and compass and make sure that you know beforehand how to use them.

Plan your route carefully before you start.

Leave a note of your planned route with a responsible person (and stick to it unless changed circumstances make it dangerous to do so).

Report your return as soon as possible.

If it appears that you are going to be seriously delayed then inform your base, or the police, as soon as possible.

Keep warm (but not too hot) at all times.

Eat nourishing foods and rest at regular intervals.

Avoid becoming over-tired.

Know some First Aid and the correct procedure in case of accidents or illness.

If you are leading a party, always go at the pace of the slowest member, and never separate (except possibly in the event of a serious accident in order to obtain help).

Obtain a weather forecast before you start out and take this into consideration at the planning stage. Notice any changes in the weather as you proceed and take these into consideration.

DO NOT:

Go out into mountainous or moorland areas on your own, unless you are very experienced; three is a good number for a party.

Attempt routes which are beyond your skill, strength or experience.

(b) *In old mining areas*:

The area to the south around Allendale and Blanchland was the scene of a great deal of mining activity. Old mine areas can provide sources of danger of their own. To help avoid accidents the Peak Park Joint Planning Board in co-operation with Derbyshire County Council has prepared a leaflet, *Mind that Mine*. It contains information on mines and draws up a Code of Conduct Near Mines:

DO walk with caution and constant care, especially when with children.

DO keep to well-used paths – shafts are often quite near.

DO look out for hummocky ground.

DON'T go near mining areas in fog, snow, dark, or stormy weather.

DON'T go near shafts, climb on shaft walls, or throw rocks down shafts.

DON'T go in the depressions of collapsed shafts or open rakes.

DON'T attempt to explore shafts or levels unless in a properly equipped party with experienced leaders.

Finally, do not damage remains in any way or collect samples of minerals or fossils in the vicinity of workings (or elsewhere).

(c) *Along the coast*:

Six of the routes go along the Northumbrian coast using coastal paths or beaches. A small brochure *Seaside safety on the East Coast* has been prepared by the Department for Transport and the Central Office of Information. This gives the following helpful checklist:

Emergency at sea or on cliffs

Be alert to people who may be in distress. You could save life. If you see a red flare, orange smoke, or a craft or person in difficulty:

Dial 999 and ask for the Coastguard. When connected give your name and the telephone number and explain where you are speaking from. Give all the information you can about the incident: what you have seen and where it is from your position as accurately as possible. This will help save time.

Stay by the telephone in case further information is needed. Ring again if the situation changes.

On the beach

Before going into the water, pay attention to any warnings displayed on the beach, or given by the beachguards.

Don't swim just after a meal, or if the water is very cold (cramp).

Don't swim off headlands (strong currents).

Be wary of undertow currents – even when the sea looks calm.

Don't let children go out on an airbed unless it is tethered to the shore by a line and watched by an adult. Children near water should *always* be supervised.

Don't touch strange objects. Hazardous items, such as flares or canisters of chemicals, may sometimes be washed ashore. Tell the coastguard or police about them.

Be wary of sandbanks where you could be cut off by the tide.

Cliff dangers

Keep well clear of the cliff edge. It may overhang and be unsafe. Remember even dry grass can be slippery.

Don't climb on cliffs unless you are properly equipped and you are in an organized party. (Some local authorities prohibit cliff climbing.)

Before walking along a stretch of beach under cliffs, find out what the tide is doing. You could get cut off.

Don't dig into soft cliff faces. They can collapse and bury you.

(d) *Weather forecasts*:

These can be obtained from a number of sources. Radio and television provide regular forecasts; written weather forecasts are put up at Information Centres; and a forecast for inland areas of the north-east may be obtained from Weathercall, telephone 0898 500 418 (24-hour, 7-day-a-week service). Marinecall forecasts (telephone 0898 500 453) give information for the north-east on the sea, state of the visibility levels, high-water times and the latest gale warnings, plus a forecast for 24 hours ahead.

How to give a grid reference

A grid reference is a very useful method of pin-pointing a position on an Ordnance Survey Map. The grid lines on Landranger and Pathfinder maps are the thin blue lines going vertically and horizontally across the map, covering it with a network of small squares.

FIGURE 3

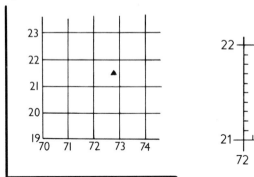

The method of determining a grid reference is as follows:

Figure 3 shows a section of an Ordnance Survey Landranger map with the position of a youth hostel marked.

Step 1: Write down the number of the 'vertical' grid line to the left (or west) of the hostel. This is 72.

Step 2: Now imagine that the space between this grid line and the next one to its right is divided into tenths. Estimate the number of tenths that the hostel lies to the right of the first grid line. This is eight. Add this to the number in Step 1, making 728.

Step 3: Add on the number of the gridline below the hostel (i.e. to the south). This is 21; so the number becomes 72821.

Step 4: Now repeat step 2 for the space between the grid lines below and above the hostel. The hostel is five-tenths above the bottom line. Add this to the number, making 728215. This figure is called a six-figure grid reference. Coupled with the number of the appropriate Landranger or Outdoor Leisure sheet, it will enable any point to be identified.

Step 5: The numbers of the grid lines repeat after 100. There will therefore be many other places in the United Kingdom with exactly the same six-figure grid reference. To overcome this problem, the maps are also divided up into large squares with sides made up from 100 of the small squares, each of which is designated by two letters; on the Landranger sheets these are given on the small diagram which shows the adjoining sheets. In the example above, if the large square is designated by SP, then the full grid reference is SP 728215. There is only one place in the United Kingdom with this grid number.

The Countryside Access Charter

The Countryside Access Charter was prepared by the Countryside Commission for practical guidance in England and Wales only.

Your rights of way are:

Public footpaths – on foot only. Sometimes waymarked in yellow.

Bridleways – on foot, horseback and pedal cycle. Sometimes

waymarked in blue.

Byways (usually old roads), most 'Roads Used as Public Paths' and, of course, public roads – all traffic.

Use maps, signs and waymarks. Ordnance Survey Pathfinder and Landranger maps show most public rights of way.

On rights of way you can:

Take a pram, pushchair or wheelchair if practicable.

Take a dog (on a lead or under close control).

Take a short route round an illegal obstruction or remove it sufficiently to get past.

You have a right to go for recreation to:

Public parks and open spaces – on foot.

Most commons near older towns and cities – on foot and sometimes on horseback.

Private land where the owner has a formal agreement with the local authority.

In addition you can use by local or established custom or consent, but ask for advice if you're unsure:

Many areas of open country like moorland, fell and coastal areas, especially those of the National Trust, and some commons.

Some woods and forests, especially those owned by the Forestry Commission.

Country Parks and picnic sites.

Most beaches.

Canal towpaths.

Some private paths and tracks.

Consent sometimes extends to riding horses and pedal cycles.

For your information:

County councils and London boroughs maintain and record rights of way, and register commons.

Obstructions, dangerous animals, harassment and misleading signs on rights of way are illegal and you should report them to the county council.

Paths across fields can be ploughed, but must normally be reinstated within two weeks.

Landowners can require you to leave land to which you have no right of access.

Motor vehicles are normally permitted only on roads, byways and some 'Roads Used as Public Paths'.

Follow any local bylaws.

And, wherever you go, follow the Country Code:

Enjoy the countryside and respect its life and work.

Guard against all risk of fire.

Fasten all gates.

Keep your dogs under close control.

Keep to public paths across farmland.

Use gates and stiles to cross fences, hedges and walls.

Leave livestock, crops and machinery alone.

Take your litter home.

Help to keep all water clean.

Protect wildlife, plants and trees.

Take special care on country roads.

Make no unnecessary noise.

Notes on the route descriptions and maps

Difficulty

The routes were selected to give a wide range of walks of both length and difficulty. This was done deliberately to make the book attractive and useful to as many kinds of walker as possible. It does make it essential, however, for the sake of both interest and safety, to give a clear indication of the difficulty of each route.

A number of factors play a part in determining the time necessary to complete a walk. The most important of these factors are distance and the amount of climbing involved, and the effect of these can be assessed by Naismith's Rule (see below). Roughness of terrain or difficulties of route-finding can also, of course, play a part, but usually these are restricted in their effects to a small proportion of the total distance involved.

The method used in this book to obtain a measure of difficulty involved three stages: (1) a calculation of the total time required for each route on the basis of Naismith's Rule; (2) listing the routes on the basis of the time needed to complete them, from the shortest to the longest; (3) a review of the list after surveying each route.

The difficulty of each route can be assessed by the reader in three ways: (1) the total distance and the amount of climbing involved, which are given at the head of each route description. Difficulties of a special nature are pointed out in the introduction to the route; (2) its position in the list – Route No. 1 is the easiest, No. 30 is the hardest; and (3) its grading.

As far as this last is concerned, all the walks have been divided into four categories – Easy, Moderate, More strenuous and Very strenuous. These are not intended to be rigid categories, but are merely a guide to the difficulties of the walks. A 'typical' walk within each category would be:

Easy. A short walk (say, up to 5 miles, 8 km) over good paths, with no problems of route-finding. Some climbing may be involved, but mostly over fairly gradual slopes with only short sections of difficult ground.

Moderate. A longer walk (up to 10 miles, 16 km) mostly over good paths but with some more indefinite sections where route-finding will be difficult. Mountain summits may be reached, necessitating climbing over steeper and rougher ground.

More strenuous. A fairly long walk (10–20 miles, 16–32 km) with prolonged spells of climbing. Some rough ground, calling for good route-finding ability, perhaps with prolonged stretches of scrambling.

Very strenuous. For very good walkers only. More than 20 miles (32 km), with much climbing, and stretches of very difficult ground calling for good route-finding ability.

Distance

These are 'map miles' which take no account of the amount of climbing involved. They are given in miles and kilometres, since both are in common usage.

Ascent

These figures are also given in both feet and metres.

Naismith's Rule

An estimate of the time required to complete each route is not given in the book, as this will vary from one walker to another. But the usual method of estimating time is by Naismith's Rule, which is:

> For ordinary walking allow one hour for every 3 miles (5 km) and add one hour for every 2,000 ft (600 m) of ascent; for backpacking with a heavy load allow one hour for every 2½ miles (4 km) and one hour for every 1,500 ft (450 m) of ascent.

For most walkers this tends to underestimate the amount of time required, and each walker should try to form an assessment of his or her own performance over one or two walks. The Rule also makes no allowance for rest or food stops, for the roughness of the ground, or for the influence of weather conditions.

Car-parks

Almost all the walks described start at a car-park or parking place. This is indicated on the first map of each route and in the information given on the starting point.

Route descriptions

The letters 'L' and 'R' indicate left and right respectively, and for changes of direction imply a turn of about 90° when facing in the direction of the walk. 'Half L' and 'half R' indicate turns of approximately 45°, while 'back half L' and 'back half R' indicate turns of about 135°. Any bearings given are magnetic bearings. It should be assumed that all stiles and gates mentioned in the description are crossed, unless there is a statement to the contrary. PFS stands for 'Public Footpath Sign', PBS for 'Public Bridleway Sign', OS for 'Ordnance Survey' and PW for 'Pennine Way Sign'.

The maps

The maps take the same numbers as the routes; where there is more than one map for a route then they are given the suffixes A, B, C, etc. Thus, Route No. 22 has three maps: 22A, 22B, and 22C, to be used in that order.

The maps are drawn to a scale of 2 inches to one mile (1:31 680). The maps have been drawn, with one or two exceptions, so that the route goes from the bottom to the top of a page. This will enable the walker to 'line-up' a map, i.e. hold it in the same direction as his route, while still holding the book in the normal reading position. The arrow on each map points to grid north.

For mountain and moorland areas it is strongly recommended that, in addition to this guide, Landranger or Pathfinder maps are carried; these should be used where difficulty of route-finding arises, if the route is lost, or where bearings have to be estimated.

Features of interest

Some information on features of interest along the way is given with each route description. The best position for seeing these

The starting points for Routes 1 to 30.

FIGURE 4

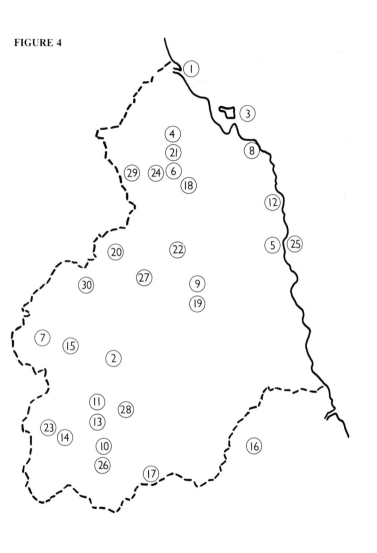

FIGURE 5

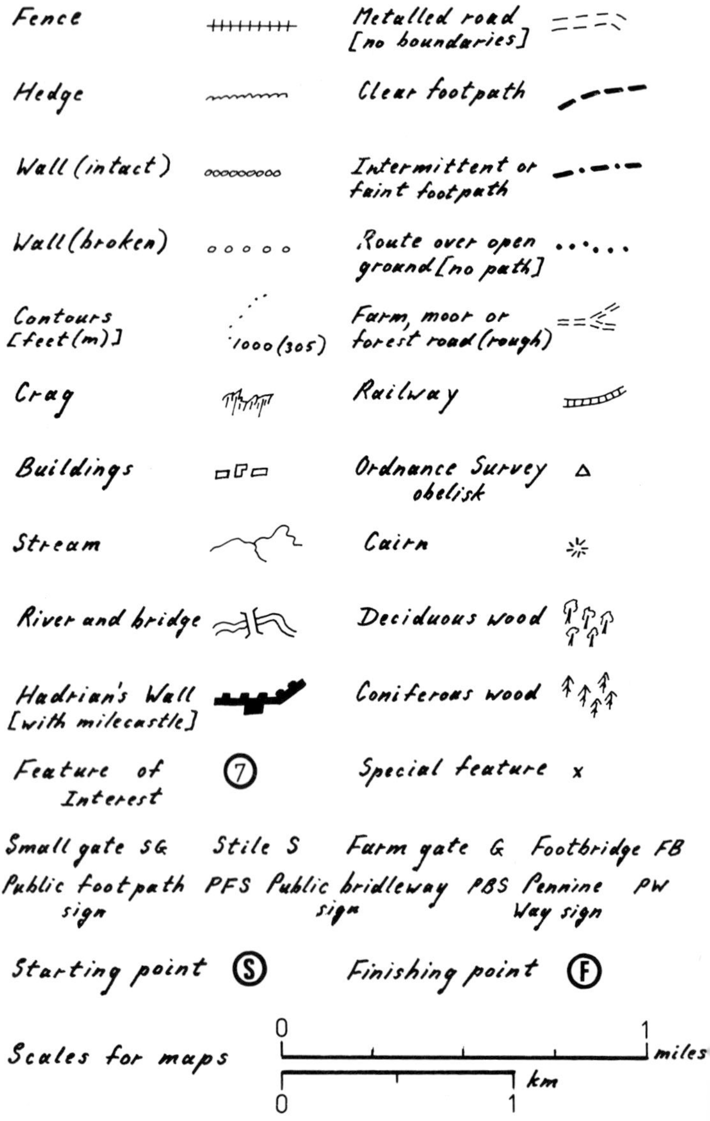

Fence	+++++++++	Metalled road [no boundaries]	= = =
Hedge	∿∿∿∿∿	Clear footpath	▬ ▬ ▬
Wall (intact)	∞∞∞∞∞∞∞	Intermittent or faint footpath	▬ · ▬ · ▬
Wall (broken)	∘ ∘ ∘ ∘ ∘	Route over open ground [no path]	·· · ·· ··
Contours [feet (m)]	1000 (305)	Farm, moor or forest road (rough)	= = ≪
Crag		Railway	▭▭▭▭
Buildings	▫▯▭	Ordnance Survey obelisk	△
Stream		Cairn	⁎
River and bridge		Deciduous wood	🌳🌳🌳
Hadrian's Wall [with milecastle]		Coniferous wood	↑↑↑↑
Feature of Interest	⑦	Special feature	x

Small gate SG   Stile S   Farm gate G   Footbridge FB

Public footpath sign PFS   Public bridleway sign PBS   Pennine Way sign PW

Starting point Ⓢ   Finishing point Ⓕ

Scales for maps

0			1
			miles

0		1	
		km	

features is indicated both in the route description and on the accompanying map.

Where appropriate, the location of a feature of interest is indicated by the number of the appropriate Landranger sheet with a six-figure grid reference. Thus, 81-991110 gives the location of Alnham church, i.e. in position 991110 on Landranger sheet No. 81.

Access

As far as is known the routes described either (a) use public rights of way, (b) cross areas over which there is a current access agreement, (c) use a concessionary path, or (d) cross land which is privately owned, but which has been opened to the general public. Three of the walks involve short sections of shoreline; in Britain the area between the tide lines is mainly owned by the Crown and access is usually allowed. In no case, therefore, is it expected that any difficulties will be encountered. Nevertheless, it must be emphasized that walkers have an obligation to behave properly when using footpaths, shorelines, or crossing areas of wild country, so that no damage is caused or any nuisance given to other people. It should also be pointed out that the position with regard to an area of land may change with time. In particular, official diversions – for example, to allow a badly-eroded path to recover – should always be followed; such diversions will normally be well waymarked.

Key to the signs used on the route maps.

The best walks

Easy routes

Route 1   Berwick Ramparts

With its three magnificent bridges, fine old houses and unique
ramparts, Berwick-upon-Tweed is by far the most interesting town
in Northumberland and one of the finest in the whole of Britain.
For that reason it would have been scandalous to have omitted a
visit there from any book of best walks. The route described here
starts alongside the river, and then follows a full circuit of the
ramparts, with occasional forays to visit interesting features a short
distance away. Berwick, however, is a town to be visited again and
again if its character is to be fully appreciated.

   Care should be taken on the ramparts, particularly if children
are with you, for the sloping grass-covered edges are not protected
and the drop from them is a fair one.

Length: 3 miles (5 km).

Ascent: Virtually none, except for a few steps and short inclines.

Starting and finishing point: The car-park at the railway station in
Berwick-upon-Tweed (75-994534). There are other car-parks
within the town.

Maps: Berwick Visitor's Guide No. 4, *Exploring Berwick*,
published by the Berwick-upon-Tweed Civic Society and
obtainable from the Information Centre in Berwick.

Route description (Map 1)
Before starting, read (1) Berwick ramparts, for a general history.
   Leave the station car-park and turn L to the main road, then L
again over the railway bridge. At a junction go L up the road to
Duns for a few yards, then L through a small white gate. A path
leads down through a park – with a splendid view of the castle, see
(2) Berwick Castle – to the river bank. There turn L along a
footpath which goes through the castle walls and underneath a

MAP 1

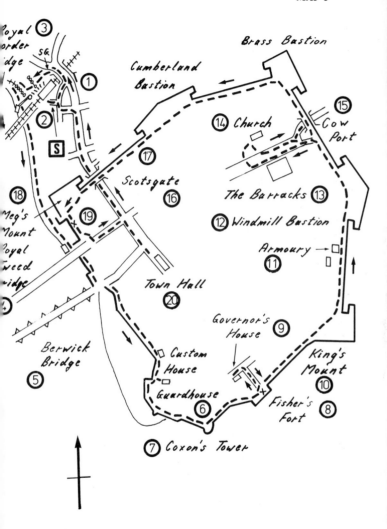

Royal
Border
Bridge

SG.

③

①

②

S

⑰

Cumberland
Bastion

Brass Bastion

⑭ Church

⑮

Cow
Port

Scotsgate

⑱

Meg's
Mount
Royal
Tweed
Bridge

⑲

⑯

The Barracks ⑬

⑫ Windmill Bastion

Armoury → ⑪

Berwick
Bridge

⑤

Town Hall

⑳

Custom
House

Guardhouse

⑥

Governor's
House

⑨

King's
Mount

⑩

Fisher's
Fort

⑧

⑦ Coxon's Tower

railway bridge – see (3) the Royal Border Bridge. Soon go under another bridge – see (4) the Royal Tweed Bridge – and along to a cobbled street.

Go along the street and cross over the road at the end with another bridge to the R – see (5) Berwick Bridge. Continue down the flagged street ahead with a wall and quay to the R, soon passing the Custom House. (Berwick is famous for its mute swans and it is usual to see many of them on the river from this point.) After the Custom House go down the first street on the L for a few yards and have a look at the building on the R with columns at the front – see (6) the Guardhouse, then return to the ramparts and turn L. Soon reach a tower – see (7) Coxon's Tower – and shortly afterwards a gun – see (8) Fisher's Fort and the Crimean gun.

Continue along the ramparts. Just after the gun turn L down a side street with a central lawn. At the end turn L for a few yards to the large house with a small porch – see (9) the Governor's House. Afterwards return to the ramparts and turn L to resume your original direction.

Pass the first bastion – see (10) King's Mount. Between that and the next, Windmill Bastion, notice the tall house on the L with lions at the front and, just beyond, a strong stone building surrounded by a tall wall – see (11) The Armoury. Pass the next bastion – see (12) Windmill Bastion – and immediately afterwards turn to the L down a street with a broad area of grass. The building on the L with the gateway and coat of arms is now a museum – see (13) the Barracks. Towards the end, cross over and go through the car-park into the churchyard to visit the church – see (14) Holy Trinity Parish Church. Afterwards walk back towards the ramparts. There have a look at the opening which takes a road under the walls to the far side – see (15) Cow Port.

Go back on to the ramparts and turn L, i.e. to resume your original direction. Keep along the ramparts, passing two more bastions, Brass and Cumberland, until they pass over the main street

Quay Walls – an area of fine houses, mostly built in the eighteenth and nineteenth centuries. The Walls were reflagged in European Architectural Heritage Year (1975).

of Berwick – see (16) Scotsgate. The car-park on the R just before
was originally a cattle market – see (17). Immediately beyond
Scotsgate there is a further bastion – see (18) Meg's Mount.
Continue along the ramparts, once again parallel with the river,
passing a white stone statue – see (19) Annie, Lady Jerningham. Just
before the Royal Tweed Bridge go up some steps on the L to the
main road and turn L. At the crossroads look to the R for a view of
the Town Hall – see (20), then turn L and walk up the road, passing
under Scotsgate. Keep walking up the L-hand side until you reach
Railway Street; there turn L back to the station car-park.

(1) *Berwick ramparts*

It appears that before the end of the thirteenth century, Berwick –
which had by then been part of Scotland for some three centuries –
had no town defences of any significance. Following its capture by
Edward I in 1296, however, a ditch, bank and wooden palisade
were provided, the latter being replaced by a stone wall one year
later. No further work of any substance, other than repairs, seems
to have been carried out until 1482 when the town came into
English hands for the last time. The inadequate nature of these
early fortifications is well illustrated by the fact that Berwick –
which was at the centre of Border troubles throughout this period
– changed hands on no less than sixteen occasions. This dismal
record must have made a deep impression, for the following
seventy-seven years saw a whole series of major works.

Apart from some early piecemeal additions, this work occurred
in two periods: the first between 1550 and 1557 under Edward VI
and Mary, and the second under Elizabeth between 1558 and
1569. It was during this second period that the ramparts were
constructed which are today such a prominent feature of Berwick;
for that reason they are often referred to as the Elizabethan or
Tudor ramparts.

The ramparts were designed to meet the threat imposed by the
development of gunpowder and the consequently increased
effectiveness of artillery. The tall and relatively thin walls of the

The southern flanker of Windmill Bastion and a section of the ramparts.

medieval castle no longer gave any real protection when prolonged
bombardment from a safe distance could so easily destroy them.
The answer lay in a combination of lower, but thicker, walls which
could absorb artillery fire without being breached and in the
provision of relatiatory fire-power. These two features were found
in the 'bastion' which is used at Berwick. In essence it consists of
an earthwork faced with a reinforced stone wall in the general
shape of a symmetrical arrow-head. Guns placed on the two flanks
were able to bring a devastating fire along the face of adjacent
parts of the fortification, while guns on the outward faces provided
offensive fire.

It was originally intended to surround the central area of the
town with a rampart reinforced with six evenly spaced bastions. In
the event, the design was modified as the work progressed and in
1569 was suspended altogether. Only two bastions, Windmill and
Cumberland, were completed in their original symmetrical form;
one, Brass, was completed but to a non-symmetrical design; and
two others, Meg's Mount and King's Mount, were only half
finished. No ramparts were built along the river, the defensive line
being provided there by the old medieval wall.

(2) *Berwick Castle*

Records indicate that there was a castle at Berwick about the
middle of the twelfth century. It changed hands several times in
the centuries following, sometimes by agreement and sometimes
by capture, but it remained with the English from 1482.
Modifications and additions were made by various owners, but all
work on it ceased early in the seventeenth century and from then
on it was slowly demolished as its stone was taken for local
building works. By 1839 the castle was already in a ruinous state
and the building of Berwick Railway Station on the site in 1844–46
merely delivered the *coup de grâce*. Nowadays the most prominent
feature is the west wall with remains of towers at each end. The
wall dropping down to the river – the White Wall – was built by
Edward I in 1297 to prevent enemy access along the river side. At

One of the flankers of Brass Bastion seen from outside the walls.

its base there is the Water Tower, built in the sixteenth century, and behind it a steep flight of steps appropriately called the Breakynecks.

The castle's greatest moment was on 17 November 1292 when Edward I met with the full Parliament of England and a large proportion of the nobility of England and Scotland in the Great Hall of the castle to decide the succession to the throne of Scotland. His decision in favour of John Balliol, Lord of Galloway, rather than Robert Bruce, Lord of Annandale – or any of the other twelve contestants – was probably sound enough, but his somewhat high-handed manner subsequently was not. Four years later, hostilities – a prelude to some centuries of bloody warfare – began on the Border.

(3) *The Royal Border Bridge*
The highest and longest of Berwick's three bridges, this magnificent brick-built structure of twenty-eight arches was constructed between 1847 and 1850 on a design by Robert Stephenson as part of the east-coast route from London to Edinburgh. Berwick Station, just beyond the bridge on the north side, was built on the site of the castle, part of which was demolished, around the same time.

(4) *The Royal Tweed Bridge (The New Bridge)*
The modern bridge of four spans built from reinforced concrete a short distance upstream from Berwick Bridge was opened on 16 May 1928 by the Prince of Wales (later Edward VIII). It carried the Great North Road over the Tweed into Berwick (the present A1 bypasses the town well to the west over still another bridge).

(5) *Berwick Bridge (The Old Bridge)*
The lovely old stone bridge of fifteen arches which links Berwick with the south bank of the Tweed was built between 1611 and

The east flanker of Cumberland Bastion; the gun mounted in position was one of a pair which could scour the front of the ramparts as far as Brass Bastion.

1634, although it was in use for a few years before its final completion. It was constructed as a more permanent replacement for a wooden bridge built in Tudor times which stood a short distance further upstream, although this was merely the latest in a succession of bridges dating from at least the twelfth century. The second arch from the Berwick bank, where the river is deepest, was made higher to allow the passage of boats, whilst the sixth pier from Berwick was given deeper recesses and a more substantial cutwater to mark the original boundary of Berwick with North Durham. Despite its narrowness, the bridge carried the Great North Road until 1928, when the Royal Tweed Bridge was opened.

(6) *The Guardhouse*
The sturdy stone building down the cobbled street just after the Custom House was originally an eighteenth-century guardhouse which stood in Marygate. It was taken down and removed to its present site in 1815.

(7) *Coxon's Tower*
This is a two-storey watchtower situated strategically at the most southerly point of the fortifications overlooking the river mouth.

(8) *Fisher's Fort and the Crimean gun*
The projecting section between King's Mount and Coxon's Tower is called Fisher's Fort; constructed originally in 1522–23, when it was called 'The Bulwark by the Sands', it was rebuilt in the eighteenth century. It held an artillery battery which was intended to control the mouth of the river. The gun near the fort is a Russian gun captured in the Crimea.

(9) *The Governor's House*
The large house facing Palace Green was the Governor's House, built in the eighteenth century. Governors, who commanded the garrison of Berwick, lived here until 1833 when the post was abolished.

The Guardhouse.

(10) *King's Mount*

This is the first bastion met with on the walk, and the point at which the medieval walls, which run along the riverside, meet the Elizabethan ramparts. It was originally intended that the bastion would have the full arrow-head shape with two flankers, but only that to the north had been completed when work was suspended in 1569.

(11) *The Armoury*

The sturdy, well-buttressed building protected by a high wall was the garrison armoury or magazine built in 1749.

(12) *Windmill Bastion*

Unlike King's Bastion, this has the full shape as intended by the original plans. The gun mountings on top of the bastion were used by coastal guns in the nineteenth and early twentieth centuries.

(13) *The Barracks (Ravensdowne)*

Although Berwick had supported a garrison since the end of the thirteenth century, no special provision was made for this and it was the custom for troops to be quartered in local inns or houses. Although no doubt popular with the men themselves and at least some of the local people, this was a source of constant complaints and in any case was felt to be bad for discipline. The construction of a barracks was approved, therefore, in 1717, the work being completed in 1721, when they were occupied. Accommodation was provided for 36 officers and 600 men in two three-storey blocks facing each other across a square, with an entrance gate on the third side. This proved to be inadequate, however, and in 1739–41 a third block of two stories was added on the fourth side of the square to serve as a storehouse. The barracks were the depot of the King's Own Borderers (later the King's Own Scottish Borderers) from 1881 until 1964. Nowadays it houses three museums open to the public: the regimental museum of the Borderers, the Borough Museum and Art Gallery and an Army

The Armoury.

museum run by English Heritage. The arms displayed over the entrance are those of George I who was on the throne at the time of building.

(14) *Holy Trinity Parish Church*

The church, described by Pevsner as 'of quite exceptional architectural interest', was built in 1648–52 during the Commonwealth period (a rare event) – partly, it is said, with stone taken from the old castle. It was the work of John Young of Blackfriars, London, largely on the initiative of Colonel George Fenwick, then Governor of Berwick. Over the years alterations and additions have reduced its original starkly Puritan design.

(15) *Cow Port*

This is the narrow, tunnel-like opening through the walls at the eastern end of The Parade between Brass Bastion and Windmill Bastion. It is the only gateway of the original Tudor ramparts still surviving in its original form. The doors on the outer end of the opening were added about the middle of the eighteenth century. The inner end was defended by a further gate and a portcullis, the groove for which can be seen. Its name derives from a medieval cowgate, through which cows were driven to pastures near here.

(16) *Scotsgate*

Originally this was similar in design to Cow Port, but was rebuilt in 1815 and again in 1858. It carried – and still carries – the traffic to and from Scotland, hence its name.

(17) *Berwick cattle market*

The large car-park outside the walls between Scotsgate and Cumberland Bastion was for a time a cattle market, opened in October 1886. There is a rather ornate plaque commemorating the

The gateway of Ravensdowne Barracks. The arms above the entrance (containing those of England and Scotland, France, Ireland and Hanover, marshalled quarterly) were the Royal Arms of George I. The arms of France were not removed until 1801 and those of Hanover in 1837.

opening on the outer rampart wall opposite the Information Centre.

(18) *Meg's Mount*

As with King's Mount, it was originally intended that this bastion, which forms the north-west corner of the fortifications, would have the full arrow-head shape with two flankers. Construction along the river towards King's Mount was never completed, however, and only the flanker towards the town had been built when work was suspended. The bastion, therefore, joins the medieval wall on the river side.

(19) *Annie, Lady Jerningham*

The white statue of a lady with two dogs just beyond Meg's Mount is of Annie, Lady Jerningham, wife of Sir Hubert Jerningham, the last Member of Parliament for the Borough, who died on 9 October 1902. The statue was designed by Sir Hubert and executed by O. P. Penachini in 1906. The couple lived at Longridge Towers about 3 miles (5 km) to the south-west of Berwick.

(20) *The Town Hall*

The prominent building with the steps, large portico, columns and tall belfry at the end of Marygate is the Town Hall, built in 1750–61. Although the design is credited to a local man, Joseph Dods, it is largely the work of Samuel and John Worrall of London. The arcaded area at the far end is the Buttermarket, where local produce was bought and sold. Apart from its use for civic functions, Borough Quarter Sessions were once held there and the second floor was the old town gaol. Part of this, used to hold felons, is still virtually in its original state (including the condemned cell and a fine display of leg irons and manacles used to hold prisoners).

The inner entrance to Cow Port.

MAP 2

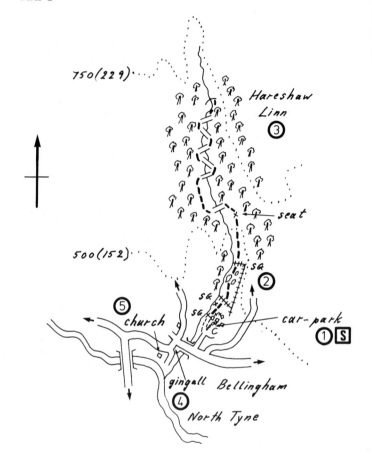

750(229)

Hareshaw
Linn ③

— seat

500(152)

sa

②

sa

⑤ church

sa

car-park

① S

gingall Bellingham

④

North Tyne

Route 2   Hareshaw Linn

Hareshaw Dene and the Linn have been enjoyed by the people of
Bellingham since at least the end of last century, for six bridges
were built and paths surfaced with cobbles around that time to
improve access to them. Today they still offer one of the most
delightful short walks in Northumberland. The way is absolutely
straightforward, along clear footpaths and through an area of
deciduous woodland noted for its beauty and for its interesting
fauna and flora. With reasonable care – particularly of children –
the way is safe as far as the Linn, although no attempt should be
made to proceed further; neither are there any escape routes from
the valley and a return must therefore be made along the same
path. A short pamphlet, *The Hareshaw Linn Walk*, is available at
the Information Centre in Bellingham and gives good information
about the trees, plants, animals and birds which can be seen there.
Note that Bellingham is pronounced 'Bellinjum'.

Length: 3 miles (5 km).

Ascent: 325 ft (100 m).

Starting and finishing point: The Hareshaw Linn car-park at
Bellingham (80–840835). From the main street in Bellingham go
down the Redesmouth/West Woodburn road. Immediately after
the bridge turn L and go along to the R of the stream to the
entrance of Bellingham Industrial Estate. The car-park is just
inside the rough road on the L.

Maps: Landranger 80; Pathfinder 522 (NY 88/98).

Route description (Map 2)
From the car-park continue down the rough road away from
Bellingham (PFS 'Hareshaw Linn'). The Border Counties Railway
crossed the river around here – see (1). Go through a small gate to
the L of a building and up the track beyond to a second small gate.
Continue along the broad path to the L of the fence, soon leaving

to the L between hillocks – see (2) the Hareshaw Ironworks. At the far end, go through a small gate leading into a wood. Keep along the clear path (partly cobbled), dropping down to a footbridge over the stream. Continue along the path, crossing over five further bridges, until the waterfall is reached – see (3) Hareshaw Linn. Return by the same path.

Before leaving, have a look around Bellingham. Go back to the main street and turn L. A short distance along find a gun on the L – see (4) the Bellingham gingall – then the town hall with a clock, and finally, just round the bend, Bellingham Church – see (5) St Cuthbert's and the 'Tale of the Long Pack'.

(1) *The Border Counties Railway*
Bellingham was served by the Border Counties Railway from 1862 to 1963 with a junction at nearby Redesmouth which had branch lines to Riccarton Junction, Hexham and Morpeth. The line was single, but there was a passing loop at Bellingham. It was never a great success, being either too late (e.g. for the Hareshaw Ironworks) or too early (e.g. for the Kielder Forest) for local developments which might have given it valuable trade.

(2) *The Hareshaw Ironworks*
A small ironworks operated in Hareshaw Dene from 1840 to 1848. Difficulty of transport was the main reason for its failure, as a railway did not reach Bellingham until fourteen years after its closure. The hillocks along the way before the wood is entered are spoil-heaps from the ironworks.

(3) *Hareshaw Linn (80-842854)*
At the Linn a small stream comes over a bed of sandstone which overlies softer and more easily erodable shales. Undercutting, due to erosion of the shales by the fall, brings occasional collapses of the sandstone lip and the growth of the gorge. As time goes on, therefore, the gorge will gradually grow longer.

The gingall.

(4) *The Bellingham gingall*

The small gun on display at the centre of Bellingham is a gingall –
a large musket, usually fired from a rest, which was used in India
and China. It was taken at the north-west fort at Taku Bay on 17
June 1900 during the Boxer Rising and presented to the town by
Commander E. Charlton RN of HMS *Orlando*. The Boxers were
members of a Chinese secret society whose name was a shortened
form of the title of their organization 'Righteous and Harmonious
Fists' and who practised a series of callisthenic exercises which
were intended to produce harmony of mind and body in
preparation for combat. After a long period of relative obscurity,
they burst into prominence in a series of uprisings beginning at
Shantung in 1898. The principal cause of the uprisings was deep
resentment at the continual interference in Chinese affairs during
the nineteenth century by several European countries, including
Britain. 'Destroy the foreigner' was their rallying cry, soon eagerly
echoed by peasant and the Empress Dowager alike.

   On 15 June 1900 the French settlement at Tientsin was attacked
and this was met by a counter-attack on surrounding forts by
contingents of troops from several foreign warships anchored in
nearby Taku Bay. It was presumably during the capture of the
north-west fort that the gingall was taken. The Boxer Rising ended
with the signing of a truce on 7 September 1901, after a successful
action by an international force. A number of leaders were
executed and a large indemnity had to be paid, but the main result
of the truce was to leave things much as they were before.

(5) *St Cuthbert's and the Tale of the Long Pack*

It was recorded by Reginald of Durham that a miracle occurred in
a church at Bellingham in the twelfth century. Whatever credence
we may give to this, it is at least reasonable to assume that he
would hardly have been mistaken about the existence of the
church. It is possible that this referred to an early wooden
structure, but it may have been the stone one that was erected in
its place towards the end of the century. Nearly four centuries

St Cuthbert's church at Bellingham.

later, in 1597, this second building was the refuge of the people of Bellingham when attacked by a party under the Earl of Buccleugh, although the choice was not a good one and it fell after a short bombardment with cannonballs. Not surprisingly in the circumstances, the church was reported to be in a ruinous state only a few years later and a major restoration had to be undertaken. It was at this restoration that the thick stone vaults in the nave and transept, which are so much admired today, were put into place. A final restoration took place in the 1860s.

To the north of the church is a long gravestone which is associated with the episode of the 'Tale of the Long Pack' which took place at Lee Hall, a short way downstream from Bellingham. According to the story, a travelling pedlar called at Lee Hall and asked permission to leave a long pack there while he went in search of lodgings. During the night a servant noticed the pack moving and, suspecting that someone had been left behind with intent to rob the house, fired at it, wounding whoever was inside. More than one version of the tale exists and the final outcome – apart from the thwarting of the robbery, of course – is in some doubt!

Route 3   Holy Island

Holy Island or Lindisfarne is the island of St Aidan and St Cuthbert, and one of the most popular tourist attractions in Northumberland. Judged purely on its merits as a walk, the way described here is slightly lacking in distinction, but no holiday in Northumberland – nor any book on best walks there – would be complete without a visit to the island. As some 100,000 people visit it each year, almost all of them between spring and autumn, winter is by far the best time to come, when peace and quietness bring out its true character. (The castle, however, is only open from April to September.) Ornithologists will also prefer winter, for Lindisfarne is an important site for over-wintering wildfowl and waders.

Length: 4¼ miles (7 km).

Ascent: None.

Starting and finishing point: The main car-park in the village (75-128421). On reaching the village turn down Green Lane, the car-park is on the L at the end of the street. There is also a large reserve car-park on the castle approach.

Maps: Landranger 75; Pathfinder 452 (NU 04/14).

Note: Holy Island can only be reached (and left) by car or on foot by crossing the Causeway – see (1) – from the mainland. This is covered at high tide and it is dangerous to attempt to cross around those times. Generally it may not be fordable for a period from approximately 2 hours before to 3½ hours after each high tide. Information about this may be obtained from local Information Centres and from notices at each end of the Causeway. The tides come in with considerable speed, and cars and people are occasionally caught by them; for this reason a refuge has been provided at around the mid-point.

Route description (Map 3)
Holy Island, as its name implies, is one of the great centres of Christendom; before visiting it, read (2) Lindisfarne and (5) Lindisfarne Priory for a general account.

Leave the car-park into the road and turn L into Sandham Lane. Turn R and walk along to a T-junction where you turn L. Head directly towards the castle – see (3) Lindisfarne Castle – running parallel with the shoreline. Just before the castle go through a small gate. The entrance to the castle is up the cobbled path to the R, but this route forks L to pass the castle on its L-hand side. Beyond the castle reach the sea wall by a bridge and continue to the shoreline, bending L to a further small gate.

Keep on the clear path which runs to the R of a fence for ¾ mile (1.2 km). Near a small lake (The Lough) reach a stile and then go ahead to a stone wall. (Half-R you will see a prominent white pyramid, and a short diversion can be made to it from this point.) Cross and turn L along a path which runs to the R of the

MAP 3

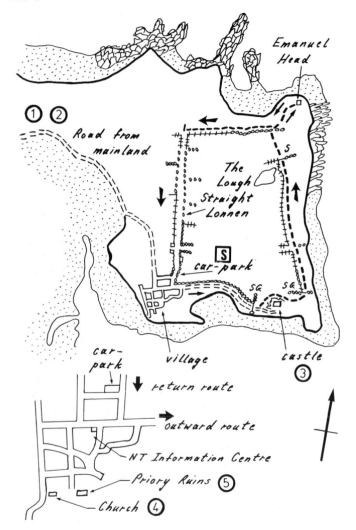

Emanuel Head

① ②

Road from mainland

The Lough
Straight
Lonnen

SB

car-park

S

village

castle

③

car-park

return route

outward route

NT Information Centre

Priory Ruins ⑤

Church ④

wall and later a fence. After nearly ½ mile (800 m) reach the end of a lane (Straight Lonnen) and turn L. Follow this back to the village, arriving down Sandham Lane by the car-park.

Before leaving, explore the small village, particularly the church – see (4) – and the Priory with its museum – see (5). Of more interest to some may be the shops, tea-rooms and public houses.

(1) *The Causeway*

The Venerable Bede described Lindisfarne as being 'twice each day enclosed by the waves of the sea and twice joined to the mainland with the ebbing and flowing of the tides'. This description is as appropriate today as it was in his time at the beginning of the eighth century, for the island is still cut off twice each day and the only way on to it, other than by boat, is across Holy Island Sands at times of low tide. The traditional way until early this century was by the Pilgrim's Causeway which ran to Chare Ends just north of the village; this was marked by a line of poles around 1860. The present causeway, which takes a shorter and more direct line to the western end of the island (called The Snook), was constructed in 1954.

(2) *Holy Island (Lindisfarne)*

Holy Island is situated about 10 miles (16 km) to the south-east of Berwick-upon-Tweed. The developed or cultivated part of the island is about 1 mile (1.6 km) square in extent, but there is a further area of dunes to the north (The Links) which extends to the west as a long peninsula called The Snook. The name 'Holy Island' came into use about the eleventh century; previously it was known as Lindisfarne, possibly derived from 'Lindis' the name of a stream on the mainland and the Celtic word 'Fahren' meaning 'a place of retreat'.

Some agriculture has been practised on Lindisfarne since at least the seventh century, but, apart possibly from the early monastic period, it has not been the main occupation of the islanders. Most of the time fishing was more important, employing a high proportion of the population. In the nineteenth century some two-thirds of the residents were employed in catching or in the subsequent cleaning of fish. This had largely ceased by the beginning of this century, however, and nowadays few boats operate from there.

A fair amount of industrial activity, mainly mining, has taken place on Lindisfarne. The kilns near the castle were built in 1860 for the burning of limestone quarried on the island; iron ore was also extracted in the seventeenth century by the Carron company from a seam between high and low water; and coal has been mined for short periods on The Snook.

Nowadays, of course, tourism has taken over as the main occupation of the island. In 1962 a small factory was built on the island for the production of mead which is sold to visitors; the same company also owns the Wine and Spirit Museum in Berwick-upon-Tweed.

(3) *Lindisfarne Castle*

Situated on Beblowe Crag, an outcrop of the Whin Sill, at the south-east corner of the island, the small castle is the most spectacular feature on Lindisfarne. It was constructed in the middle of the sixteenth century as an artillery fort to guard the small harbour at a time of Border troubles, part of the stone coming from the ruin of the old priory. It was taken on two occasions: the first during the Civil War when it acted as a Royalist base for land and sea operations in the north-east until taken by the Parliamentarians in 1645; and the second in dramatic circumstances in 1715 during the Stuart uprising. The armaments were removed in 1819 and it was later used as a coastguard station. Fortunately, it was purchased in 1902 by Edward Hudson, the founder of the magazine *Country Life*, and beautifully restored as a private house by Edwin Lutyens. It is now in the safe keeping of the National Trust to whom it was given in 1944, with a collection of oak furniture, by Edward de Stein and his sister, Gladys de Stein.

The statue of St Aidan, the first Bishop of Lindisfarne and an evangelist whose followers re-established Christianity in Northumbria.

(4) *The Parish Church of St Mary*

The church was built in the twelfth century as a separate building from the priory; additions were made later on two occasions and there was a major restoration in Victorian times.

(5) *Lindisfarne Priory*

In 635 a monastery was established at Lindisfarne by Aidan, a monk from Iona off the west coast of Scotland, under the protection of Oswald, a Christian convert who had his capital at nearby Bamburgh. (A previous monk, Corman, had returned home after finding the Northumbrians 'uncivilized people of obstinate and barbarous temperament', but apparently Aidan was made of sterner stuff!) Under him and his successors, the most notable of whom was Cuthbert who was Bishop for two years from 685, the monastery flourished and Christianity was brought not just to Northumbria, but also after 654 to the neighbouring Kingdom of Mercia.

In the following century and a half the monastery flourished – as did the Christian church generally. The arrival of Viking longships off the Dorset coast and the subsequent murder of the Reeve of Dorchester in 789, however, marked the end of that era; a conclusion confirmed by the sacking of Lindisfarne and the murder or capture of most of the monks on a January morning four years later. The latter event, in particular, sent a shock-wave of horror throughout the whole of Christendom.

The monastery was re-established and continued until 875 when is was deserted before the threat of a further Viking attack. The See founded by Aidan some two and a half centuries earlier, had come to an end. Carrying the body of St Cuthbert and the head of St Oswald, the monks moved first to Chester-le-Street and then later to Durham.

Following the Conquest a Norman bishop, William of Saint-Calais, was appointed to Durham in 1081 and Lindisfarne came under the jurisdiction of the Prior and convent of Durham. On

The ruins of Lindisfarne Priory. Lindisfarne Castle can be seen in the background.

their initiative a priory was built on Lindisfarne which was occupied until the Dissolution in 1537. From then onwards the buildings gradually decayed, partly from neglect and partly by deliberate plundering, and they were little more than ruins from the seventeenth century onwards.

The ruins which can be seen today are those of the priory founded in the eleventh century, no remains existing of the earlier buildings associated with Aidan and Cuthbert.

Route 4   Doddington Moor

A short but very pleasant route, which reaches the summit of Dod Law and then returns to the starting point over Doddington Moor to the north. The views from Dod Law are exceptionally good and would justify a visit on their own account, but most walkers will probably find the enigmatic 'cup-and-ring' markings near the summit area to be the most interesting part of the walk. The village of Doddington, which has an unusual church and the remains of a bastle, is worth a short visit before you wend your way home.

Length: 3½ miles (5.5 km).

Ascent: 500 ft (150 m).

Starting and finishing point: Doddington, about 3 miles (5 km) north of Wooler on the B6525, Berwick-upon-Tweed road (75-999325). Cars may be parked on a grass verge by the side of the main road, just opposite a row of cottages and a telephone box.

Maps: Landranger 75; Pathfinder 475 (NT 82/92) and 476 (NU 02/12) – almost entirely on the latter.

The decorated doorway on the west side of the Norman church at Lindisfarne Priory; this was the main entrance which would be used only on important ceremonial occasions. The gate was added early last century.

Route description (Map 4)

From the parking place, cross the road and turn R towards Wooler. By the old cross – see (1) the Bonny Dod Well – go L up the road signed 'Wooler Golf Club'. After a few yards, immediately after the houses on the R where the road bends, go R over a stile (PFS 'West Horton/Dod Law/Weetwoodhill'). Head up the grassy slopes half L (no path). Soon go over a crossing path and continue to the edge of an area of bracken. Follow a path which goes uphill through the bracken alongside a line of hawthorn bushes to a stile in a fence. Beyond the stile the path continues to rise up the hillside, with superb views opening up on the R.

Soon reach a cottage – see (2) the Shepherd's Cottage. Pass the cottage on the R and immediately afterwards turn L, going by the old kennels and the wall of a small enclosure. At the far corner go half R up the hill on a path, keeping to the R of some small crags. At the top reach a broad moor road and turn L for a few yards to find some marked stone slabs on the R – see (3) Doddington Moor. Retrace your steps along the moor road, continuing to the Ordnance Survey obelisk at the summit of Dod Law for a magnificent all-round view.

Again retrace your steps back to the gap in the fence. Go through and turn R and walk alongside the fence until you reach a stile after 50 yards (45 m). Go over and down the path directly ahead (i.e. in the direction of the yellow arrow on the stile). The path descends gradually across the moor to reach a fence junction. Cross the stile to the R and head towards the small group of trees on the ridge directly ahead.

At the trees, turn L and follow the edge of the field with a wall on your R until you reach a stile. Cross and keep in the same direction across a large field, heading to the L of a small hill with rocks (actually a quarry) and gradually leaving the wall. Go by the hill to a gate (PFS 'Westwoodhill') which leads into a lane. Turn L and follow the lane for 1¼ miles (2 km) back to the centre of Doddington.

As the walk is so short, spare about half an hour at the end for a

MAP 4

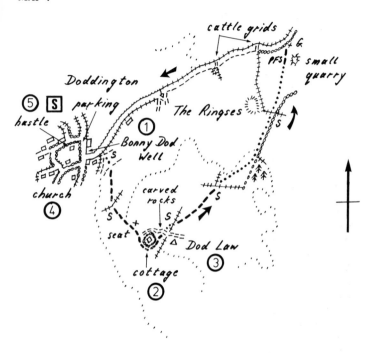

Doddington

cattle grids

G

PFs

small quarry

The Ringses

S

⑤ S
bastle

parking

① Bonny Dod Well

S

S

carved rocks

S

S

church

④

seat

cottage

②

Dod Law

③

short tour of Doddington – see (4) the Graveyard Watch and the rotating church, and (5) the Doddington Bastle.

(1) *The Bonny Dod Well (75-999324)*

This was originally a natural spring which supplied the village with water. The present cross was erected in 1846 by the Earl of Tankerville who was Lord of the Manor – on the design of the then incumbent, the Revd William Procter – when the old spring had got into rather a bad state. The water issued from the three openings in the base into the stone trough.

(2) *The Shepherd's Cottage (75-005316)*

This small cottage in a superb position just below the crest of the hill and facing out over the flat valley of the Till was occupied until the 1960s.

(3) *Doddington Moor*

The hilltop of Dod Law contains much evidence of prehistoric settlement. One camp, just to the north of the Shepherd's Cottage, is about ½ acre (0.2ha) in area and consists of a D-shaped main enclosure with a small annexe to the north-west; another further to the east of similar shape occupies about 1½ acres (0.6ha). The former contained a number of huts and was probably a farmstead with provision for stock enclosure, whilst the latter was perhaps used purely for stock. There is a third even further to the east on the opposite side of the Ordnance Survey obelisk, and just under a mile to the north-east on the other side of the moor is the hillfort of The Ringses made up of three ramparts. Probably more interesting to the visitor, however, are the so-called 'cup-and-ring' carvings which can be found on several rock faces. They consist of small hollows inside one or more concentric rings or rectangles, sometimes attached to straight or curving lines. Similar carvings have been found in Yorkshire, Dorset, and in parts of Scotland and Wales. They were probably carved about 2200–1400 BC, but their purpose is unknown.

The Bonny Dod Well at Doddington.

(4) *The Graveyard Watch and the rotating church (75-996322)*
The church of St Mary and St Michael was originally built in the
twelfth century with a nave and chancel and a further chamber or
tower to the west; as usual the altar was at the east end of the
church. By the early part of the nineteenth century the church was
in need of work and in 1838 the incumbent, the Revd William
Procter, commissioned Ignatius Bonomi to restore it. One feature
of this work was that the building was repaved 3 ft (about 1 m)
above its original level. At the end of the century further work was
carried out, in which the church was turned about so that the altar
is now at the WSW end. The reason for this is not known.

The small tower in the south-eastern corner of the churchyard
was a watchtower erected in 1826 to deter would-be body-
snatchers!

(5) *The Doddington Bastle*
The ruin in the centre of the village, half concealed by trees, is the
remains of a bastle (see page 322) built in 1584. Originally a
building of three stories with walls one yard thick, it has obviously
deteriorated considerably. So, for that matter, has Doddington
itself, which was once a much larger and more important village
than it is nowadays. The development of textile machinery which
put hand-loom weavers out of work, and the enclosure of
Doddington Moor early in the nineteenth century, are two factors
blamed for this.

Route 5   The mouth of the Aln

From its source near Alnham, at the eastern extremity of the
Cheviot Hills, the Aln heads generally eastwards until it makes its
exit through a series of tortuous meanders into the North Sea at
Alnmouth. This lovely walk explores the final mile or two of the
river between Alnmouth and Lesbury, returning to the starting
point along the beach and over a ridge which gives a bird's-eye

The Shepherd's Cottage below Dod Law. Some well-defined 'cup and ring'
carvings can be found at the top of the hill just behind the cottage.

view of the town and coast. Lacking in length and with little
climbing – and with a beach, ice-creams and teashops at the end! –
this is an ideal walk for that lazy summer afternoon when the
bigger and more demanding routes fail to inspire. *Note*: A short
section of shoreline used on this route may be impassable or
inadvisable at high tide or in bad weather. It is recommended,
therefore, that you obtain information about the tides and weather
before you start, and that you take these into consideration.

Length: 4½ miles (7 km).

Ascent: 250 ft (80 m).

Starting and finishing point: The car-park near the beach at the end
of The Wynd at Alnmouth (81-250107). A fee is charged for parking.

Maps: Landranger 81; Pathfinder 477 (NU 21/22).

Route description (Map 5)
Leave the car-park, go on to the beach and turn R. Walk along the
beach, soon curving to the R into the mouth of the Aln. Cross the
dunes and go up some steps on the right to the road; there turn L
down Riverside Road. On the opposite side of the river you will see a
prominent hill with a cross – see (1) Alnmouth. Soon the road swings
R by a children's play area; at the end of the play area go L through a
stile (PFS 'Lovers Walk to Duchess Bridge') and along a footpath to
the river bank. Keep by the river until you reach a bridge.

   Go up some steps into the road and cross to the opposite side,
then turn L along the footpath. Keep on the footpath for nearly ¼
mile (400 m) to the entrance to Alnmouth & Lesbury Cricket
Club; turn R through the small gate immediately beyond this.
Follow the path to the L of a hedge and passing the cricket
pavilion, soon going through a small gate and bending to the R
behind some houses. Continue beyond the last house for 75 yards
(70 m), then go L to a small gate which leads into a lane. Turn R
over a footbridge and up a path to reach the road in Lesbury
opposite the church – see (2) Lesbury.

MAP 5

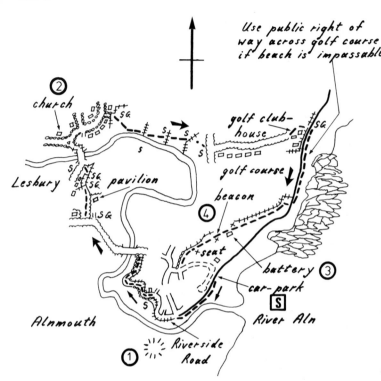

Use public right of way across golf course if beach is impassable

② church

Lesbury

pavilion

golf club-house

golf course

beacon

seat

battery ③

car-park

S

River Aln

Alnmouth

① Riverside Road

Turn R and follow the road through bends, over a crossroads and up a hill. At the top of the hill, where the road bends L, go R at a PFS ('Foxton Hall/Alnmouth') and up a path to the R of Hawthorn Cottage to a small gate. Go ahead by a fence and then, where this bends L, walk slightly R down the field to reach the river at a bend. Follow the path at the edge of the field, with the river to the R, to a ladder stile. Go over and up half L by a fence and a row of hawthorns; where these end continue up the field in the same direction to a second ladder stile. Cross the next field keeping in the same direction to another stile, then go up L to reach a road. From these fields there are good views to the R of the Aln meandering over its flat flood plain.

Go down the lane opposite (PFS 'Foxton Hall') until you reach the club-house of the golf-course. There go to the L of the members' car-park down a path which leads to the beach. Turn R along the beach, walking over the sands or long 'pavements' of rock. (If the beach is covered it is possible to use a public footpath which goes through a gap to the R just before the club-house, by a green and then across the fairway to the beach – but, otherwise, the beach is much better.)

Go along the beach for about ¼ mile (400 m) until you reach a pile of concrete blocks at the edge of the dunes with the first of several breakwaters in sight. Go back about 60 yards (50 m), then L (i.e. R to your original direction) up a narrow path to reach a fence. Turn L and follow the fence (there are some caravans on the opposite side) which soon bends R across the fairway of the golf-course, away from the beach. On the opposite side of the fairway you should pick up a clear path which continues up the ridge, with the fence still to the R (rather obscured by bracken in summer). The path goes along the ridge, with lovely views to the L of the sea and ahead over Alnmouth, soon passing to the R of a small fortification – see (3) the Percy Artillery Volunteers – and then a tall metal beacon – see (4) the Armada celebrations.

The lovely estuary at Alnmouth. The small hill on the far side of the river was the site of St Walaric's chapel built in the twelfth century.

At the end, drop down to reach a road at a junction. Go L down the road back to the car-park.

(1) *Alnmouth*

Settlement at Alnmouth goes back to very early times for there is an earthwork on Beacon Hill to the north of the town and a carved Saxon cross has also been found there. Its history as a seaport dates from the twelfth century and by the eighteenth and nineteenth centuries it was one of the most flourishing ports on the Northumbrian coast, with a lively trade in grain and timber. John Wesley visited it in 1748 and several times later; since he described it as a '. . . small seaport, famous for all kinds of wickedness', no doubt he considered his services to be much in demand. John Paul Jones, in command of ships of the American Navy, also paid it a visit in 1779 and bombarded the town. The small green hill on the opposite side of the Aln, known locally as Church Hill, was originally on the north side of the river and the site of St Walaric's Chapel, built in 1147. A great gale in 1806 was responsible not only for destroying the remains of the chapel but also for changing the course of the river. Nowadays, Alnmouth is largely a seaside resort, a delightfully unspoilt place with superb sands and two golf-courses.

(2) *Lesbury*

Lesbury was Lechesbiri about 1190 and Lescebyry in 1254, both names meaning the 'place or town of the leech or physician'. St Mary's Church, reached during the course of the walk, contains some twelfth-century work, but was extensively restored in Victorian times.

(3) *The Percy Artillery Volunteers*

The small fortification near the path as it climbs over the ridge was a battery '. . . erected by His Grace Algernon Duke of Northumberland, KG for the use of the Percy Artillery Volunteers . . .' and completed on 12 March 1861. There is a small stone plaque on the front which records the event.

The Aln, looking up-river towards Lesbury.

(4) *The Armada celebrations*

The tall metal structure also passed on the ridge was one of the string of beacons which were lit around the country to celebrate the 400th anniversary of the victory over the Spanish Armada, held in 1988.

Route 6   Happy Valley

A delightful route which follows lovely grassy paths high above Coldgate Water to North Middleton and then returns along the opposite bank of the river to the starting point. There should be little problem with route-finding, as the outward part of the route is well waymarked with yellow arrows and the return route keeps generally close to the river on a clear path. Prospective walkers will be delighted to know that there is a tea-room at Colgate Mill, strategically placed at about the midpoint of the walk (open July–September). Other areas of the country have their own 'Happy Valleys'; in this case the name may have been the invention of ladies at nearby Middleton Hall at the beginning of this century.

Length: 4½ miles (7 km).

Ascent: 325 ft (100 m).

Starting and finishing point: A wide grass verge at the roadside near Skirl Naked (75-977250) on the Wooler side of the bridge. There is ample room for cars. An alternative starting point is the National Park car-park near Middleton Hall (75-995257), but this will necessitate a walk down a quiet country lane before Happy Valley is reached, adding 1½ miles (2.5 km) to the total distance, with very little to show for it.

Maps: Landranger 75; Pathfinder 475 (NT 82/92).

The bridge at Skirl Naked at the confluence of the Carey and Harthope Burns. The parking area, which is the start of Route 6, is at extreme right.

MAP 6

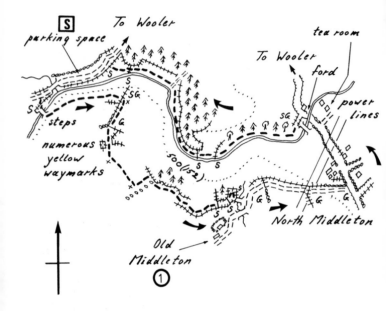

S

parking space

To Wooler

tea room

To Wooler

ford

power lines

steps

numerous yellow waymarks

500 (152)

North Middleton

Old Middleton

①

Route description (Map 6)
From the parking area walk down to the nearby bridge and cross
it. Immediately after the bridge, where the fence ends on the L, go
L over a stile (PFS 'Middleton Old Town/Nth & Sth Middleton')
and on to a footbridge. On the opposite side go up some steps and
along the clear path which goes across the hillside, overlooking the
river and parking area. Soon go through a small gate in a fence
and, after a few yards, turn R up the hillside keeping by the fence
to a gate. Continue to climb until the path curves to the L to run
once again across the hillside.

   Eventually at a broken wall and a small post (yellow arrows)
turn L downhill until you reach a fence. Turn R and follow the
path to a stile at the corner of a wood, then alongside the wood to
a further stile at the far end. There follow the fence on the L
around the edge of the field until you reach a third stile. Go
through and drop down half L to the footbridge a few yards away,
then up to a farm road. (This farm road leads R to the site of Old
Middleton – see (1).) Turn L through a gate and go down the farm
road until you reach the road at North Middleton.

   Turn L and follow the road, passing some houses and a large
farm, until you reach a ford after ⅓ mile (500 m). The Happy
Valley tea-rooms are to the R, just before the ford. Coldgate Mill
is now a private house with a few remains of the old mill itself.
Cross the river over the footbridge to the L of the ford (the ford
can be dangerous in times of flood). On the opposite bank do not
go to the road, but instead turn L on the clear path. Now follow
this path for 1¾ miles (3 km) keeping generally with the river until
a road is reached. There turn L for a short distance to the car-
park.

(1) *Old Middleton (75-990241)*
The small cottage, now in a state of ruin, indicates the site of the
village of Old Middleton or Middleton Old Town. Once
considered rare, lost or deserted villages are now known to be
common in the British countryside. Pestilence, devastation in war,
deliberate eviction by greedy landowners intent on increasing their
wealth or surrounding their houses with parkland, climatic

changes, natural disasters and even deliberate destruction in order
to further some great engineering project are some of the factors
which have played a part in the abandonment of villages, even in
quite recent times. Old Middleton is only one of the many
thousands of villages or hamlets which have disappeared down the
ages, unfortunately in most cases leaving us little or no record of
the life that was once lived there.

Route 7   The Duchess Trail and the Devil's Lapful

The Kielder Forest is one of the largest man-made forests in
Europe. It is appropriate, therefore, that at least one walk should
be found there. Of the many available, this is a particularly good
route which starts at Kielder Castle and climbs up into the forest
to visit two burial mounds, the Devil's Lapful and the Deadman.
Most of the way is along forest roads and waymarked trails which
give easy walking, but there are two descents along fire-breaks
which are of ankle-twisting propensity owing to ruts and fallen
timber. The route coincides for part of its way with two Forestry
Commission trails: the Duchess Trail and the Historic Trail;
leaflets for these are available at Kielder Castle.

Length: 4¼ miles (7 km).

Ascent: 400 ft (120 m).

Starting and finishing point: The car-park at Kielder Castle
(80-631934).

Maps: Landranger 80; Pathfinder 509 (NY 69/79); Kielder Water.
Northumberland Leisure Map (this shows almost the entire route).

Route description (Map 7)
For a better appreciation of the forest and the work of the
Forestry Commission, see (1) Kielder Forest, before starting.
   Leave the car-park by going into the road, and turn R down the
hill. At the bottom turn L along the path which leads to Kielder

Happy Valley.

Castle. There is an excellent exhibition on the history, work and natural history of the Kielder area in the Information Centre; see also (2) Kielder Castle. At the front of the castle go to the R to a notice 'Duchess Trail 1 Hour' (this walk will take longer) and from there to the L, down to the river bank. Go along the river bank until you come to a bridge.

Cross and take the path to the R (yellow arrow). Keep on this excellent path – part of the Duchess Trail, see (3) – as it enters the trees; information about the various tree species is provided on small plaques. Soon reach a broken wall – there is a rugby field down to the R, see (4) – and follow the path through a gap and uphill. Higher the path bends to the L and contours the hillside at a higher level.

Reach a wall and walk along its R-hand side. When the wall ends, continue for a few yards, then turn R uphill on a narrow path to reach a higher forest road. Turn R. After ½ mile (800 m), at a T-junction turn back half L. Later turn back half R at the first forest road on that side. At the top cross a fire-break and continue along a level section. The pile of stones on the R in a small clearing is the Devil's Lapful – see (5).

Continue along the forest road from the Devil's Lapful for about 300 yards (270 m), then turn R down a fire-break. (If you miss this you will find the forest road bending to the L soon afterwards.) Care is needed in the descent, for the long grass may conceal broken branches and ruts. Continue descending until you reach a forest road; there turn R. This leads to a T-junction. Go on to the L for about 200 yards (180 m) and then turn R down a second fire-break.

Descend into a small valley and then ascend on the opposite side to reach another forest road. (Just before you reach the forest road there is another cairn to the right – see (6) the Deadman.) Turn R and after about ¼ mile (400 m), where the forest road bends to the L, leave it to the L into a fire-break, as indicated by an orange arrow. Take a lovely path down into the forest following the arrows, and on to a small gate on the opposite side. Go through and half L down the field, to a gate and road at the bottom. Go R down the road to a T-junction.

MAP 7

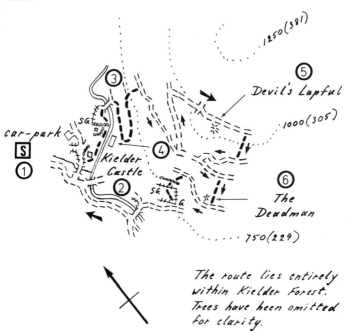

The route lies entirely
within Kielder Forest.
Trees have been omitted
for clarity.

Go L over a bridge and immediately turn R along a path on the L-hand bank of the river. Soon reach a road and go half L to a minor road which leads up to Kielder Castle and the car-park.

(1) *Kielder Forest*: see page 39.

(2) *Kielder Castle (80-632935)*
Kielder Castle, which is situated on the hillside above the confluence of the Kielder Burn and the North Tyne, was built as a hunting lodge by William Newton for Earl Percy, the Duke of Northumberland, in 1772–5. It was of a quadrangular plan – possibly to the Duke's own design – but was altered somewhat in the following century. The castle was acquired by the Forestry Commission in 1930 and now houses a restaurant, a book and souvenir shop and an exhibition on Kielder Forest. The Border Counties Line, opened by the North British Railway Company in 1862 from Riccarton Junction just over the Border to Hexham, had a station at Kielder about ⅓ mile (500 m) to the west of the castle. The line was single-track, but there was a passing loop at Kielder. The route of the line beyond Falstone, which closed in 1958, has long been submerged beneath Kielder Water, but the great ornate viaduct which carried the railway over the North Tyne still survives.

(3) *The Duchess Trail*
The trail is based upon a drive which was constructed by a Duchess of Northumberland so that she could while away the time while her husband was out hunting.

(4) *The rugby field* between the Duchess Trail and the river was the scene of a particularly vicious football match which was held towards the end of the eighteenth century. As the shooting was then particularly poor – probably owing to a disease which affected the birds – a whole-day game with an unlimited number of players was arranged to entertain the party, in addition to wrestling and

Kielder Castle.

various sports such as the long and high jump. At the end of the day eight people are reported to have lost their lives and several others died over the next week or two from their injuries.

(5) *The Devil's Lapful (80-642928)*

The great mound of stones to the right of the forest road is called the Devil's Lapful. It is at least 200 ft (60 m) long with its highest point at the far end, where it is about 40 ft (12 m) wide. Unfortunately sheepfolds have been built along the near side as you reach it, which have partly obscured the outline of the mound. It was probably built as a simple burial place for a notable member of a tribe or family in Neolithic times between 3500 and 2500 BC. In the days before the planting of the forest, the cairn would have been a conspicuous feature on the bare hillside, and paths came to it from all directions.

(6) *The Deadman (80-638922)*

Unlike the Devil's Lapful, this is a round cairn 60 ft (18 m) in diameter and nearly 5 ft (1.5 m) high. Although it has been opened in the centre there is, unfortunately, no record of what remains were discovered there. The Devil's Lapful was already old when this was built, probably in the Early Bronze Age, 1700–1400 BC.

Moderate routes

Route 8   Budle Bay

This is a lovely route which consists of two quite separate parts: the first along the coast from Bamburgh to Budle Bay with fine views over the Lindisfarne National Nature Reserve; and the second along field paths back to the starting point. Some time must be saved for Bamburgh, however, with its superb castle and church, and for a visit to the Grace Darling Museum. The first part of the route is best taken along the beach followed by Harkess Rocks, but this way may be impassable at high tide or in bad weather, and the road should then be used.

Length: 6½ miles (10 km).

Ascent: 200 ft (70 m).

Starting and finishing point: The large car-park by the castle at Bamburgh (75-183349).

Maps: Landranger 75; Pathfinder 465 (NU 13/23).

Route description (Map 8)
The magnificent castle at Bamburgh, which towers over the car-park, is open to the public – see (1) Bamburgh Castle for information about it – but leave it until your return.

   Leave the car-park by going into the road, and turn L. Go round the bend and then cross over to a footpath with a PFS 'Lifeboat Cottage ¼'. This goes alongside the castle, with the playing-fields to the L. At the end of the castle wall turn down to the beach. On the beach turn L and walk along it for ⅔ mile (1.1 km) until you reach a lighthouse – the rocks nearby have a white stag painted on them. (For those who prefer it, or if the tide makes the beach impassable, there is an alternative start along the road. For this, do not go down to the beach, but instead take the L-fork at the end of the castle wall; at the road turn R and follow it to the lighthouse.) Looking back half R along this section you should have a good view of several islands; these are famous for their seabird populations – see (2) the Farne Islands.

Go into the road and continue along it until you reach the entrance to the golf-course by the club-house. Continue ahead (PFS 'Budle Point ¾') along a clear path across the course – beware of golfers. Soon pass a quarry and then later a wall corner, both on the L. Go along by the wall until you reach a gate in a corner which takes you on to a metalled road. Go L, with caravans to your R, soon reaching a gate which leads into another road. The large bay, Budle Bay, over to your R, is part of an important nature reserve – see (3) Lindisfarne National Nature Reserve.

Go through the small gate almost directly across and follow a wall up a rough pasture. Where the wall meets a fence, go through a gate and head half R diagonally across a large field. At the end enter a road through a gate. Turn R and walk along the road for ¾ mile (1.2 km) to a road junction. Before the junction there is an information board on the R and an excellent view over Budle Bay. At the junction turn L along a quiet lane away from the main road.

After ½ mile (800 m), in a dip with woods on each side, go L through a small gate (PFS 'Drawkiln Hill') and up half R. At the top the path bends L to the R of a fence to reach the edge of a field after about 200 yards (180 m) – note the limekiln over to the R. Keep on the path on the L-hand side of the field to a gate, then go half L to another gate which leads into a wood. Go up through the wood to a gate at the top, then keep in the same direction to still another gate which leads into a caravan park. Go through the park, keeping to the bottom edge by a hedge, to a small gate at the far end which leads into a road.

Go L in the road and follow it to a T-junction; there turn L and after 50 yards (45 m) R through a gap. Take the path which runs to the L of a fence. At the end go over a fence in a corner and on, to the R of a row of trees, to a stile to the R of a wood. Pass the wood to the R, keeping roughly parallel with it until you reach a stile in a hedge. Go through into a lane and turn L. At the main

MAP 8

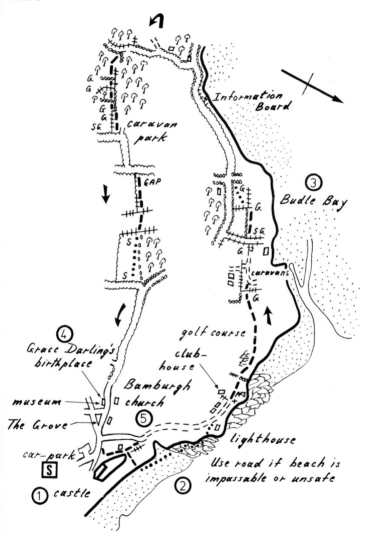

caravan park

Information Board

③ Budle Bay

GAP

caravans

golf course

club-house

④ Grace Darling's birthplace

Bamburgh church

museum

The Grove

⑤

lighthouse

car-park

Ⓢ

① castle

②

Use road if beach is impassable or unsafe

road turn R and follow it back to Bamburgh, keeping on the grass verge on the R.

As you go through Bamburgh watch out for some of the features associated with the local heroine, Grace Darling – see (4). On the opposite side of the road from the churchyard you will find her birthplace marked with a small plaque. Just beyond is the Grace Darling Museum. After finding these, cross the road to the small gate leading into the churchyard and walk down the L-hand side, passing in turn her grave and the memorial to her. Pay a visit to the church – see (5) – before leaving by the main entrance. Cross the road and after a few yards turn R down the road which runs along the top end of the central wooded area (The Grove). At the end turn L, so that you walk down towards the castle on the R-hand side of the road. You will find the house where Grace Darling died about half-way down. Keep on down the R-hand side of the road until you reach the car-park where you started.

(1) *Bamburgh Castle (75-183351)*

The immense natural strength of the long flat-topped and steep-edged ridge of the Whin Sill, which runs roughly parallel with the shoreline at Bamburgh, must have been obvious to anyone with half an eye for the siting of fortifications, and it has been in use in one way or another since prehistoric times. The great castle which dominates the small village of Bamburgh today, however, was the product of a long process of intermittent building in the twelfth and thirteenth centuries. The earliest castle probably consisted of the square keep and a bailey occupying half of the total area. Later came the enclosure of the entire area by the construction of an outer bailey and then a western bailey, although the main curtain walls of the castle were extended to include only the first of these. The entrance to the castle in its final form was at the south-eastern corner and consisted of an outer barbican and drawbridge in addition to the main gateway.

Since that time the castle has been extensively altered and

The lighthouse between Harkess Rocks and Budle Point, which is passed on Route 8. The Stag Rock is immediately before the building.

restored, the first time following its purchase by Lord Crewe in 1704 and the second time by Lord Armstrong after 1890. Some of these changes have been strongly criticized. The grounds and some rooms of the castle are open to the public for part of the year and are well worth visiting.

(2) *The Farne Islands*

The Farne Islands, which can be clearly seen to the north-east of Bamburgh, mark the most easterly visible reach of the Whin Sill. The number of islands varies with the state of the tide from fifteen to about twenty-eight, and there are in addition a number of dangerous rocks just under the surface. Apart from some small outliers they are divided into two groups, the Inner and Outer Farnes, separated by the deep Staple Sound about ¾ mile (1.2 km) wide. According to the Venerable Bede, St Aidan used to visit the Farne Islands to find the solitude necessary for his meditation and St Cuthbert lived there for nine years from AD 676 and again from 687 until his death. The cell where St Cuthbert lived was probably the spot where a church was built in 1370; this was restored in 1844–8 and is now known as St Cuthbert's Church. Near the church stands Prior Castell's Tower which is a pele tower erected in about 1500. As the Farne Islands are a danger to shipping, several lighthouses have been built there. High Lighthouse on the Inner Farne, at the extreme south-west corner of the group, was built in 1809 and is still working, but unmanned. The Longstone Light at the far north-east corner of the Outer Farne, built in 1825 to replace a less well-placed one on Brownsman, is still fully manned.

For most visitors, however, the main attractions of the Farne Islands are the seabirds and the seals. The best time to see the former is in May and June at the height of the breeding season, and the latter in November and December, when calves can be seen. There are eider on the Inner Farne – known as 'St Cuthbert's chickens' because of his love for them; puffins with their large and multi-coloured beaks; crowded colonies of guillemots; cormorants on outlying Megstone; shags, terns, gulls

Stag Rock.

and fulmar petrels. The seals which frequent the Farne Islands are the Grey or Atlantic seals which, although common here, are among the rarest in the world. It was very appropriate that the islands were acquired by the National Trust as the result of a public appeal in 1925. Inner Farne and Staple Island are open to visitors who can reach them from nearby Seahouses.

(3) *The Lindisfarne National Nature Reserve*

This highly important reserve covers an area of 8,150 acres (3300 ha) from Goswick Sands in the north to the Bamburgh side of Budle Bay in the south, and includes part of Holy Island. Of this about 88 per cent is mud-flat with small areas of sand, sand-dune and salt-marsh. Visitors are allowed to all parts of the Reserve, but are advised to consult the reserve notices which indicate danger areas on Goswick and Cheswick Sands (unexploded ordnance) and Fenham Flats (soft mud). Particular care should be exercised during the seabird breeding season from early April to end July. In the summer months eider bring their young here from the Farne Islands to enjoy shelter and plentiful food, but it is the over-wintering population of waders and wildfowl which is of the greatest interest. The wigeon flock is one of the largest in the country and that of pale-bellied Brent geese the largest outside of Ireland, but other birds are present in impressive numbers.

(4) *Grace Darling and the wreck of the Forfarshire*

Grace Horsley Darling, the fourth daughter of William Darling, the keeper of the Brownsman and then later the Longstone lighthouse on the Farne Islands, was born on 24 November 1815 in a small cottage opposite the church in Bamburgh. When she died on 20 October 1842, at the tragically early age of twenty-six from tuberculosis, she was famous throughout Victorian England. Even today she is remembered with great affection in her native village.

Her fame rests solely on the events of 7 September 1838 when the steamship *Forfarshire*, on passage from Hull to Dundee (which it did four to five times each month) with about sixty passengers

Bamburgh Castle.

and crew, struck rocks at the most westerly point of Big Harcar in the Farne Islands. The accident appears to have been caused by a combination of engine failure and misjudgement by the captain in very difficult circumstances. The accident occurred at four o'clock in the morning and was observed shortly afterwards by the Darling family who were living on the Longstone Lighthouse in the Farne Group further to the east. Using the family coble – an open rowing-boat 21 ft (6.4 m) long and 6 ft (1.8 m) wide – and taking advantage of the shelter of the Harcars, Grace and her father succeeded in reaching the wreck and in rescuing five survivors. Later William Darling made a second trip – this time with two survivors and without Grace – and rescued a further four. The entire operation took only about two hours.

Without belittling the contribution made by Grace Darling, it is likely that the initiative and seamanship which made the rescue possible came largely from her father. Another rescue party was involved that night – also showing courage and skill of the highest order – and the crew of the steamship managed to get one boat away, which saved the lives of another nine people. Nevertheless, it was Grace's contribution which was most noticed and which made her a national figure almost immediately. She received an enormous amount of attention; her bravery – and that of her father – was recognized by the award of several medals; and a public subscription list was opened for her. Her story was then – and later – made the subject of numerous plays, poems, articles and books. Even today, interest in her shows little sign of abating.

(5) *The Church of St Aidan (75-178350)*
The present church was built towards the end of the twelfth or the beginning of the thirteenth centuries as an Augustinian monastery church, probably on the site of the earlier Saxon church where St Aidan died in AD 651. With the dissolution of the monastery it

The memorial to Grace Darling in the graveyard of St Aidan's church; this was built to replace the original which was damaged by a gale in 1893. Grace Darling's remains lie in the family grave a few yards away towards the road.

MAP 9

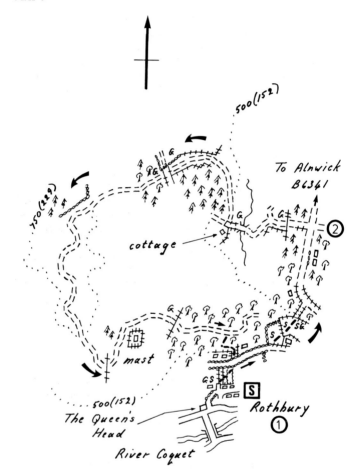

500(152)

To Alnwick
B6341

750(229)

cottage

②

mast

500(152)

The Queen's
Head

Ⓢ Rothbury

①

River Coquet

became the parish church. Its most interesting feature is a vaulted crypt below the south end of the chancel.

Towards the west wall of the churchyard is a memorial to Grace Darling; this is the second on the site, since the original, erected in 1844, was removed in 1885 owing to weather damage. The actual grave – and that of her father, mother, sister and brother – is a few yards away towards the road.

Route 9   The Rothbury Terraces

This is a short and easy route which follows some of the old carriage-ways of the Cragside estate. With the exception of the final descent to the finishing point at Rothbury, where care is needed in locating the correct point to strike down a steep wooded hillside, the route-finding is easy and the walking surface excellent. The outstanding feature of the walk, however, is the extensive view over the Coquet valley to the Simonside Hills south of Rothbury and further away to the Cheviot Hills. The route passes the main entrance to Cragside, which is owned by the National Trust, but the house and extensive grounds deserve a long stay and are better left to another day.

Length: 6 miles (10 km).

Ascent: 800 ft (240 m).

Starting and finishing point: The centre of Rothbury (81-056017). There is ample parking both in the main street and in car-parks.

Maps: Landranger 81; Pathfinder 500 (NU 00/10).

Route description (Map 9)
From the centre of the town walk eastwards along the B6341 Alnwick road, turning L up a side road immediately after the Queen's Head. The road soon bends half R uphill and then R at the top. Immediately after this second bend, go L up a path between a fence and hedge. At the top go through a small gate

and follow a clear path which slowly climbs across three fields to a higher road. Turn R and walk along the road.

Immediately after the wood end on the L, go L over a ladder stile and follow a grassy path which goes half R up a large field. Soon cross a stile above a house and continue to climb to a small gate at the top of the ridge. Continue in the same direction, descending steeply through a wood to reach a road. Turn L uphill.

After ½ mile (800 m) turn L down a forest road immediately opposite the entrance to Cragside – see (2). Follow the road as it goes to a gate and then bends down into a valley. In the valley, cross a bridge and go up to a cottage on the L. Go through the gate directly opposite the cottage (PFS 'Crocky's Heugh') and up a moor road. This soon curves to the L around a coniferous wood and on to a gate. Go through the gate and then through a second gate directly opposite.

The way is now quite clear. Keep on the firm moor road for 2½ miles (4 km) as it runs around the top of the hill. This moor road was one of the carriage-ways laid out in the Cragside estate for the Armstrong family. Eventually pass a prominent mast – a TV aerial erected to improve reception in Rothbury – and continue to a gate which leads into a deciduous wood. Go through the gate and follow the lovely path beyond. After about ⅓ mile (500 km) watch carefully for a flat-topped rock outcrop just inside the wood on the R; there are several initials and dates cut into the rock surface. (If you miss this, note that shortly afterwards the path bends sharply to the L.)

Turn R off the path and, passing the rock outcrop, descend steeply through the woods, taking care to avoid further outcrops lower down the slope. At the bottom reach a crossing path and there turn L, passing some houses. This path leads to the road that you came along earlier. The return path to Rothbury is on the opposite side of the road to the R.

Rothbury is a pleasant enough place to finish the walk, although it lacks features of great interest. There is, however, a good Information Centre and a church worth a visit – see (1).

The entrance (south) front of Cragside, most of which was built in the period 1872–4.

(1) *Rothbury*. Information on the history and features of the town is given on page 213.

(2) *Cragside (81-074022)*
The history of Cragside began in 1863 with the purchase of 20 acres (8 ha) of land by Sir William Armstrong from the owner Archdeacon Thorp. On this he erected a two-story lodge which could be used for occasional periods in the summer time – for the rest of the year his main residence was at Jesmond Dene in Newcastle. Soon after its completion, about 1866, the Armstrongs decided to make Cragside their main residence, and commissioned the architect Norman Shaw to design a much larger house. Work on the new house began in 1870 and was complete by about 1874, but further alternations and additions were made until Armstrong's death in 1900, by which time the house was substantially as it is today.

Throughout the remainder of his life Armstrong continued to add to the estate, and the original 20 acres (8 ha) had grown to 1729 acres (700 ha) by the end of the century. Thirty-one miles of carriage-ways and paths were laid out, five lakes – four of considerable size – were created, and seven million trees (mostly conifers) planted, which transformed the previously bare rocky hillside into a well-forested one. After Armstrong's death the estate went to his great-nephew and then through his descendants; finally, in 1977, passing to the Treasury along with some of the estate in part-settlement of death duties. It was handed over to the National Trust who opened it to the public after considerable restoration.

William Armstrong – later 1st Baron Armstrong of Cragside – trained and practised originally as a solicitor, but at the age of thirty-seven set up the firm of W. G. Armstrong & Company on the Tyne, which specialized in hydraulic machines. The latter part of the nineteenth century saw the firm grow into a huge industrial concern with a principal interest in armaments; after amalgamations it became Vickers Armstrong in 1927. This success

The suspension bridge, Allen Banks.

was due not only to Armstrong's business acumen, but also to his interest and ability as a scientist and engineer. These interests were reflected in the work at Cragside, which was the first house in the world to be lit by electricity derived from water power.

Route 10   Allen Banks

The course of the River Allen from the confluence of its two tributaries to its junction with the South Tyne near Bardon Bridge is through a deep, wooded, limestone gorge of immense beauty and great ecological importance. It is appropriate, therefore, that much of it is now in the safe keeping of the National Trust and part has been designated as a Nature Reserve under the guardianship of the Northumberland Wildlife Trust. This walk – one of several that could be worked out in this area – follows the river through some of its finest moments. Although the banks are beautiful at any time of the year, spring and autumn are probably the best. On fine summer weekends the paths hereabouts can be very busy and Plankey Mill is a popular spot for picnics – see (1).

Length: 6½ miles (10.5 km).

Ascent: 600 ft (185 m).

Starting and finishing point: The National Trust car-park near Ridley Hall (87-798641). Drive along the A69 from Bardon Mill towards Haydon Bridge, turning right along a minor road after about 1 mile (1.6 km). Follow this over the South Tyne and then under a railway bridge, taking the left fork immediately afterwards. The car-park is on the right after ¼ mile (400 m) (toilets). A small donation is requested for parking – and should be given to support the Trust in its fine work.

Maps: Landranger 87; Pathfinder 546 (NY 66/76) and 547 (NY 86/96).

The River Allen.

MAP 10

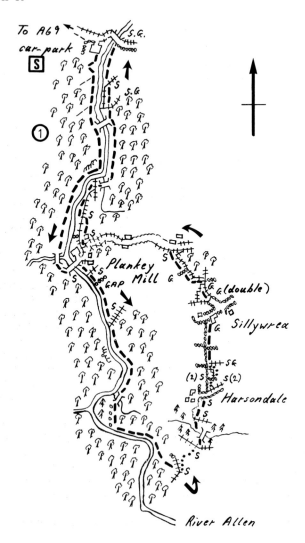

To A69
car-park
S

S.G.

S

S.G.

①

Plankey
Mill

GAP

G

G (double)

Sillywrea

G

SG

(2) S   S(2)

Harsondale

S

S

S

River Allen

Route description (Map 10)
Take the clear path from the far end of the car-park, reaching the
river bank after a few yards. Follow this path, ignoring all side
paths, for nearly ½ mile (800 m) until a suspension bridge over the
river is reached. Do not cross, but continue on the same side for a
further 1 mile (1.6 km) to a second suspension bridge (Plankey
Mill).

 Cross the bridge. Immediately on the other side, go R over a
stile and follow a path through meadows along the L bank of the
river. The path crosses three fields and then enters a wood over a
stile. Keep by the river, later moving higher to the L to find a very
clear path which gradually rises high above the river. Soon, where
the river bends to the R, go over a small footbridge and then
alongside a broken wall. Where the wall ends, reach the river
again and turn L. Keep on the clear path as it rises slowly, away
from the river, eventually reaching a stile in a fence on the far side
of the wood.

 Cross and then turn L for a few yards to a corner; there turn R
and head directly up and across the open area towards the far
reach of the wood. Enter over a stile and follow a clear path which
descends to a footbridge, then rises to a stile at the far side.

 Go straight ahead to a hedge corner and then to the R of the
hedge to reach a road near a farm, Harsondale. Turn R. After
150 yds (140 m), where the road bends, go over a stile on the L
and up the field, keeping by the L-hand wall. At the top go over a
stile and turn R to a second stile in a fence. Cross, turn L and
follow the fence around a corner to a wall. Follow this wall down
the hillside to the farm of Sillywrea, going through a gate between
the house and a barn.

 Turn R along the lane past the barn, turning L after a few yards
through double metal gates into a side lane. At the end of the lane
enter a field through a gate and go down the field, curving to the R
to a gate at the bottom. From the gate go ahead along the bottom
edge of the field, keeping to the L of a fence. Continue to follow
this fence as it curves to the L around a wood, eventually reaching
a lane.

 Turn L and follow the lane which leads down to the suspension

bridge over the Allen at Plankey Mill which was crossed earlier.
Do not go all the way to the bridge but turn back half R along a
rough lane, about 125 yds (115 m) before reaching the buildings.
After 50 yds (45 m) go L over a stile and along a path to a ladder
stile to the L of a ruin. Beyond, follow the clear path which keeps
to the R of the river for 1½ miles (2.5 km), eventually to reach a
road bridge. Go under the bridge and up R to a gate which leads
into the road. Go R over the bridge and along the road back to the
car-park.

(1) *Allen Banks*
185 acres (75 ha) of land was given to the National Trust by the
Hon. Francis Bowes-Lyon in 1942, along with covenants over a
larger area of the Ridley Hall estate nearby. Further small areas
have been given or purchased since that time, including the old
kitchen garden of the Hall which now forms the car-park where
this walk starts.

Route 11   The Wall: Steel Rigg to Housesteads

Few would challenge seriously the assertion that the section of
Hadrian's Wall from Steel Rigg to Housesteads is the finest along
its entire length. It is also the one section where visitors are
allowed to walk along the top of the Wall. This superb circular
walk combines the whole of this section with a long parallel course
to the north which allows the full glory of the Wall and the
immense strategic importance of the Whin Sill to be appreciated to
the full. Adequate time must be allowed for a visit to Housesteads,
without which the walk would be incomplete.

Length: 7 miles (11km).

Ascent: 750 ft (225 m).

Spring tooth-harrowing using Clydesdales, Jock and Farmer, at Sillywrea
in the Allen valley.

Starting and finishing point: Steel Rigg car-park, just north of Twice Brewed on the B6318 Newcastle upon Tyne–Haltwhistle road (86-750676).

Maps: Landranger 86; Pathfinder 546 (NY 66/76); OS Historical Map & Guide 'Hadrian's Wall'.

Route description (Map 11)
Read the section on Hadrian's Wall – see page 33 – before you start the walk.

Leave the car-park by going into the road and turn R. At the bottom of the hill turn R along a farm road and over a ladder stile (PFS 'Hotbank'). Follow the farm road by a wood and go on to its end at another ladder stile. On this section there is a superb view, over to the R of Crag Lough and the long undulating craggy ridge of the Whin Sill – all looking very much as it must have looked to hostile tribesmen as they approached it from the north more than 1½ millennia ago. The two large crags which form the scarp face of the Whin Sill are well-known climbing crags – see (1).

After the stile, keep in the same direction along a path with a wall to the L. Soon pass a barn on its R and continue – initially by a wall and then across an open field – to a stile in a wall. The path now goes ahead to a ditch, bends R and then L to cross the ditch, and heads up the field to a stile in a fence by a gate. Now take the path across the field, aiming for the L-hand edge of the hill to the L of the farm (i.e. not the path which heads towards the wood). This reaches a stile in a fence with a farm road on the opposite side.

Go L along the farm road; this soon bends R and later fades away. Keep in the same direction along the top of a low ridge parallel with the Whin Sill, ignoring any paths going off to the L. You should pass to the L of a coniferous wood and by a limekiln – see (2) – and a small quarry, eventually to reach a ladder stile in a wall. After the stile follow the farm road which leads in the same direction. (Do not take the farm road to the L indicated by arrows – this is the Pennine Way, heading to the north.) The farm road dwindles to a path and leads to a coniferous wood which is entered

MAP 11

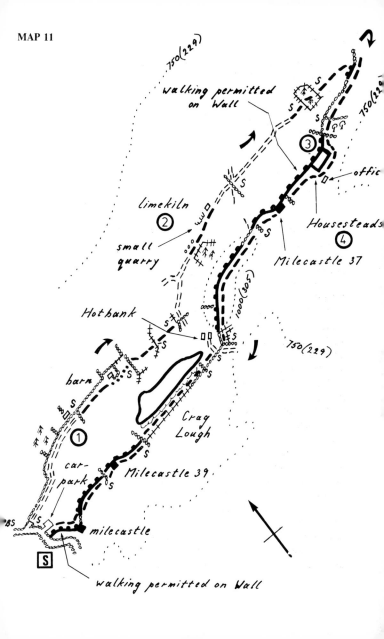

750(229)

walking permitted
on Wall

750(229)

S

S

S

office

③

limekiln

② Housesteads ④

small
quarry

Milecastle 37

Hothank

750(229)

1000(305)

S

S

S

barn

Crag
Lough

①

car-
park

Milecastle 39

BS

S

milecastle

S

walking permitted on Wall

over a stile. Follow the path through the wood, to leave it over a stile on the opposite side. Beyond, follow a path roughly in the same direction. This gradually goes down to the R of the ridge, heading at the end up to the R to a ladder stile and small gate in Hadrian's Wall.

Turn R and climb, keeping the Wall on your R. Follow the Wall over three tops, then down to a ladder stile in a corner. Go through a wood, leaving it at the far end over a further ladder stile. Now keep to the L of the Wall as it descends into a valley – see (3) the Knag Burn Gateway. Rise up on the far side to the fort of Housesteads – see (4). Go to the L, following the walls of the fort, until you come to the office/museum at the south-west corner. Visitors to the fort should pay an entrance fee at this office.

After the visit leave by the West Gate and turn R up to the Wall. (Walkers who do not wish to visit the fort should bypass it to the L to reach the Wall on the far side.)

See page 165 for the remainder of the route back to the Steel Rigg car-park.

(1) *Rock climbing on the Whin Sill*
Two considerable exposures of the Whin Sill can be seen as you walk parallel with the Wall. The first, Peel Crag, starts a short distance to the left of the car-park and the second is directly over Crag Lough. Climbs on both were recorded by Marcus Beresford Heywood in the journal of the Climbers' Club in 1912, but nothing more was noted until the 1940s. The main development took place in the period 1940—1970 and few climbs have been added since then; the 1970s and 1980s, in fact, saw a considerable drop in the popularity of both crags. Today there are nearly 200 routes of up to about 85 ft (26 m) in length, with some longer traverses. The climbs become harder in wet weather as the friction of the rocks reduces considerably.

(2) *Limekilns (86-779690)*
The spreading of chalk to improve land for pasture or for the growing of crops was known in Roman and medieval times and

Limekilns near Hotbank Crags.

was a common technique in the eighteenth and early nineteenth centuries. (In some areas, e.g. Hertfordshire, the practice was even reported as late as the First World War.) From the sixteenth century, however, this was supplemented by the use of burnt lime (quicklime), produced as the name implies by the heating or 'burning' of limestone. In the early days the limestone was burnt on open fires or in simple kilns produced by covering the fire with a layer of turf, a practice which survived until last century. By the eighteenth century, however the use of stone-built limekilns was widespread and in some areas virtually every farm had one in operation. Eventually, however, lime became available on a large-scale commercial basis, and with the improvement in transport the small local kilns fell gradually out of use. Superb examples of now disused limekilns, which were fed from limestone outcropping in the Wall area, can be seen on this walk and to the south near Crindledykes. The limestone and coal were fed in alternately from the top over a fire and the burnt lime was removed from the base.

(3) *The Knag Burn Gateway (86-791689)*: see page 248.

(4) *Housesteads (86-790688)*: see page 246.

Route 12   Dunstanburgh Castle

Dunstanburgh Castle, a mile or so north of Craster, has been in a ruinous state since Elizabethan times. In an area particularly rich in castles it remains, nevertheless, one of the most attractive; at its best on winter days when cold sea-mists envelop its shattered towers and walls. Starting from the small fishing village of Craster, this route takes in a magnificent section of the Northumbrian coast which includes the castle and two important seabird colonies. The walk passes the entrance to Howick Hall gardens which are open to the public each afternoon between Easter and September for a small fee.

Length: 8 miles (13 km).

Ascent: 350 ft (110 m).

Starting and finishing point: The car-park in the old quarry at Craster, a short distance along the road from the harbour (81-256197). A small parking fee must be paid. There are toilets and a National Trust Information Centre.

Maps: Landranger 75 and 81; Pathfinder 477 (NU 21/22).

Route description (Maps 12A, 12B)
See (1) Craster, before you leave, for a short account of the quarry area which is now a nature reserve.

Leave the car-park by going into the road, and turn R. Walk down to the harbour – see (2) the Memorial Harbour – and take the road to the L, soon going through a small gate. Go along a lovely green path with the seashore to the R. After just over ½ mile (800 m), go through another small gate and nearly ¼ mile (400 m) later, a third small gate. On the shore immediately to the R of this last gate you should see the remains of a ship – see (3) the wreck of the *Nova Scotia* – which can be reached at low tide. Over to the L is an area of marshy ground which was once a small harbour – see (4). After the gate keep on the path which slowly rises up to another gate which admits you to the castle. The castle is in the care of English Heritage and is open to the public – see (5) Dunstanburgh Castle.

After visiting the castle return to the entrance gate and turn R (i.e. L to your original direction), and walk along the path which passes the castle to the L. Soon reach the seashore again and look to the R for a superb view of a large seabird colony – see (6) Gull Crag. Then turn L and walk up the path parallel with the beach and heading away from the castle; as you go, notice the strange folded rock on the beach a few yards along. It is known as the Greymare Rock from its shape and colour. Keep on the good coast path for ¾ mile (1.2 km), parallel with the shore and to the R of a golf-course – see (7) the National Trust and Embleton Links. You should pass two pillboxes; about 100 yards (90 m) after

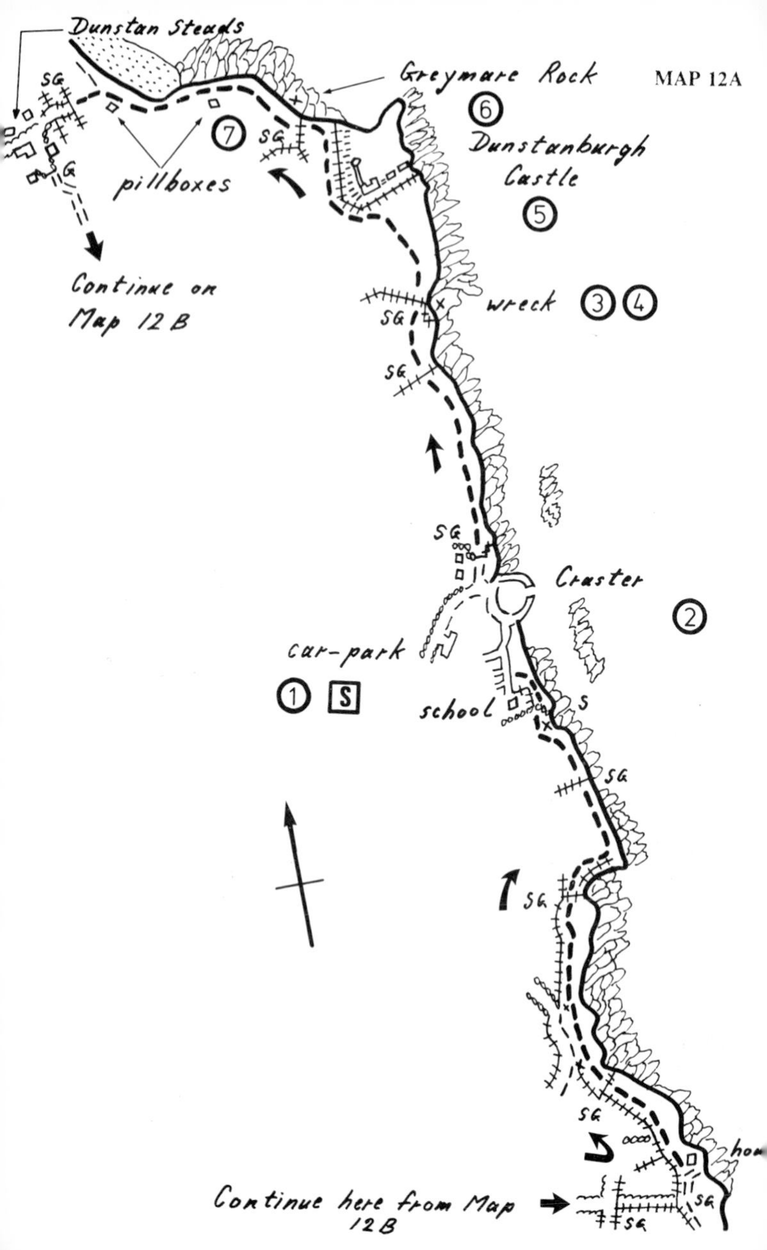

Dunstan Steads

Greymare Rock

Dunstanburgh Castle

⑥

⑤

wreck ③ ④

SG

pillboxes

SG

⑦

SG

Continue on
Map 12 B

SG

SG

SG

Craster

②

car-park

school

① S

S

SG

SG

SG

SG

SG

hou

SG

SG

Continue here from Map
12 B →

MAP 12B

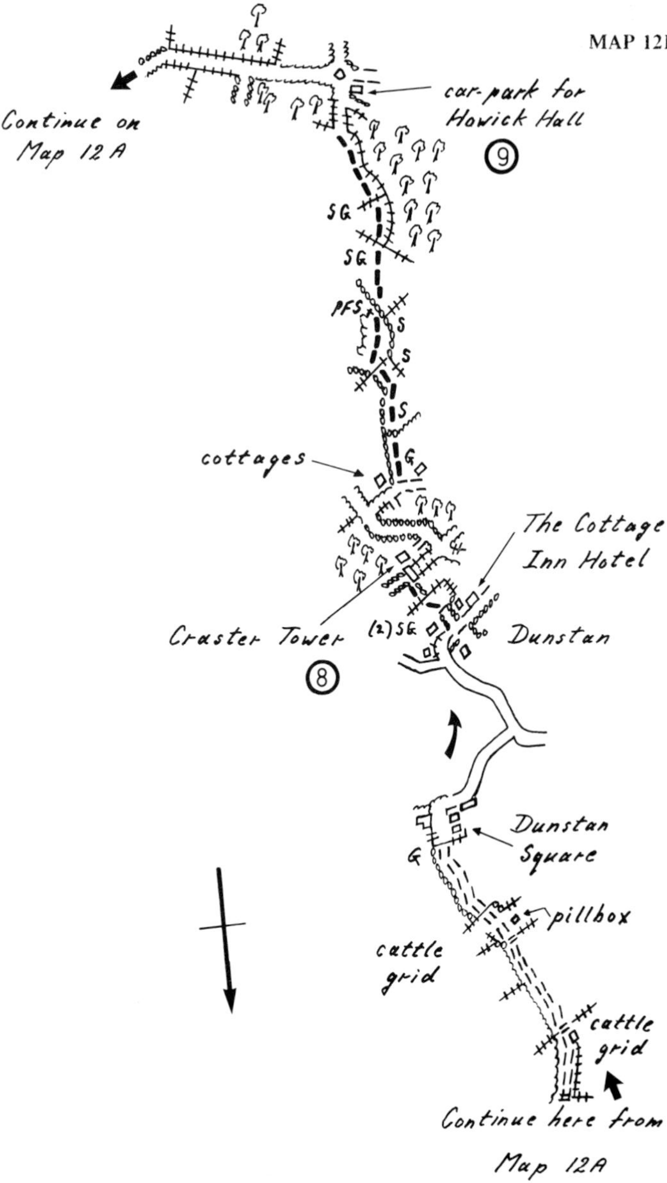
car-park for
Howick Hall
9
Continue on
Map 12 A
SG
SG
PFS
S
S
S
G
cottages
The Cottage
Inn Hotel
Craster Tower
(2) SG
Dunstan
8
G
Dunstan
Square
pillbox
cattle
grid
cattle
grid
Continue here from
Map 12A

the second reach a crossing path and turn L towards a large farm.
The path crosses a fairway (caution!) to the end of a road.

Go down the road until you reach a large farm, Dunstan Steads;
there turn L down a lane immediately before the buildings. Go
through the farmyard and the gate at the opposite end, then down
the concrete-surfaced road beyond. Follow this for 1 mile (1.6 km)
to the farm of Dunstan Square – just before the end there is an
unusual pillbox to the R made from cement-aggregate-filled
sandbags.

Go through the farmyard and into the road which immediately
bends R. Follow the road to a T-junction, then turn L. At the next
junction continue ahead to the hamlet of Dunstan.

Just before the Cottage Inn Hotel go L at a PFS ('Craster
Tower'). The path runs in front of a row of cottages to a small
gate, then half L across a field to another gate in a corner and by a
wall to a road. Turn R under an arch – Craster Tower is to the L,
see (8) – and down to a crossroads; there turn L. After a second
bend go R up a rough farmroad at a PFS ('Howick Hall Gates')
towards Keeper's Cottage.

Immediately after the row of cottages, go L through a gate and
up a path by a hedge. Cross a stile at the top and go up the next
field, still by the hedge, finally bending L with the hedge to a
ladder stile. From the stile go half R, keeping to the R of a long
crag. The path gradually approaches a ladder stile in a wall (PFS
'Howick Hall'). After the stile go slightly to the L across a field to
a small gate. Cross and follow the broad path, keeping to the
R-hand side of the field. Eventually reach a corner and turn R up
a farm road. This leads to the car-park and entrance gates of
Howick Hall – see (9). The entrance fee should be paid at the
small hut in the car-park.

Turn L and follow the road, passing a side turn, until it reaches
a T-junction. There go directly ahead through a small gate (PFS
'Coastal Path Craster') and on to a further small gate near to the
sea. Then turn L.

Go along the path parallel with the sea, passing a house to the
L. The path is quite clear, soon running just to the R of a road.
Beyond the road the path approaches a small gate at a prominent

cliff. Go through it and follow the path up to the R above the cliff. At the end the path bends L and runs parallel with the beach once more. Continue until you reach the old school building in Craster. There go over a ladder stile to the R and along by the school ground to a playing-field at the end. Turn L to a road and then R. Follow this road to the harbour at Craster, then turn L back to the car-park.

(1) *Craster (81-257198)*

Kippers and roadstone are the two products most associated with Craster, although the second of these is now no longer produced.

The roadstone was hard and durable quartz-dolerite, extracted from quarries in the centre of Craster which now house the car-park. From there the stone was taken in tubs on an overhead ropeway, over the village to two tall hoppers at the end of the southern jetty of the harbour, to be removed from there by coasters. The concrete base of the hoppers is still there, but the upper parts were removed during World War II as it was thought that they might serve as landmarks to the Germans in the event of invasion (production of stone had ceased just before the war). Since then the quarries have been established as a nature reserve under the care of the Northumberland Wildlife Trust and dedicated to the memory of Dr Lawrence Arnold, a distinguished ornithologist and botanist, in recognition of his work for nature conservation.

Kippers are produced by the smoking of herring, a fish which occurs in great numbers in the North Sea. Although efforts had been made to develop the British fishing industry since the seventeenth century, these were not really successful until the beginning of the nineteenth, which saw the building of large numbers of herring-luggers. The British herring industry reached its peak just before the First World War, since when there has been a great decline. This trend can be seen in Craster where the late-nineteenth-century fleet of forty-seven cobles and herring drifters has shrunk to its present strength of some four or five. Kippers, however, are still smoked in Craster, in a factory just opposite the harbour.

(2) *Craster Memorial Harbour (81-260199)*

The harbour at Craster was constructed in 1906 in memory of
Captain John Charles Pulleine Craster, 46th Punjabis, who was
killed in action during the Tibetan Expedition in June 1904. The
expedition was one of the more shameful incidents in British
colonial history. Largely owing to the urgings of Lord Curzon,
then Viceroy of India, the British Cabinet agreed in 1903 to a
military invasion of Tibet. This was based on the belief that it was
necessary to thwart Russian ambitions in the area, although it is
clear that such fears were totally unfounded. To make matters
worse, the leader of the expedition, Colonel Younghusband, was
never properly instructed as to the object of the advance and
under what circumstances it was to be terminated. On 11
December 1903 the expedition crossed the border and succeeded
in reaching the capital Lhasa by the following August. Major
engagements took place at Gyantse and at Lhasa, but a
combination of British Maxim guns and artillery was sufficient to
make them both little more than organized massacres. The loss of
life among the Tibetans was very heavy, among the British troops
very light. The signing of an Anglo-Tibetan Treaty in September
1904 – which was almost immediately allowed to lapse after
protests by several other European nations – brought about an end
to the affair.

The two small islands, which lie on each side of the harbour
approach are Little Carr and Muckle Carr. They are composed of
limestone, and hold beacons.

(3) *The wreck of the Nova Scotia (75-258212)*

The wreck which is visible at low tide is all that remains of a Polish
trawler, the *Nova Scotia*, driven ashore in 1958.

(4) *The Castle Harbour*

About ¼ mile (400 m) south of the castle entrance, a deep narrow
inlet served as a small harbour. The entrance is now blocked, but

The original gatehouse of Dunstanburgh Castle. This was replaced by a
new entrance on the north side of the castle in the time of John of Gaunt.

its position is marked by an area of marshy ground on the land side.

(5) *Dunstanburgh Castle (75-257219)*

The immense potential of the hill, on which Dunstanburgh Castle now stands, for the placing of a fortification must have been obvious from the beginning, and it is likely that there were settlements there in the second century and again in Anglian times. The present building was not begun, however, until 1313 when Thomas, Earl of Lancaster and High Steward of England, whose father had been given the land by Henry III in 1269, gave orders for the work to be started. It took about three years to complete. Earl Thomas himself, however, made little use of it, for he was executed at Pontefract after the Battle of Boroughbridge in 1322. The castle played a part in the Wars of the Roses when it was held for the Lancastrians, but was taken on two occasions: the first time by a Yorkist army in 1462 and the second time in 1464. Largely as a result of this, the structure was in a ruinous state by 1536 when the Royal Commissioners of Henry VIII inspected it, and has remained so to this day. It was given to the State in 1930 and is now in the care of English Heritage.

(6) *Gull Crag (75-258221)*

The long, dark, curving cliff which terminates at Castle Point is the nesting place in the spring and early summer months of large numbers of seabirds, in particular kittiwakes.

(7) *The National Trust and Embleton Links*

A large area of dunes and foreshore, including the golf-course, around Embleton Bay to the north of Dunstanburgh Castle, was given to the National Trust in 1961 by Sir Ivan Sutherland. A further substantial area of foreshore has also been leased from the Crown Estate Commissioners.

Lilburn Tower, built about 1325 for John Lilburn, Constable of Dunstanburgh.

(8) *Craster Tower (81-251196)*

Craster Tower consists of a tower house which was built before 1415 – since it was mentioned in a list of all the castles of Northumberland compiled in that year – and a wing which was added in 1769. The Craster family are said to have lived there since the thirteenth century.

(9) *Howick Hall (81-248175)*

The hall was built by Sir Henry Grey in 1782 with a drive that led to the south front. This was changed, around the beginning of the next century, by the building of a new entrance hall to the north, so that the drive could approach from that direction. Of great interest also are the extensive and beautiful gardens – possibly at their best in spring when the daffodils are out – which are open to the public in the afternoons from Easter to September. There is a car-park by the entrance where the entrance fee is paid.

Route 13   Vindolanda and the Wall

Apart from Hadrian's Wall, the Tyne Gap is notable for two other features: the Stanegate established by the Emperor Trajan, and the Military Road built at the end of the eighteenth century. This route combines them both with a superb section of the Wall and a visit to one of the Stanegate forts, Vindolanda. On no account should Vindolanda be missed, as the site is an excellent introduction to the Wall.

Length: 7½ miles (12 km).

Ascent: 1300 ft (390 m).

Starting and finishing point: Car-park at the Once Brewed Visitor Centre on the B6318, Newcastle upon Tyne–Haltwhistle road (86-752669).

Maps: Landranger 86; Pathfinder 546 (NY 66/76); OS Historical Map & Guide 'Hadrian's Wall'.

Route description (Map 13)
Before leaving, see the small exhibition at the Visitor Centre and read the section on Hadrian's Wall (page 33). The building just behind the Visitor Centre is the Once Brewed youth hostel – see (1).

Leave the car-park into the road and turn R downhill away from the main road. Cross the Brackies Burn and rise through bends. At the top of the hill immediately after the farm, Smith's Shield, turn L on to a side road (sign 'Hadrian's Wall/Vindolanda') – see (2) Transhumance. Keep on this narrow road for 1 mile (1.6 km) until you reach the Roman fort of Vindolanda. A visit to the fort is strongly recommended; particularly interesting are the reconstructions of a section of the Wall – see (3) Vindolanda.

Pass the car-park and entrance, and continue to follow the road, now rough and between walls, down into a valley. At the bottom, before the rise starts, go through the gate on the L to see a Roman milestone – see (4) the Stanegate. Then continue up the road, passing another car-park for the fort, to a T-junction. There turn L. From here there is a good view to the L of the Wall and the Whin Sill and back over Vindolanda. Keep on the Newbrough road, passing a road to the L after ½ mile (800 m) and another road to the R after ⅓ mile (1.1 km). About 100 yds (90 m) after the second junction turn L along a farm road and follow this to the farm of Crindledykes.

Go through a gate into the farmyard to the R of the house, and immediately R through a second gate. Follow the farm road down as it curves L to a third gate. Keep on the farm road as it goes over a large area of rough pasture, up to and over a small ridge with a cliff to the R. Beyond the ridge the farm road becomes narrower and goes up to a ladder stile which leads on to the B6318 – see (5) the Military Road. Go through the gate half R on the opposite side of the road and up the farm road which leads to the fort of Housesteads – see (6) Housesteads.

DO NOT PASS BY WITHOUT PAYING A VISIT TO HOUSESTEADS. A small entrance fee should be paid at the office/museum on the L as you reach the fort.

After viewing, go through the West Gate, i.e. on the L side as

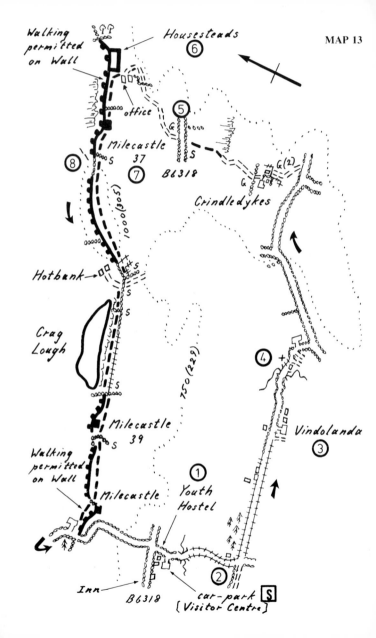

MAP 13

Walking
permitted
on Wall

Housesteads
⑥

Walking permitted on Wall

office

Milecastle
37

⑧

⑦

S

1000 (305)

⑤

S

S

B6318

Crindledykes

G(2)

G

Hotbank

S

S

S

Crag
Lough

750 (229)

S

④

+

Vindolanda
③

Milecastle
39

S

Walking
permitted
on Wall

Milecastle

①
Youth
Hostel

②

Inn

B6318

car-park
(Visitor Centre)

[S]

you view the fort from the office, and turn R up to the Wall. (If
you have insisted on ignoring my recommendation to visit the fort,
go up the L-hand side of the fort from the booking office, passing
the West Gate.) Climb on to the Wall and turn L (PFS
'Hotbank'). (As this is National Trust property, walkers are
allowed to use the top of the Wall in some parts.)

Keep on the top of the Wall until you reach a milecastle – see
(7) Milecastle 37 – then descend to its L-hand side. Keep to the L
as you follow the Wall through two dips – at the second of these
(Rapishaw Gap) the Wall is replaced by a drystone wall for a
distance – see (8) the Pennine Way. Keep following the wall as it
climbs to a hilltop and then bends to the L to descend by the farm
of Hotbank. The view half R over Crag Lough and the great cliff
of the Whin Sill is breathtaking and the finest along the Wall –
Roman legionaries and auxiliaries on duty on this section more
than 1,500 years ago probably found it much the same and just as
beautiful.

At the bottom the Wall bends to the R. Keep following it, soon
going over a ladder stile. Immediately go R over a second ladder
stile and keep on in the same direction to a third stile which leads
into a wood. Go through the wood and along the top – Crag
Lough is down to the R – until you reach a further ladder stile.

*At the time of writing major work is being carried out on the
section of Wall following, and the route may be changed: if so,
follow any signs.* Descend into dip to R of wall, crossing over at
the bottom. Rise up steps to the L of the wall, and go over the top
of a hill to a further gap with milecastle (39). The path goes over
to the R of the Wall to bypass the milecastle before returning to
the L.

After the milecastle go up some steps to the L of the Wall and
over the top of a hill, soon dropping down to a ladder stile in a
dip. (You have to work hard on this route!) Rise up again and
over another hilltop. On the far side the path goes to the R of the
Wall, dropping down to a temporary bridge, then up to meet the
Wall again on the opposite side. Keep by the Wall until you reach
a ladder stile which permits access to the top. Then walk along the
top until you reach the road at Steel Rigg. Turn L and follow the
road down to the car-park at Once Brewed.

(1) *Once Brewed youth hostel (86-752669)*
Apart from Rock Hall near Alnwick, this is the largest youth
hostel in Northumberland. It was re-opened in October 1987 after
extension and modernization which had started the previous year;
the work was made possible by financial support from the
Countryside Commission and Dr Daniel Rutenberg. It is an
extremely popular hostel, not just with Pennine Way walkers – the
Way comes along the Wall only a short distance away – but also
with school and other parties visiting the Wall area.

(2) *Transhumance*
For many centuries a common farming practice in hill areas of
England and Wales was for a farmer and his family to spend the
winter in milder lowland areas and then move for the summer
months with their cattle to higher common grazing grounds. In the
winter the family would live in a stouter and more permanent
building, but in the summer would occupy a small and simple hut
near to the pastures. The fields around the main farm in the valley
would thus be left ungrazed to produce hay for winter feed. In
England the custom ceased in the eighteenth century, but in Wales
it survived until the middle of the nineteenth. The last recorded
case of this practice (called transhumance) was in Snowdonia in
1862. The summer dwelling was called an 'hafod' in Wales and a
'shieling' in the north of England. The word 'shield' is common on
the Wall (Shield on the Wall, Gap Shield, Cawburn Shield, High
Shield, Smith's Shield) and marks the position of these shielings,
as does the word 'hafod' in Welsh place-names.

(3) *Vindolanda (86-770663)*
Built as one of the forts of the Stanegate around AD 90, it was
abandoned for a time when Hadrian's Wall was constructed. It was
reoccupied, however, in the middle of the second century and then
remained in use for nearly 300 years. The site is now owned and
managed by the Vindolanda Trust, a registered charity. The Trust

Sheep gathering in the area of the Wall. The Whin Sill can be seen in the
distance.

began a major excavation campaign in 1970, and the main finds
from this can be seen in the adjoining museum at Chesterholm.
The fort is also worth visiting for the excavated area of the civilian
settlement (*vicus*) – the best example available at present – and the
replica of parts of the Wall. For opening times contact
Chesterholm Museum, Bardon Mill, Hexham, Northumberland,
NE47 7JN. Telephone: Hexham (0434) 344277.

(4) *The Stanegate*

Under the governorship of Agricola or his successors, an east-west
road, called the Stanegate, was built through the Tyne Gap to link
the forts at Corbridge and Carlisle which guarded important river
crossings on the two great Roman roads that ran into Scotland.
Movement along this road was guarded by forts at Chesterholm
and Nether Denton, approximately one day's marching distance
apart. Following the withdrawal from Scotland, this road acquired
greater importance as it then marked the line of the frontier
between the Tyne and Solway. It has been thought that an
elaborate system of forts, fortlets and watchtowers was established
along the line of the Stanegate – that is, prior to the building of
Hadrian's Wall – to guard and to control movement across the
frontier, but the evidence for this is poor at the moment.

  The narrow road from the vicinity of Smith's Shield to beyond
Vindolanda, where the road bends to the south-east, marks the
line of the Stanegate. It is also joined again a short distance
further along, just before the route leaves along the farm road to
Crindledykes.

(5) *The Military Road*

The B6318 which runs to the south of the Wall is known as the
'Military Road'. The origin of this name is to be found in the
events of the 'Forty-five' uprising when General Wade, who was
commanding an English force at Newcastle on the east coast,
found that there was no road across country which would enable
him to close with the Scottish force under Charles Edward Stuart
(the Young Pretender or Bonny Prince Charlie) coming down the
west coast. As a result the rebel force succeeded in reaching as far

south as Derby before prudence dictated a retreat. The Military Road was authorized after the uprising to avoid any further problem along the same lines, but there was also considerable pressure from local landowners and tradespeople for its construction on commercial grounds. It was built in the 1740s by civilian labour and operated eventually as a turnpike with tollgates. From Newcastle it was built on the line of the Wall – and with Wall material – to a few miles beyond the fort of Carrawburgh, thus effectively destroying most of the Wall in the process. The difficulty of taking the road along the Whin Sill saved the centre section of the Wall from a similar fate.

(6) *Housesteads: see page 246.*

(7) *Milecastle 37 (86-785687)*
These fine remains were excavated in 1852 by John Clayton (1792–1890), who owned Housesteads and Vindolanda and part of the centre section of the Wall. Further excavations were carried out in 1907 and 1933. It was built by Legion II Augusta and occupied until the fourth century. This particular milecastle is known as a 'short axis' type because its north-to-south axis is shorter than the east-to-west axis. Of particular interest is the north wall which is the highest section of original Wall still standing.

(8) *The Pennine Way*
The Pennine Way, which has been following the line of Hadrian's Wall since Greenhead, finally leaves it at Rapishaw Gap and heads north towards the Scottish border. Walkers at this point who are on the Way are now on the last three or four days of a journey which probably began just under two weeks or so before, at Edale in Derbyshire. The Pennine Way, which is still the longest and toughest of Britain's National Trails, was the brainchild of Tom Stephenson, the first full-time secretary of the Ramblers' Association, and was opened in 1965.

Route 14   Featherstone Castle

Featherstone Castle is situated in lovely parkland a short distance
to the south-west of Haltwhistle, in the valley of the South Tyne –
a pleasant area of farmland, woods and steep, narrow, twisting
roads. This lovely – but only moderately long – route explores
some of the area's finest corners. In contrast to the Pennine Way,
which crosses rough moorland less than a mile to the west, the
walking here is largely over pastures, with one beautiful stretch
along the river. The old track of the branch line which ran from
Haltwhistle to Alston – now well grassed-over – is followed for a
short distance.

Length: 9½ miles (15 km).

Ascent: 550 ft (170 m).

Starting and finishing point: Haltwhistle (86-705639).

Maps: Landranger 86; Pathfinder 546 (NY 66/76) and 559 (NY 65/
75).

Route description (Map 14)
From the centre of the town – see (1) Haltwhistle – walk along the
A69 road towards Carlisle (there is a pavement all the way) until
you reach a road on the L signed 'Plenmeller/Whitfield/Alston'.
Turn L along it. Immediately before the bridge over the river, turn
R down a narrow lane. Follow this as it drops down to a bridge
and then rises up to the farm of Wydon. Continue on the road
(now rough) through the farm to a gate, and then beyond by a wall
to a second gate. In the next field the farm road bends to the L to
a further gate. Finally, go up the next field, keeping by a fence to a
fourth gate.
    Go half R across a large pasture towards a wood. At the wood
you should pick up the source of a small side stream and continue
on its R bank, passing a water trough, until you reach a stile in a
fence – i.e. do not enter the wood, but go to the R along its

MAP 14

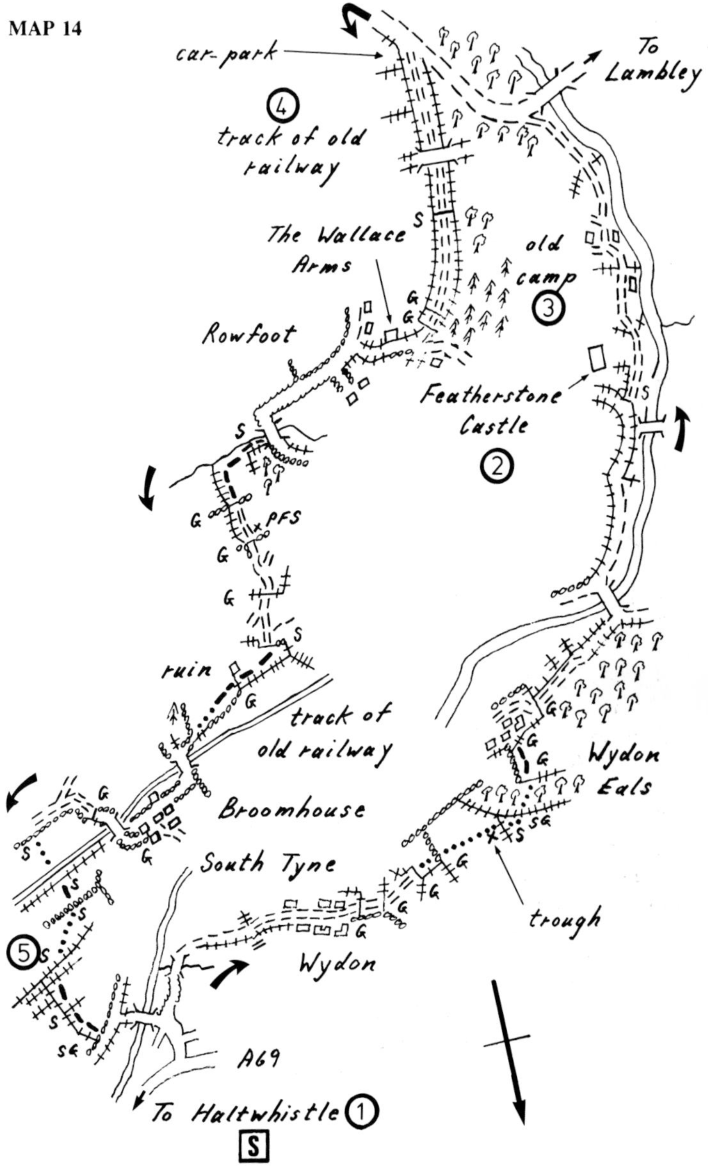

car-park

④
track of old
railway

To Lambley

old
camp ③

The Wallace
Arms

S

Rowfoot
G
G

Featherstone
Castle

②

S

S

G

PFS

G

G

S

ruin
G

track of
old railway

Wydon
Eals

G

Broomhouse

G
G

trough

South Tyne

S

S

⑤ S

Wydon

A69

To Haltwhistle ①

S

boundary. After the stile, continue along the edge of the wood by
a fence for about 150 yards (140 m) until you reach a small gate.
Go through it and descend half R through the wood, following the
direction of the yellow arrow, to reach a gate at the bottom. Go
through and to the R of a wall until you reach the farm of Wydon
Eals. Go into the farmyard and half R to a gate by a barn which
leads into a road.

Go through the gate ahead and down the road. After ½ mile
(800 m) reach a junction; there turn L down to a bridge over the
South Tyne. Immediately over the bridge turn R (along the
Featherstone Station/Coanwood road) and walk for another
½ mile (800 m) until the road bends to the L. Here turn R over a
stile by a gate and walk along the wide path parallel with the river.
Follow this path for 1 mile (1.6 km), until you reach a road. On
the way you will pass a large house – see (2) Featherstone Castle –
and then some semi-ruined brick buildings – see (3) Camp 18.

Turn L up the road until you reach a Nature Trail car-park on
the L. Turn into the car-park, leaving it at the far end along the
railway track. This track was originally the Alston Branch of the
Newcastle and Carlisle Railway – see (4) the Alston Branch. Keep
on the track for ¾ mile (1.2 km), until you reach a road. Go into
the road and turn R, soon passing the Wallace Arms. At a
T-junction turn L and follow the road until it bends L and drops
down to a bridge over a small stream. Immediately after the bridge
go R over a ladder stile (PFS 'Broom Houses/Linn Shield').

Go along the valley – parallel to the stream with a wood to the L
– until you reach a fence; there turn L and follow the fence as far
as a gate in a wall. (Do not go through a gate in the fence reached
earlier.) Go along the farm road from the gate to a second gate
(PFS 'Broom Houses'). The farm road now rises to some trees and
another gate. Immediately after this go L at a junction; this leads
to a fence corner and then a ladder stile. Go ahead to a fence;
there bend R to go parallel with the old railway track. Keep with
the fence until you reach a gate in a corner by a ruin.

Continue slightly L, aiming for the L-hand edge of some trees.

Tractor at work near Wydon Eals in the South Tyne valley.

At the trees continue in the same direction, aiming for the point where further trees meet the track; there you will find a ladder stile. Go along the lane between the wood and the track, soon turning L over a bridge and along to a farm. Go into the farmyard, turning L by a PFS ('Linn Shield'), then immediately R through a gate which leads into a walled lane. Follow this over a bridge and up to a gate; then keep by the wall on the L until you reach a ladder stile. Cross and drop down to the railway track and a further ladder stile. Go up the field to a gate and stile at the top. There is a good view of Haltwhistle from here – also see (5) Bellister Castle.

Now go half R down the large field until you reach a stile in the fence at the bottom. (*Note*: there are two stiles in this fence. Your stile is the R-hand one. If you make a mistake and take the L-hand stile, then it can be recognized because the path beyond *immediately* goes L, whereas your path drops down through bushes half R to a stile.) From the stile go ahead to a fence and follow it, keeping to the R-hand edge of two fields, to a road. Turn L and soon R to cross a bridge over the South Tyne. This brings you to the A69, where you turn R for the centre of Haltwhistle.

(1) *Haltwhistle (86-710643)*

This small market town was called Hautwisel in old documents of 1240 and Hawtewysill in Assize Rolls of 1279. The name probably meant 'the junction of streams by the hill', for the Haltwhistle Burn joins the South Tyne not far away, but other derivations are possible. It is an excellent place to start a walk, for there is car-parking and a railway station with good links to other centres between Newcastle and Carlisle. There are, moreover, excellent tea-rooms to revive your spirits when you finish. Those who prefer other types of spiritual uplift may find the Church of the Holy Cross, which was built in the thirteenth century, more to their liking. It contains medieval gravestones to the Thirlwall and Blenkinsop families and another which bears a long verse to John Ridley, 'The Lord of Walltown', who died in 1562. There is also

Featherstone Castle.

an old pele tower in the centre of the town – now part of the Red Lion Hotel, which will provide spiritual uplift of a third kind.

(2) *Featherstone Castle (86-677609)*

Situated on a haugh (i.e. an area of flat land by a stream) in a great curve of the South Tyne, the castle can be seen both from this walk and from the road which rises steeply up the hillside behind, although the buildings themselves are not open to the public. The oldest parts are on the west side; in particular, a strong tower-house built in the fourteenth century, which was a time when owners of manorial residences felt the need for some protection. Most of the rest was added early in the nineteenth century by Thomas Wallace, although the castellations give it the look of an older building.

The castle took its name from the Featherstonehaugh family who were the original owners and who held it for twelve generations from early in the thirteenth century. One member of the family was indirectly involved in a famous literary hoax perpetrated upon Sir Walter Scott. A poem written by a friend, Robert Surtees, describing the violent death of Albany Featherstonehaugh in a sixteenth-century border feud, was passed off as an old Northumbrian ballad to Scott, who unfortunately used part of it in his poem *Marmion: a tale of Flodden Field*, published in 1808, adding in a footnote that it '. . . was taken down from the recitation of a woman eighty years of age, mother of one of the miners of Alstonmoor'! With friends like that, who needs enemies?

(3) *Camp 18 (86-673603)*

The gateway, just beyond the castle, was the entrance to Prisoner of War Camp No 18 which housed thousands of German officers between 1945 and 1948. There are also several brick buildings further along, and the foundations of a number more. The gateway contains a plaque to Captain Herbert Sulzbach, OBE, an

Some of the old buildings of Prisoner of War Camp No 18, near Featherstone Castle.

interpreter at the camp, who '. . . dedicated himself to making this camp a seed-bed of British-German reconciliation'.

(4) *The Alston Branch*

The railway branch line from Haltwhistle to Alston was completed in 1852, although part of it had been opened for traffic the previous year. At Lambley it met a further line which served the collieries to the east towards Brampton Junction, but extensions to the south beyond Alston to Nenthead and into the Wear Valley, which had been proposed, were never built. The line had four stations on its 13-mile (21 km) length, apart from the two terminal stations. In its day it carried lead from the mines around Alston, coal from Lambley and agricultural produce from the South Tyne valley, although it was never an outstanding commercial success. Despite much opposition, the line was closed in 1976. In its day it was a very scenic route, the outstanding feature being a great nine-arch viaduct at Lambley.

(5) *Bellister Castle (86-701630)*

The castle lies a short distance from the route, but part can be seen during the final stages. It consists of two attached buildings set together on a mound: the first, the remains of a square pele tower built in the fifteenth century; and the second, a large three-storied house with two towers, mullioned windows and castellations, built in 1669. The contrast between the tower, built primarily for defence, and the house, intended mainly as a dwelling-place, reflects the changed circumstances along the Border between the two periods.

   The estate, along with three farms and several cottages, was acquired by the National Trust in 1976 as a bequest from Mr Edward Donaldson Jackson. The castle and estate are not open to the public except on public rights of way.

Route 15   Kielder Water

Kielder Water, one of the largest man-made lakes in Europe, lies at the heart of Kielder Forest, near to the western boundary of

MAP 15

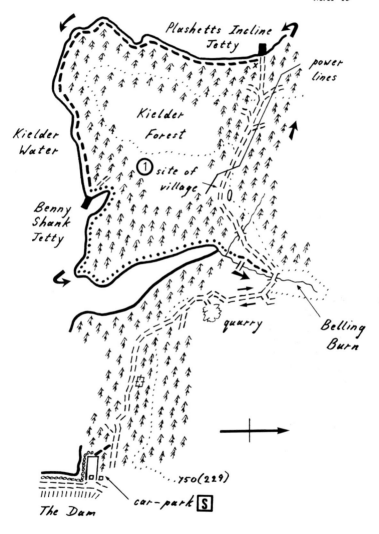

Plushetts Incline
Jetty

power
lines

Kielder
Forest

Kielder
Water

① site of
village

Benny
Shank
Jetty

quarry

Belling
Burn

750(229)

car-park S

The Dam

Northumberland. This route combines a long forest walk, which passes the site of an old colliery village, with a superb section along the north-east shore of the Water. The forest section along broad forest roads gives easy walking; the shore, by contrast, is difficult, with fallen branches and undergrowth to contend with, and about two-thirds of the total time should be allowed for it. Part of the way along the shore, from Plashetts Incline Jetty to Benny Shank Jetty, is extremely well waymarked, but little difficulty should be found in following the rest, for generally it stays within narrow limits between the shore and the tree-line. Although distant signs of civilization are evident throughout, the sense of isolation is remarkable.

At present between mid-March and the end of October a ferry calls at Plashetts Incline and Benny Shank Jetties; the walk can be reduced in length, therefore, by taking the ferry back from either of these two points. If possible, contact Bellingham (0434) 240436 beforehand to ensure that the ferry is running.

Length: 9 miles (14 km).

Ascent: 500 ft (150 m).

Starting and finishing point: Hawkhope car-park at the northern end of the Kielder Water dam (80-708883).

Maps: Landranger 80; Pathfinder 521 (NY 68/78); Kielder Water Northumberland Leisure Map.

Route description (Map 15)
For the history of Kielder Water and Forest, see pages 42 and 39.

Leave the car-park from the far end and follow a narrow path to a wide forest road. Turn L and follow this, ignoring any paths or other forest roads off it, for 1½ miles (2.4 km) until it crosses a broad bridge over a river (the Belling Burn). Continue along the

Plashetts Incline Jetty.

forest road, soon going by a small lake and into an open area by power lines. This open area is the site of the old colliery village – see (1) Plashetts Colliery Cottages. Continue along the forest road until you reach a three-way junction; there take the centre road which drops down to the L of power lines, with superb views ahead over the Water, until you arrive at a jetty on the shore. This is Plashetts Incline Jetty; a return can be made from here using the ferry when it is in operation.

Turn L in front of the Information Board and follow the path parallel with the shoreline. The route to Benny Shank Jetty follows the shore of the Water, keeping between it and the tree-line. Orange waymarks have been placed throughout, and footbridges built over side streams where required. After 2 miles (3 km) reach Benny Shank Jetty; a return can also be made from here when the ferry is operating.

At the picnic tables at the jetty turn L and walk up the L-hand side of the inlet, crossing over to the opposite side when it is convenient and safe to do so. Turn R down the opposite side and again continue between the tree-line and the shore, soon turning L with it into The Belling Inlet. Eventually reach a footbridge which crosses the Belling Burn at the head of the Inlet; do not cross, but continue along by the river until you reach a wide bridge and forest road. This is the bridge crossed earlier. Cross and follow the forest road back to the starting point.

(1) *Plashetts Colliery Cottages (80-685896)*
From the evidence of surface exposures it was thought likely that substantial coal deposits existed around the valley of the North Tyne south-west of Kielder. Difficulties of transport hindered any early exploitation, however; it was confined – apart from some fairly insignificant use by local families – to two small drift-mines on the Lewis Burn south of the river and by the Plashetts Burn to the north. The opening of a railway line through the valley in 1862, with stations at Kielder and Plashetts, allowed the possibility of more intensive commercial development, and a Plashetts Coal

The northern shore of Kielder Water.

Company was granted a lease to work the area of the Belling Burn. A small colliery was opened and several cottages were built for the miners and their families, the coal produced at the colliery being taken down on a branch line from the workings to Plashetts Station where it was sent away on mainline trains. The enterprise proved unprofitable, however, and in 1884 a new company took over the lease, only to be replaced in turn by a third company five years later. This last company met with greater success and continued to operate until the early 1930s.

With the upturn of fortune, the work-force increased and rows of cottages were built to house them and their families. Most of them were situated about mid-way along the branch line on the west side of the Belling Burn. At its height there were some sixty-four cottages with perhaps 200–300 people. There was also a school, a Methodist chapel, a village hall and a store. Eventually the original mine by Belling Burn was closed down and a new mine, New Hollin Colliery, with a separate branch line, opened just above Plashetts Station.

The site of the village, the line of the colliery railway and the incline down to Plashetts Station can all be found, although virtually all trace of the workings and buildings themselves have now disappeared.

Route 16 The Derwent Walk

The massive closures of railway branch lines which took place in the 1960s presented local authorities with a wonderful opportunity to create walking and riding trails. Some authorities pursued this objective vigorously and deserve the highest praise; others did nothing and let the opportunity slip through their fingers. The Derwent Walk, on the line of the old Derwent Valley Railway, is an example of what could have been done by all. It is a magnificent walk through lovely deciduous woodlands, best seen in the early spring after bud-break or in the autumn when the rich browns and reds are a tonic to the soul. At any time it is worth

Benny Shank Jetty.

doing. Tall viaducts, a long, deep, cutting near Rowlands Gill, and the remains of several old station platforms are the principal railway memorabilia. This is the only route in the guide which falls entirely outside Northumberland.

Several excellent leaflets are obtainable from Department of Environment, County Hall, Durham, DH1 5UQ, telephone: Tyneside (091) 3864411; and Thornley Woodlands Centre, Rowlands Gill, Tyne and Wear, NE39 1AU, telephone: Rowlands Gill (0207) 545212.

Length: 11 miles (18 km).

Ascent: 650 ft (200 m).

Starting point: The Swalwell Visitor Centre in the Derwent Walk Country Park between Blaydon and Whickham (88-199620).

Finishing point: Consett (88-101523).

Maps: Landranger 88; Pathfinder NZ 05/15 and NZ 06/16.

Public transport: At the present time there is a bus service between the start and finish of the route; information about the way to the bus stop at Consett is given at the end of the route description. A good alternative arrangement is for two car-owners to combine and leave cars at each end.

Route description (Maps 16A, 16B, 16C)
Before starting the walk read (1) the Derwent Valley Railway, and (2) the Derwent Walk Country Park.

At the entrance to the Visitor Centre area, facing the building, go through a squeeze stile by a gate on the L. This leads to another squeeze stile and then up to the railway track. There turn R.

Apart from a short section at Rowlands Gill, further route description is unnecessary as the way along the track is perfectly

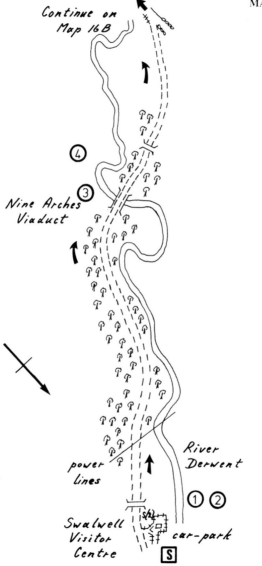

Continue on
Map 16B

④

③ Nine Arches
Viaduct

River
Derwent

power
lines

① ②

Swalwell
Visitor
Centre

car-park

S

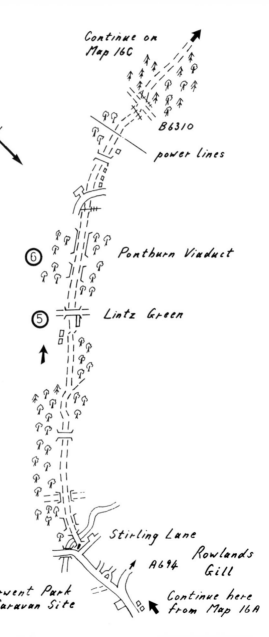

MAP 16B

Continue on Map 16C

B 6310

power lines

Ponthurn Viaduct

⑥

⑤ Lintz Green

Stirling Lane

Rowlands Gill

A 694

Continue here from Map 16A

Derwent Park Caravan Site

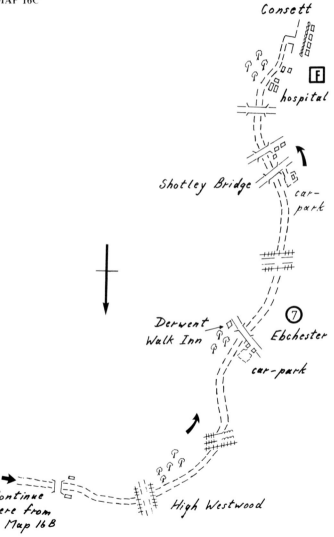

Consett

F

hospital

Shotley Bridge

car-park

⑦ Ebchester

Derwent
Walk Inn

car-park

Continue
here from
Map 16 B

High Westwood

clear until the end is reached at Consett. Only the main features of interest are mentioned therefore.

0 miles, 0 km: Swalwell Visitor Centre. This was opened in 1981 on the site of the former station. Toilets.

1¾ miles, 3 km: Nine Arches Viaduct – see (3). A lovely view can be obtained from here over the Gibside estate – see (4).

3 miles, 5 km: Rowlands Gill. Reach the road and cross to the pavement opposite. There turn L and follow the road to a junction after 250 yds (230 m). Cross back over the road and take the L-hand fork signed to Gibside Chapel. Just before a bridge cross Stirling Lane and immediately turn R on a path. This bends L across a bridge and back on to the track.

5 miles, 8 km: the small station of Lintz Green (platforms still extant) was the scene of an unsolved murder – see (5) the Lintz Green Murder.

5¼ miles, 8.5 km: soon after Lintz Green station the trail passes over two viaducts, the second of which is the Pont Burn – see (6).

7 miles, 11 km: High Westwood. The site of one of the stations on the original line.

8½ miles, 14 km: Ebchester Station. The Roman road of Dere Street crossed the railway line around the station area – see (7) Dere Street and Vindomora. Of more interest to walkers who arrive here around mid-day will probably be the Derwent Walk Inn just over the bridge.

9¾ miles, 16 km: Shotley Bridge. This was the last station on the line before Consett. Toilets and picnic area.

11 miles, 18 km: the trail reaches a road in Consett. For a bus back to Swalwell, turn L along the road, taking the first turn to the R after 150 yds (140 m). Follow the road down to a T-junction and cross to a bus stop on the opposite side.

(1) *The Derwent Valley Railway*

Under the spur of proposals (the Newcastle Derwent & Weardale Bill) from a group of rival railway companies for a line to Newcastle which would use the Derwent Valley, the North Eastern Railway Company put forward plans (the Blaydon & Conside Bill) for a line through the valley from Consett to

Newcastle. After a period of parliamentary in-fighting and some shrewd diplomatic moves on the part of the NER, however, the former proposals were withdrawn and the latter became law on 17 July 1862. The contract for the line was given to the firm of Morkill & Prudham of Duns who submitted the lowest tender of £150,036 (later increased to £163,000), and work began in 1865. Although the line was only approximately 11 miles (18 km) long, some considerable engineering work was required, notably viaducts over the Derwent at the northern end, in Swalwell over the Hexham turnpike, on each side of Rowlands Green and near Lintz Green. Some substantial cuttings had also to be dug. Despite this, the line was opened to goods on 18 June 1867 and to passengers six months later.

Commercial traffic included coal from the many collieries in the valley, milk from local farms to Tyneside, timber, bricks, iron ore and paper products. Passenger traffic came from the seven stations on the line and increased almost continuously until 1914, with twenty-one trains each day in the two directions. After 1920, however, a sharp decline set in, largely owing to the provision of bus services in the valley. By 1953 the position had deteriorated to such an extent that passenger services were withdrawn altogether, followed by commercial traffic in 1962.

(2) *The Derwent Walk Country Park*

The track of the Derwent Valley Railway between Swalwell and Consett, which had closed in 1962, was purchased by Durham County Council and, after work by that authority and Gateshead and Tyne & Wear, opened for walkers, cyclists and horse-riders as the Derwent Walk in 1972. This necessitated clearance of growth from the track, the repair of viaducts and bridges, the reinstatement of the drainage system, and the repair of bordering fences. Some planting was also carried out. Since then adjacent areas have been purchased and the whole has been designated as a country park with a total area of about 400 acres (162 ha). Visitor centres have been provided at Swalwell and near Thornley Wood, and there is a caravan- and camping-site at Rowlands Gill. In addition to the trail itself, several local history and nature trails are

open to walkers only, and special events are occasionally held there. The eastern section to Rowlands Gill is in the care of Gateshead Metropolitan Borough Council and the western section in that of Durham County Council. The Country Park and Walk are open at all times.

(3) *Lockhaugh (or Gibside or Nine Arches) Viaduct (88-181599)*
To the east and west of Rowlands Gill the line had to be brought across the Derwent, partly to bring it through the village and partly to avoid the grounds of Gibside Hall. This necessitated the building of two large viaducts. The first of these was 500 ft (152 m) long with nine arches of stone and brick, and reached a height of 80 ft (24 m). Originally intended for single-line working, it was widened later to take a second track.

(4) *Gibside Chapel (88-179588)*
The chapel, which has been in the care of the National Trust since 1965, was designed by James Paine on the commission of Sir George Bowes, owner of the Gibside estate. Work began in 1760, but was not completed until early in the nineteenth century. The main feature of the chapel is the imposing front elevation with its double staircase, portico and central dome. The figure on the top of the tall column nearby – erected in 1757 – is 'British Liberty'. Excellent views of the chapel, the statue and the Gibside estate generally can be obtained from the Nine Arches Viaduct.

(5) *The Lintz Green Murder (88-150567)*
The small station at Lintz Green was the scene late on the evening of Saturday 7 October 1911 of an unsolved murder. The victim was the stationmaster, Mr George Wilson, who was shot through the left breast a few minutes after seeing to the departure of the 10.45 p.m. passenger train from Newcastle to Consett. Although several passengers, his daughter and the booking clerk were on the scene almost immediately, there was no sign of his assailant and

Lintz Green Station on the Derwent Walk; the scene of an unsolved murder in 1911.

nobody was ever charged with the crime. Mr Wilson, who died almost immediately, was unfortunately unable to speak. There was some indication that robbery may have been the motive, although if so it was unsuccessful as the murdered man had almost no money on him.

(6) *The Pont Burn Viaduct (88-146565)*
This was the largest viaduct on the line, with a length of 600 ft (183 m) and a height of 120 ft (37 m); each of the ten arches had a span of 60 ft (18 m).

(7) *Dere Street and Vindomora (88-106548)*
The great Roman road of Dere Street (see page 312) crossed the Derwent near Ebchester; its course now largely coincides with the line of the B6309. Where it crossed the river the small fort of Vindomora was built around AD 80, initially of clay and timber. After rebuilding with stone, the fort remained in occupation until the end of the fourth century.

Route 17   Blanchland Moor

Blanchland Moor, at the southern extremity of Northumberland where it meets its neighbour County Durham, is a superb area of heather moor, defined on the west by Devil's Water, to the south and east by the Beldon Burn, and to the north by the conifers of Slaley Forest. This superb route, which seeks out the best of the moor, follows old mine ways and packhorse trails, with a short stretch of pathless moor. Blanchland, where the route starts, is one of the loveliest and most interesting villages in the county and worth a visit on its own account.

Length: 9½ miles. (15 km).

Ascent: 1200 ft (360 m).

The old platform at Shotley Bridge Station; there are toilets and a picnic area to the right.

Starting and finishing point: The car-park in Blanchland
(87-965504). This is about 100 yards (90 m) from the centre of the
village.

Maps: Landranger 87; Pathfinder 560 (NY 85/95) and 570
(NY 84/94).

Route description (Maps 17A, 17B)
It is better to leave Blanchland until your return when you can also
enjoy the delights of the local tea-room, but see (1) Blanchland, to
whet your appetite.

Leave the car-park into the road and turn L. Follow the minor
road for ½ mile (800 m) to the farm of Shildon – see (2) – where
the metalled surface ends. Continue along the farm road ahead,
soon passing a barn, until you reach the next farm, Pennypie
House. As might be expected from its name, this has quite an
interesting history – see (3). Do not follow the farm road up to the
farm, but go through the gate ahead and continue along a moor
road with a small wood to your R.

After 100 yards (90 m), at the end of the wood where the moor
road bends, leave it to the L, keeping virtually in the same
direction and head up the moor to the R of a line of shooting
butts. If your direction is correct you will reach a ladder stile in a
wall. Cross and head half L up the moor beyond (no path). Go
over the top of the fell (Burntshieldhaugh) and down the other
side for a very short distance until you meet a clear crossing path.
Turn L along it. This is the line of an old packhorse trail – see (4)
Carriers' Way.

You should have no difficulty following the path, which is very
clear and partly in a holloway, as it runs along the edge of the fell
keeping more or less at a constant height. Soon pass a hut, and
then cross a wall at a gate. Later reach a fence and continue with
the fence to the L under some electricity cables to a stile. Cross
the stile and go up half L to a stone hut. Just after the hut you will
reach a wide moor road.

Turn R and follow the moor road until it peters out. Here keep
in the same direction over a stretch of pathless moor contouring

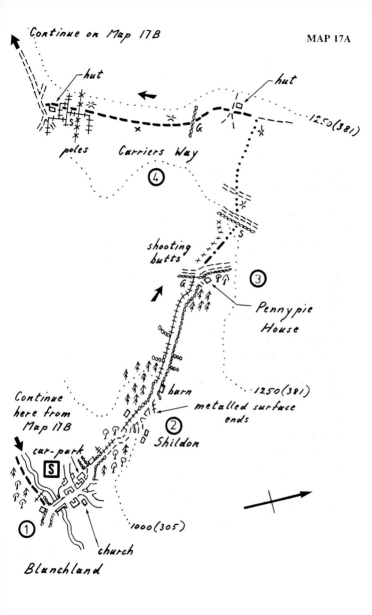

Continue on Map 17B

MAP 17A

hut

hut

1250 (381)

poles

Carriers Way

④

shooting
butts

③

Pennypie
House

1250 (381)

barn

metalled surface
ends

②

Shildon

Continue
here from
Map 17B

car-park

S

①

1000 (305)

church

Blanchland

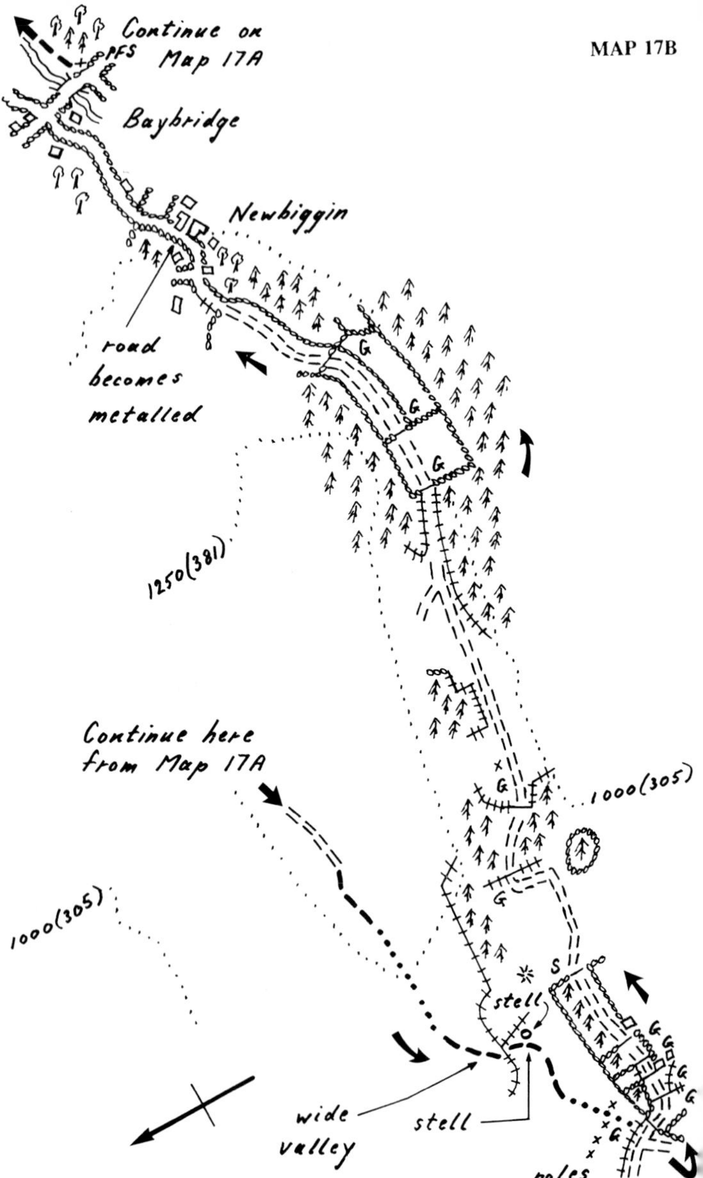

Continue on Map 17A

PFS

Baybridge

Newbiggin

road becomes metalled

1250(381)

Continue here from Map 17A

1000(305)

1000(305)

G

G

G

G

G

G

G

G

S

stell

stell

wide valley

poles

the slope. (Do not be lured down the slope to the R towards a coniferous wood and a stream valley.) After ¼ mile (400 m) you should reach the edge of a wide valley where it makes a meander. Here go down to the R to a shelf which can be seen slanting down and across the L-hand side of the centre spur of the meander. This will lead you down to the floor of the valley where you will meet a fence. Leave the path to the L and cross the fence over a wet area and up to the R of a stell (i.e. by crossing the valley floor). At the stell, bend to the R up an obvious path which goes to the top of the moor. On the moor keep in the same direction (again no path), keeping roughly parallel with two woods to the L. After ⅓ mile (500 m) reach a gate at the far L-hand corner of the moor by the second wood. Go through it into a moor road.

Immediately turn L through a gate and follow the farm road, soon reaching a deserted farm (Riddlehamhope). Go by the farm, continuing along the farm road. Keep on this lovely way for nearly 3 miles (5 km) until the way becomes metalled by the farm of Newbiggin; then go along the metalled drive for ½ mile (800 m) to a main road at Baybridge.

Turn R and follow the road over the river (Beldon Burn), entering County Durham. After 70 yards (60 m) go L through a gate (PFS) and along a path through a delightful wood to the R of the river. Soon reach a road near Blanchland and turn L down and over the bridge into the village. Go through the arch by the post office and up the road ahead, back to the car-park.

(1) *Blanchland (87-966504)*

In 1165 an abbey of Premonstratensian monks was established in Blanchland on land which had been given to them by Walter de Bolbec. The monks or canons of the Order – which took its name from the original abbey at Prémontré, near Laon, Île de France – wore white gowns and were noted for their strictness. Building continued until the early part of the sixteenth century, but much of the abbey and its estate was destroyed by the Scots in 1327, and it was finally closed by Henry VIII as part of the Dissolution in 1539. By the time John Wesley preached there in 1747, most of it was in a ruined state.

The Blanchland estates became the property of the Forster family and then Lord Crewe around 1700, passing into the care of the Lord Crewe Trust on his death in 1721. It was the Trustees of that charity who began the creation of a model village in 1752, possibly using the layout of the abbey buildings as a guide.

The result is a credit to them, for Blanchland is now widely regarded as one of the prettiest and most interesting villages in Northumberland. The main feature is the massive crenellated gatehouse which was originally the main entrance into the abbey; it now houses the village post office which still uses a Victorian postbox. The Lord Crewe Arms Hotel, named after the village's benefactor, was built on the site of the Abbot's Lodge and guest house, and contains some of the original stonework; while the church was built from the remains of the abbey church, its unusual shape being the result of the building of new walls to bring the various parts together.

(2) *Shildon (87-961511)*
Numerous remains of the old lead-mining industry, e.g. spoil-heaps, smelt-mill chimney and engine house, can be seen around the cottages.

(3) *Pennypie House (87-950518)*
This was once an inn on a drove road which came down from the direction of Slaley Forest to a crossing over the Beldon Burn at Baybridge. It is said that pies were on sale here at a penny a time, for passing drovers or local mineworkers – hence its curious name.

(4) *Carriers' Way*
This was an old packhorse route between East Allendale and the South Tyne valley.

A corner of Blanchland. The large, square, crenellated building on the right was the main gateway into the abbey; it now holds the village post office.

Route 18   Bewick Moor

Although fairly small in extent, Bewick Moor is a rough and lonel
wilderness of heather- and bracken-covered slopes, and occasiona
rocky outcrops. It is also a place to stir the imagination, for
prehistoric man lived here and left us remains of hillforts and
burial mounds and those strange, enigmatic cup-and-ring marking
that still baffle archaeologists. This magnificent walk crosses the
moor twice, the first time by the lonely ruin of Blawearie and the
second on a course further to the east. The finish is along the
hillside above Old Bewick which offers one of the finest views in
Northumberland. Route-finding beyond Blawearie is not too easy
and needs care. On the return across the moor there is no path fo
about 2 miles (3 km), but a succession of clear 'aiming points'
should keep you on the right track.

Length: 10 miles (16 km).

Ascent: 950 ft (290 m).

Starting and finishing point: Old Bewick, 6 miles (9.5 km) south-
east of Wooler (75-066215).

Maps: Landranger 75; Pathfinder 476 (NU 02/12).

Route description (Maps 18A, 18B)
There is very little at Old Bewick, but the church is worth visiting
either now or on your return – see (1).

From the centre of Old Bewick go up the lane between a large
barn and the post office (PBS 'Blawearie/Quarry House'), soon
passing through a gate. Keep on the rough moor road, going
through two further gates, until you reach a ruined cottage after
1⅓ miles (2 km) – see (2) Blawearie. Just before the ruin have a
look at the large circular cairn on the L of the track – see (3).

Keep on the moor road as it bends to the L, passing the ruin.
Shortly it grows more distinct and reaches a yellow transport
container. Do not go right up to the container, but bend R just

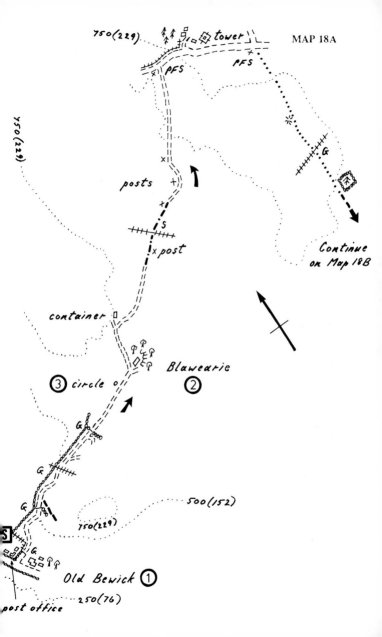

MAP 18A

750(229)   tower

PFS   PFS

750(224)

posts

S

x post

container

Blawearie

③ circle ○   ②

G

G

G

500(152)

750(229)

S

G

Old Bewick ①

post office   250(76)

G

Continue
on Map 18B

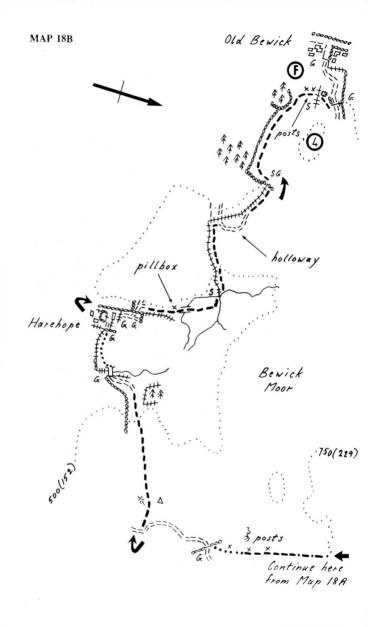

MAP 18B

Old Bewick

Harehope

pillbox

holloway

posts

Bewick Moor

500 (152)

750 (229)

¾ posts

Continue here from Map 18A

before with the moor road. Faint at first, the way becomes clearer as it bends to the L. Later, however, it deteriorates to an intermittent track as it crosses a small hill and descends by a post to a gate and stile in a fence. Keep in the same direction up a hill to a post at the top, and then on to a further post near a marshy hollow. Beyond, the track bends L and then R to another post. The moor road is now clear once again; continue along it until you reach a metalled road. (The posts on this section have yellow arrows on the opposite side as you reach them. In general, between the container and the road, head for the R-hand of two tall towers which can be seen in the distance.)

Turn R and walk along the road, passing the tower. After ½ mile (800 m), opposite a road junction, turn R (PBS 'Eglingham') and head up the moor, aiming for a prominent cairn on a hilltop. The way to the cairn is over dense heather with no sign of a path. From the cairn, head for the R-hand edge of the wood ahead, soon passing through a gate in a fence. Go down the side of the wood, continuing in the same direction from the far corner. After ⅔ mile (1.1 km) reach a farm road (over this last section from the wood a gate will be seen on the skyline; this is a good point to aim for).

Go R through the gate and along the farm road. After ⅓ mile (500 m) you should see an Ordnance Survey obelisk on the top of a small hill to your R; there the farm road bends L then R and drops down towards a wood. Immediately after the bends, leave the farm road on a grassy path which goes across the hillside down to the L of the obelisk. There are several path junctions, but aim for the L-hand edge of the wood ahead. At the corner of the wood reach a broad farm road and follow it down to a bridge over a stream.

Cross the bridge and go up half L to a wall which is then followed towards a farm. At the top, go through a gate and then through a second gate to the L of a row of cottages. At the end of the row turn R for a few yards and through a gate. Go up by the wall, soon turning L through a gate; on the opposite side continuing in the same direction, but now to the L of a fence. Soon the path starts to bend L away from the fence around the base of a hill and on the L side of a large flat area. At a World War II pillbox the path bends to the R to a small footbridge and then across the flat area to a stream.

Turn L and follow the path on the L bank of the stream until you reach a stile in a fence. Turn L and follow a path up the hill keeping to the R of the fence. At the top, at a crossing fence, turn R uphill to a moor road. There turn R (following the blue arrow), soon rising up a well-defined holloway. At the top go over to the fence on the L and follow it as it bends to the L along the edge of the hill, with superb views over to the L. The hill-top ahead contains an important hillfort – see (4).

Soon reach a small gate in a wall. Go through and immediately turn L downhill. Drop down the hillside until you near a wood, then turn R on a path to contour the hill, keeping between the wall on your L and rhododendron bushes slightly higher on your R. Pass a wood on the R, keeping in the same general direction (passing two posts with blue arrows) until you reach a stile in a fence (rather concealed). Pass to the R of some sheep pens and then go on, still contouring the slope, until you meet the farm road that you came up earlier, at a gate. Turn L through the gate and follow the moor road down and back to Old Bewick.

(1) *Old Bewick (75-066216)*

The name 'Bewick' is derived from the Old English *beo-wic* and means 'bee-farm'. A short distance to the north of the village an old cross at a fork draws attention to a small church, half hidden in trees, which lies appropriately by the Kirk Burn. Founded in the eleventh or twelfth centuries by Matilda, wife of Henry I, in memory of her father Malcolm who was killed nearby at Alnwick, it later passed into the control of Tynemouth Priory. It was restored in the fourteenth century after damage by the Scots, again in the seventeenth century, and then finally in 1867. Its most attractive features are the arches in the chancel and apse which go back to Norman times.

(2) *Blawearie (75-085224)*

Although only at a modest altitude and not very far from other habitation, Blawearie is nevertheless an exposed and isolated place. It was originally built as a shepherd's cottage, but has not been occupied for more than forty years. Nearby among the trees is a sandstone outcrop with steps, which originally formed part of a small garden.

(3) *Bronze Age circle (75-082223)*

The stone circle to the left of the track as you approach Blawearie is actually the original retaining wall of a mound, the centre of which was removed at some point in the past (probably for use in wall building). It contained four burial chambers (cists), each of which was dug into the ground, lined with slabs and covered with a capstone; three of these can still be seen on the side of your approach. On excavation no human remains were found, presumably owing to decay, but a food vessel and a necklace with over 100 jet beads were discovered, which suggest that at least one of the dead was a woman. The remains are now in the British Museum. The circle dates from the early Bronze Age, about 1700–1400 BC.

(4) *Old Bewick hillfort (75-075216)*

The hillfort stands in a highly strategic position on the highest point of a promontory which overlooks Old Bewick – and also much of the countryside around. It consists of two separate enclosures, built side by side, each with its own ditch and wall system. A semicircular bank and ditch have been built on the north side – where presumably an attack would most likely have come – to enclose both of them. All in all, it would have been a formidable place to attack. Near to the eastern wall of the fort are some cup-and-ring markings similar to those on Doddington Moor and elsewhere (see page 104).

Route 19   Simonside

This is a lovely route which explores the hill area immediately to the south of Rothbury. The walk falls into three distinct parts: a long climb up Garleigh Moor to the Lordenshaw-Great Tosson road, then forest trails and roads which take you below Simonside, and finally fieldpaths alongside the Coquet which will bring you back to Rothbury. The route uses public rights of way throughout, with the exception of the forest section where forest trails are followed. (*Note*: These trails may be closed to the public on several days each year: this will be indicated by notices in the car-park (81-038995). On those occasions omit the forest section by continuing down the road to Great Tosson where the route can be resumed.) The rocks at Simonside, wonderful views to the north over the Coquet valley and the distant Cheviot Hills, a pele tower and a folly are some of the main attractions, apart from the walking itself which should be enjoyable throughout.

Length: 10 miles (16 km).

Ascent: 1250 ft (380 m).

Starting and finishing point: Rothbury (81-057017). There is parking at the centre of town and in car-parks.

Maps: Landranger 81; Pathfinder 500 (NU 00/10) and 511 (NZ 09/19).

Route description (Maps 19A, 19B)
From the centre of Rothbury go down the B6342, Cambo Road, opposite Barclays Bank. Cross the bridge over the River Coquet and go up the steps directly ahead. At the top turn R and walk along the road. At the far end go L through a small gate and follow a path half R to a fence corner and gap. Continue by the fence, gradually leaving it to the L to a small gate leading into a road (PFS 'Rothbury'). Turn L and, at a fork, go R up a side lane (i.e. by 'Woodfold Juniper').

Pass a prominent tower – see (1) Sharp's Folly – and about ¼ mile (400 m) later go L through the second of a pair of gates (slightly hidden yellow PFS). Go up to the R of a hedge (no path) to a stile at the top; then go slightly R, crossing a stream by an old gatepost and going up to a stile on the skyline at the joining point of a wall and a fence. Ahead are two hills; aim slightly R between

MAP 19A

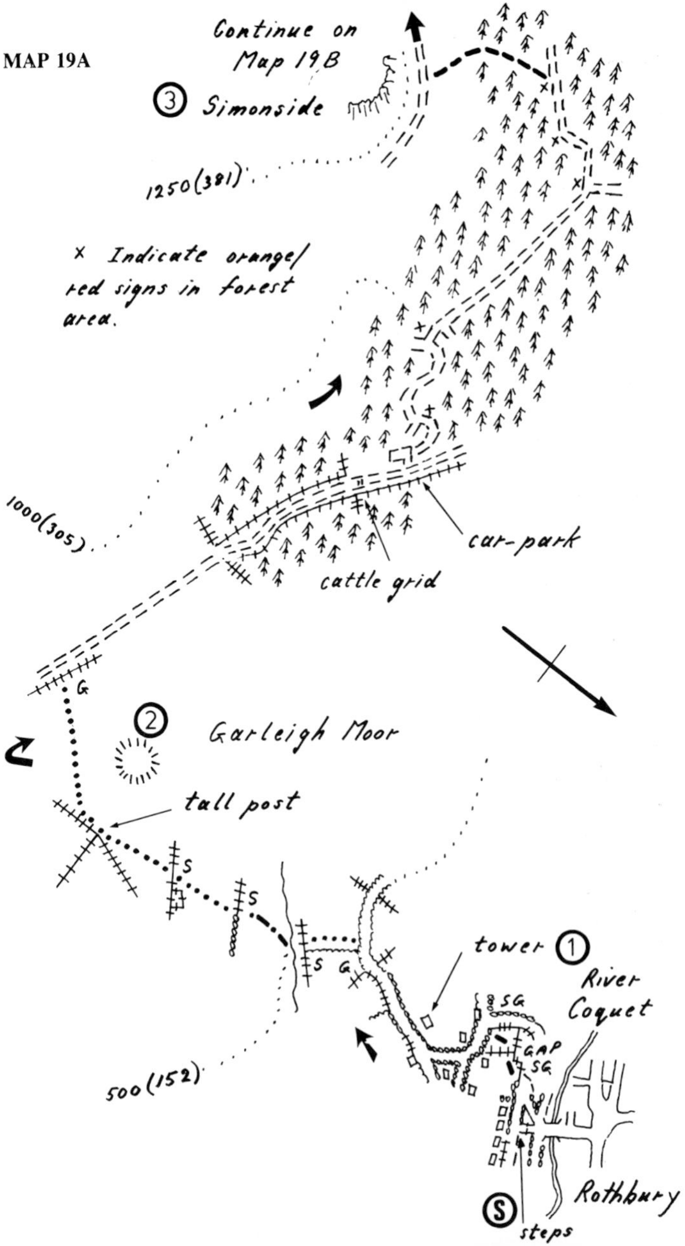

Continue on
Map 19B

③ Simonside

1250 (381)

× Indicate orange/
red signs in forest
area.

car-park

cattle grid

1000 (305)

G

② Garleigh Moor

tall post

S

S

S G

tower ①

River
Coquet

SG

GAP
SG

Rothbury

Ⓢ

steps

500 (152)

MAP 19B

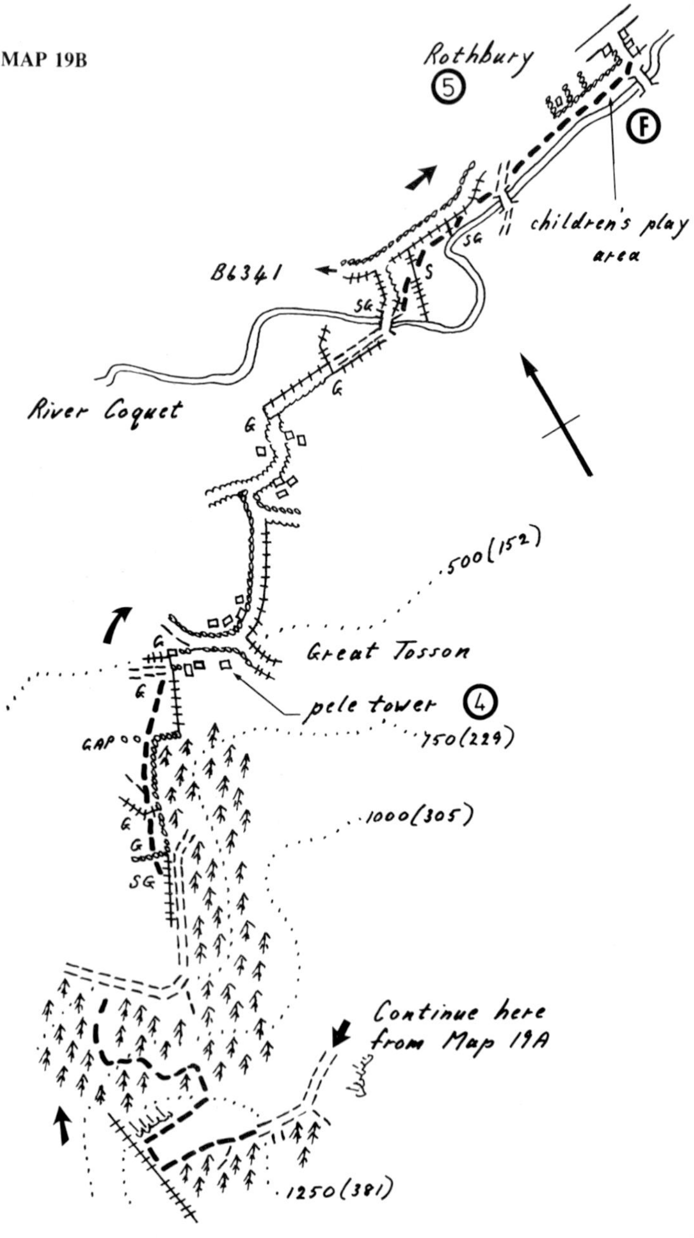

Rothbury
(5)

(F)

children's play
area

B6341

SG

S

SG

G

River Coquet

G

G

500 (152)

Great Tosson

G

pele tower   (4)

G

750 (229)

GAP

1000 (305)

G

SG

Continue here
from Map 19A

1250 (381)

the two in the direction of a few shrubby trees. By the trees go over a stile and then up the moor beyond, aiming midway between the two hills and keeping to the R of more shrubby trees. You should aim to reach a small gate at the junction of three fences where there is a tall post. *Do not go through the small gate*, but walk up by the fence for about 150 yds (140 m), then leave it half R. Cross the open moor keeping to the L of a prominent hill (no path) until you reach a road – the hill-top is the site of a hillfort, see (2). Turn R.

Walk down the road for 1 mile (1.6 km) until you reach a Forestry Commission car-park on your L. Enter and immediately turn into a forest road on the R (red/orange/green and 'Forest Walk' signs – these are Forestry Commission waymarks). Follow the forest road, ignoring a branch to the L where the 'green' trail leaves. At the next junction go R and then L at a fork; at a second fork go L again up a narrow rocky path (i.e. following the red/orange waymarks throughout). Where the forest ends, go to the L up a path which crosses the moor to a higher forest road. Turn R along it. To the L is the prominent rocky hill of Simonside – see (3) for an account of the climbing there.

At the corner of the forest, immediately below the crags, go ahead with the forest to your L, following the orange waymarks. Keep on the path which runs parallel and to the R of the forest edge, ignoring all side paths, until you reach a fence after about ½ mile (800 m). Turn R and descend alongside the fence (the moor on the opposite side of the fence is private), soon bending to the R to run along the top of a small cliff. At the start of the forest turn L and descend steeply through the forest, still following the orange waymarks. Eventually reach a grassy forest road and turn R.

Follow the forest road which soon bends L, with the forest clearing on the L to give lovely views. Immediately before the forest starts again on the L, i.e. where the forest road bends to the R into it, go through a small gate (yellow arrow) and follow the path running just outside the forest edge. Cross two gates and then, at the corner of the forest, go through a wall gap and turn half R, dropping down the hillside to a farm road where it reaches a gate. Go to the R through the gate and along the road to a fork (Great Tosson); there go L. In the village note the ruin over to the right – see (4) the Great Tosson pele tower. At a T-junction turn L along the Rye Hill/Little Tosson/Bickerton road, and shortly afterwards at a further junction keep ahead to Tosson Mill.

Pass some houses and go along to a gate. Go through and to the R between fences, soon passing through another gate and over a bridge. Immediately after the bridge go R through a small gate and cross a field to a stile on the far side. Keep in the same direction, crossing a small plank bridge and going through a small gate up to a road. Turn R and walk along the road, leaving it to the R down a path after about 90 yards (80 m). Keep on the L bank of the river, passing a bridge, until you reach a children's play area. At a further bridge at the far end of the area turn L up a narrow path which will bring you back to the centre of Rothbury. For information about the town, see (5) Rothbury, below.

(1) *Sharp's Folly (81-058008)*
The tall round castellated tower by the side of the lane was built by Archdeacon Thomas Sharp who was rector of Rothbury from 1720. It was intended as an observatory for the Archdeacon, who dabbled in astrology, but also had the additional benefit of providing work for some of the unemployed masons of the town. Thomas Sharp's son, John, was one of the Trustees of the Lord Crewe Trust who were responsible for the restoration of Bamburgh castle in the middle of the eighteenth century (see page 129).

(2) *Lordenshaw (81-055993)*
The hill-top to the right as you head up the final part of Garleigh Moor towards the road is the site of an oval hillfort with a total area of about one acre (0.4 ha). The defences consist of three banks, of which the inner one is about 6 ft (1.8 m) high in places, and an outer counterscarp bank with entrances at the east and west ends. Within, a number of hut circles can be found, some built into the defences. A short distance away there are a number of rocks inscribed with cup-and-ring markings (see page 104).

(3) *Simonside (81-024986)*

The sandstone crags below the summit of Simonside were mentioned in the Climbers' Club Journal of 1902 and were therefore, along with Great Wanney further to the south, the first crags in Northumberland to receive attention. Some famous climbers who came here before the Second World War were Geoffrey Winthrop Young, Marcus Heywood and Jack Longland. Development has been fairly continuous, but has intensified since about 1970. Today there are more than 100 routes, up to about 60 ft (18 m) in length, on the main face and on outliers.

(4) *Great Tosson pele tower (81-029005)*

The ruin to the right of the road as you go through Great Tosson was a pele tower built in the fifteenth century. Although little now remains, it was once a fairly substantial building with walls of rubble and ashlar facings 8 ft (2.4 m) thick.

(5) *Rothbury (81-055016)*

Although perhaps lacking any outstanding buildings of great age or interest – apart, of course, from Cragside only a mile or so away – Rothbury is a town of considerable charm which has been described justifiably as the capital of Coquetdale. From 1872 it was served by a single-track railway branchline which connected at Scot's Gap with the Wansbeck Railway which ran from Morpeth to Redesmouth, but this closed down for passengers in 1952 and for freight eleven years later. At one time Rothbury had also its own annual race-meeting which was held on the flat haughs by the river, but after more than 200 years these were discontinued in 1965, despite considerable protest. The Church of All Saints in Rothbury was largely rebuilt in 1850 on the site of a thirteenth-century church, but do not let this put you off, for it contains one remarkable feature well worth seeing: a font made up from a bowl of 1664 and a base which is the bottom part of an Anglo-Saxon cross-shaft of about AD 800. The shaft is carved with wonderful decorative patterns, with a lion and long-tailed beasties, and an Ascension which is claimed to be the earliest such carving in England.

More strenuous routes

Route 20   Windy Gyle

Apart from The Cheviot itself, the mountain top of Windy Gyle is
probably the best-known summit in the Cheviot Hills. It is also
one of the few places to exceed the magic figure of 2,000 ft (610 m)
which is usually considered to mark the point where mere hills
finish and real mountains begin. Only its relatively isolated
position, at a remote point on the Border Fence, prevents it from
being more often visited. The superb route follows the line taken
by packhorse trains and drove herds: The Street on the outward
journey and Clennell Street on the return. There should be little
difficulty in route-finding, as the way uses clear paths throughout.
The views and the quality of the route are magnificent all the way.

Length: 10½ miles (17 km).

Ascent: 1750 ft (540 m).

Starting and finishing point: Near Barrow Burn in the Coquet
valley (80-860115). From Alwinton continue up the narrow road
through Coquetdale. Reach Barrow Burn – several houses and a
school – and then go on for about ½ mile (800 m) to a small
bridge and the confluence of two streams (the Coquet and the
Rowhope Burn) where a rough road goes off to the R. Cars may
be parked on the small area between the two roads.

Maps: Landranger 80; Pathfinder 487 (NT 81/91).

Route description (Maps 20A, 20B)
From the parking area cross the bridge and immediately go over a
stile on the R. Follow the clear path up the spine of the ridge,
keeping to the R of the fence. Resist the temptation to cross,
keeping instead on the same side of the fence, which soon turns R.
About 250 yards (230 m) after the bend, go over a stile and
continue climbing, but now to the L of the fence, until you reach a

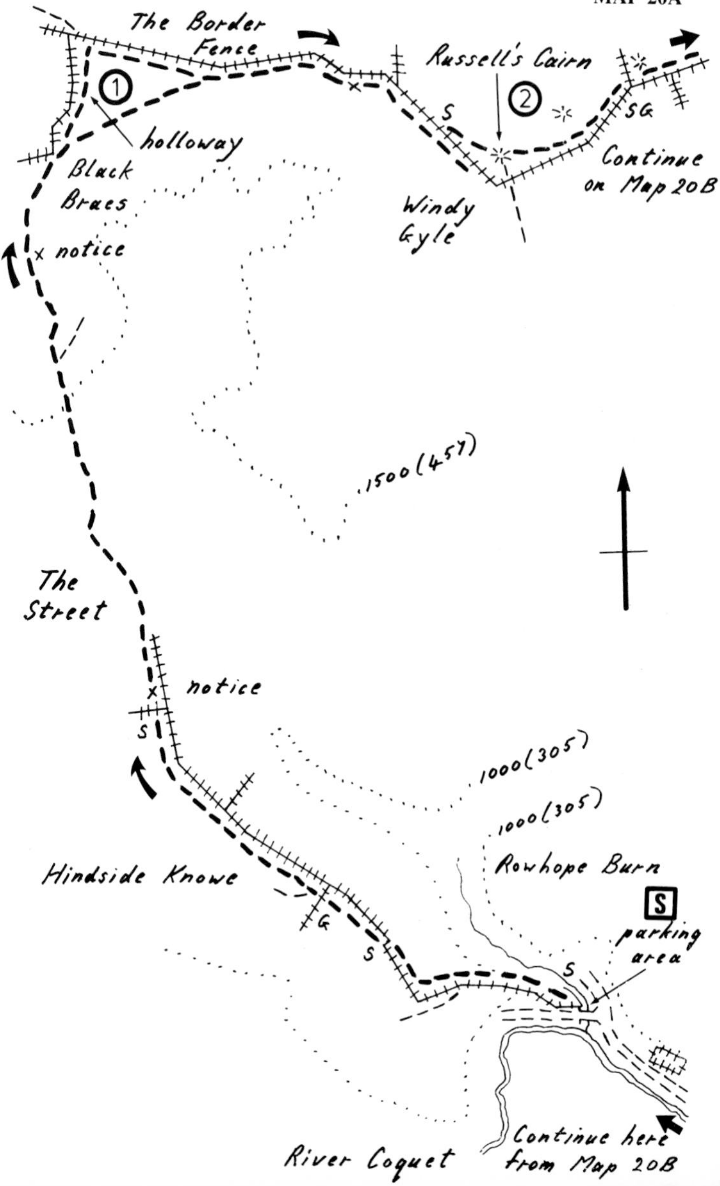

The Border Fence

Russell's Cairn

①

holloway

②

Black Braes

S

SG

× notice

Continue on Map 20B

Windy Gyle

.1500(457)

The Street

× notice

S

1000(305)

1000(305)

Rowhope Burn

Hindside Knowe

S parking area

G

S

S

River Coquet

Continue here from Map 20B

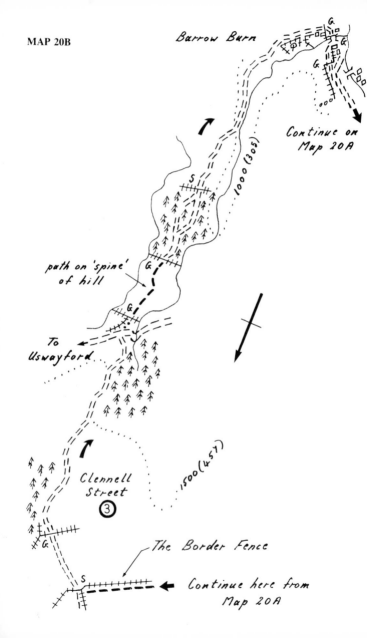

MAP 20B

Barrow Burn

1000 (305)

Continue on
Map 20A

S

path on 'spine'
of hill

G

G

To
Uswayford

G

1500 (457)

Clennell
Street

③

The Border Fence

S

Continue here from
Map 20A

gate just below the top of the hill. Go up the clear path beyond, forking R after 50 yards (45 m) so that you pass the hill-top on the R, keeping by the fence. On the far side the path descends, soon bending to the R with the fence. Cross a stile by a red notice 'KEEP TO THE PATH   UNCLEARED MILITARY TARGET AREA   DO NOT TOUCH ANYTHING   IT MAY EXPLODE AND KILL YOU'. (Please take notice of this, if for no better reason than to avoid spoiling the day for the next people to come along!) See page 49 for information about the Otterburn Training Area.

Soon afterwards the fence ends, but the way is still clear, keeping in the same direction and then bending round to the L behind a small hill. On the far side the path drops down to a col and then rises up steeply. At the top of the steep section a more gradual climb commences, until the corner of a fence is reached. This is the Border Fence separating England (your side) from Scotland (the other side).

Continue in the same direction, keeping the Fence to your L and ignoring the clear path heading half R over the moor. (This is the Pennine Way, which will be joined again shortly.) The route alongside the Fence goes through a superb holloway produced by the passage of many packhorse trains and drove herds over the centuries – see (1) The Street. At a corner do not go through the gate ahead, but bend R and continue to follow the Fence.

After 1¼ miles (2 km), cross over to the other side of the Fence (this and once or twice on Route 30 are the only times that you will stray north of the Border in this book), and continue up by the Fence. Soon the path heads away from the Fence, half L towards the summit cairn of Windy Gyle. The mound of stones is called Russell's Cairn – see (2) to find out why. Near to the summit there is also a memorial cairn.

Return to the Fence and turn L. Follow the Fence for 1 mile (1.6 km) until you reach the point where the Fence bends half L for a short distance and joins another fence coming in from the L. Go over the ladder stile on the R (i.e. back to the English side) and leave the Fence down the obvious broad track; this is the route taken by another old way – see (3) Clennell Street. The crossing point was the Hexpethgate where it is thought Lord

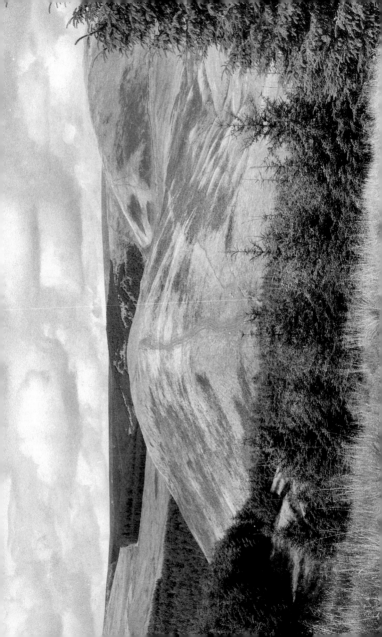

Francis Russell was killed. Descend along the track until you come to a gate. Go through and keep on the broad moor road, with a forest over to the L, for 1¼ miles (2 km) until you reach a rough farm road. This leads to the lonely farm of Uswayford.

Cross and go ahead to a gate. Go through and up the path on the spine of the hill ahead, with steep slopes falling away on each side into stream valleys. Go over the top of the hill and down to a gate which leads into a coniferous forest. Walk up the forest road, turning R at a fork at the top of the hill. Follow the lovely grassy path which soon bends to the L down hill and up to a ladder stile.

Go over and follow the moor road for 1 mile (1.6 km) until the buildings at Barrow Burn are reached; there pass the first two buildings (Deer Conservation Unit) to a gate. This leads into a farm road which goes down to a further gate and a footbridge. Pass the farm to the R, and go on to a road, then go along it back to the starting point.

(1) *The Street*

'The Street' is the name given to the clear path which goes from Barrow Burn in Upper Coquetdale over Black Braes and the main ridge of the Cheviots, which is crossed near Mozie Law, and down to Hownam in the valley of the Kale Water. The name was probably derived from the Old English word *straet* which was a common one in Saxon land charters. (It is not known for certain what it meant, although it is usually considered to imply a deliberately constructed road, often a Roman road.) Whatever the origin of The Street, it has probably been in use for a very long time, more recently by packhorse trains and by drove herds. Nowadays, it gives a superb walk, as those who follow this route will quickly discover.

(2) *Russell's Cairn (80-855152)*

The massive cairn on the summit of Windy Gyle is a Bronze Age mound, but is named after Lord Francis Russell who was killed in

Looking towards the Border Ridge from Middle Hill. The prominent hill in the centre, which has Barrow Burn to the left and Usway Burn to the right, is descended on Routes 20 and 27.

a Border fracas hereabouts – probably at Hexpethgate where Clennell Street crosses the Border ridge – on 27 July 1585. It is known that the incident occurred on a day of truce (see page 48) when Ker of Ferniehirst, the Scottish Warden of the Middle March, was due to meet with his opposite number, Sir John Forster, but the exact circumstances are still in doubt. The Scottish account laid the blame upon a young English lad named Wanless who started the affair by stealing a pair of spurs, but the English account puts the blame fairly and squarely on the Scottish party who were accused of a deliberate attack. Whatever the truth of the affair, poor Russell was certainly dead by the end of it. He seems, in fact, to have been singularly unlucky in such matters for it was he who was taken prisoner in a similar incident on 7 July 1575 at the Redeswire (near Carter Bar) when Sir George Heron, the deputy Warden of the Middle March, was killed.

(3) *Clennell Street*: see page 283.

Route 21   The north-east Cheviots

Although never moving more than 3–4 miles (5–6 km) from Wooler, nor attaining any real height, this lovely walk is an excellent introduction to the Cheviot Hills. Most of the way is along well-defined tracks, but there is a short section around Tom Tallon's Crag where a compass would be useful. The views over the low-lying country to the north, particularly during the second half of the walk, are superb.

Length: 11 miles (18 km).

Ascent: 1500 ft (460 m).

Starting and finishing point: The bus station, High Street, Wooler (75-992281). The Tourist Information Office is at the corner of the station area.

Maps: Landranger 75; Pathfinder 475 (NT 82/92).

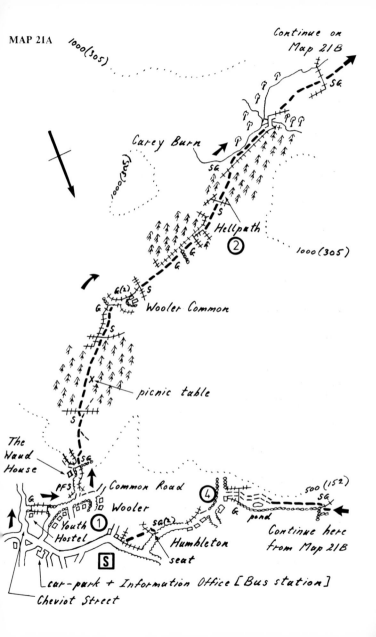

MAP 21A

1000(305)

Continue on
Map 21B

SG

Carey Burn

SG

Hellpath

② 1000(305)

Wooler Common

G(2) S

G

S

picnic table

S

The
Waud
House

SG

PFS Common Road

G Wooler

④ 500(152)

SG

Youth ① pond
Hostel

SG(2) G

Humbleton Continue here
seat from Map 21B

S

car-park + Information Office [Bus station]

Cheviot Street

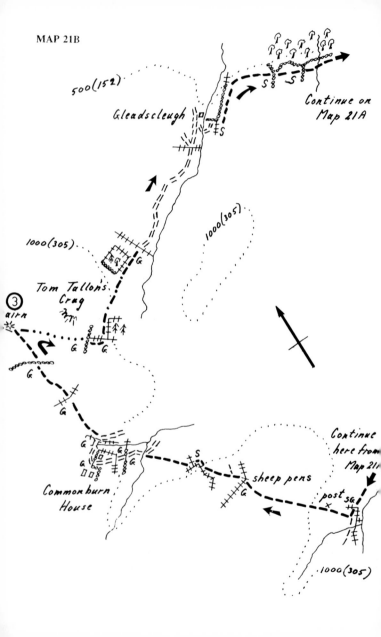

MAP 21B

500 (152)

Gleadscleugh

Continue on
Map 21A

1000 (305)

1000 (305)

Tom Tallons
Crag

③
cairn

Commonburn
House

sheep pens

Continue
here from
Map 21A

post

1000 (305)

Route description (Maps 21A, 21B)

From the bus station entrance cross the road and turn L. Cross
Ramsey's Lane and bend R up Cheviot Street. Just after the '30
mph' signs, go R along a footpath (PFS) to the L of the drive to
the youth hostel – see (1) Wooler youth hostel.

Follow the footpath – with good views to the R – until you reach
a road (Ramsey's Lane); there turn L. At the top, just before the
road junction (Common Road and High Fair), go L up a farm
road (PBS 'Waud House/Wooler Common/Broadstruther').

At a white cottage (Waud House) go ahead through a small gate
and then R over a footbridge (i.e. following the blue arrows). The
path goes down the valley by a fence for a short distance, but soon
bends R up the hillside. Head directly for the forest, going L at the
fork just before it. Enter the forest over a stile and continue on a
clear path, soon leaving it again over a stile on the opposite side.
Keep by the fence to a gate leading into a farm road. Turn R and
walk down to the farm (Wooler Common), passing it on the L
through two gates by some sheep pens.

Go up by a fence to a stile (blue arrow) and then up to the
corner of a forest. Continue along the R-hand edge of the forest,
soon going through a gap between two blocks. After the gap,
continue by the fence on the L until it bends away, then keep in
the same direction over the moor, aiming for a further forest.
Enter the forest over a stile and follow a superb path as it descends
towards a stream (Carey Burn) – see (2) Hellpath.

At the bottom go through a small gate and walk by the stream
until you can cross over a footbridge just after a stream
confluence. Immediately, go over the fence ahead and follow the
path which rises uphill. Over the hill the path runs roughly parallel
with the stream on the L, soon passing through a small gate and
later another small gate at a fence corner. After the second of
these, go R at a post (a yellow arrow indicates 'Walk No. 5').

Follow the path as it rises up the moor. As the path starts to
descend on the far side of the ridge, aim for the R-hand edge of
the fence ahead where there are some sheep pens. Go through a
gate by the pens and take the path half L. You should soon reach
a fence; there go round the corner on the R to a further stile. Now

keep in the same direction, aiming towards a farm (Commonburn House), until you reach a farm road. This crosses a stream and goes up to a gate; from there continue along it to a gate between the farm and a cottage. Enter another farm road and turn R.

Go over a bridge and through a gate; 60 yards (55 m) further on, leave the road to the L up a clear track. Soon go through a gate in a fence and then later a second gate in a wall. Keep in the same direction across the moor on a path between banks of heather, until you reach a prominent cairn with a path coming in from the R. Directly ahead across the valley is the prominent hill of Yeavering Bell with its well-developed fortifications – see (3) Yeavering Bell.

There is no clearly defined footpath over the next section of the route. From the cairn turn back half R towards the prominent crag on the hill ahead (Tom Tallon's Crag). Do not go to the crag, but aim to pass it to the R by contouring round the slope. (After a short distance a wood will become visible to the R of the crag; aim for a point about midway between the crag and the wood.) If your aim is good you will reach a gate in a wall. Go through it and follow a path on the other side parallel with a fence to the L. At a fence junction – opposite the wood to the R – go L through a gate. Go alongside a fence until it turns R, then continue in the same direction, aiming for the R-hand side of a wood. Go past the wood and on to a gate where you should pick up a moor road.

Follow the moor road down until you reach a large house (Gleadscleugh). Immediately before the house, turn R and drop down, turning R at a wall after a few yards. Follow the path over a stream and up, swinging back half L to a gate. Do not go through the gate, but instead go R uphill over a stile to a wall corner. Turn L round the corner and follow the wall on a clear path. Later the path leaves the wall and crosses the hillside to the R. Continue on this path across the hillside over two ladder stiles. At the next wall go through a small gate to the R and along a clear path which later goes by a pond and on to a road. There is a comfortable seat directly opposite to rest your weary bones – see (4) Memorial seat.

Waud House.

Turn L, then R at a road junction and pass through the small
hamlet of Humbleton. At a second seat, after about ¼ mile
(400 m), go R through a small gate and follow a path to the R of a
fence. Where the fence bends R, go up to a small gate and then
across a field. This leads into a road; there turn R and follow the
road back to Wooler.

(1) *Wooler youth hostel (75-991278)*

The first hostel at Wooler was opened on 18 June 1932 by Sir
Charles Trevelyan, Lord Lieutenant of Northumberland and
President of the Northumberland and Tyneside Regional Group of
the Youth Hostels Association. It consisted of the buildings on
opposite sides of the track at the old railway station (closed for
passengers two years earlier); that on the east platform housed
twelve males and that on the west platform six females. They
obviously believed in keeping them well apart in those days! The
present hostel was built for the Women's Land Army in 1940, but
was acquired by the YHA in 1954 for £1,000. The basic structure is
still unchanged, but working parties made some alterations to the
interior to bring it up to hostel standards. Wooden floors were put
into the dormitories, and a partition to separate male and female
sleeping-areas. Further improvements have been made since then.
The wall murals, which are one of the features of Wooler hostel,
were the work of Jim Mackenzie of Stakeford, near Choppington,
who was staying there convalescing after breaking a leg in a
motorbike accident.

(2) *Hellpath (75-959258)*

The superb path which descends through the forest towards the
Carey Burn is known as Hellpath. Readers expecting a gory tale of
strife, perhaps at the time of the Border troubles, will be sadly
disappointed, however, as the name is probably no more than a
corruption of 'hillpath'.

Humbleton Hill from the forest area near Earle Whin.

(3) *Yeavering Bell (75-929293)*

The two summits of Yeavering Bell and the saddle between them are surrounded by a massive stone rampart which once stood 8 ft (2.4 m) high on a base 10–12 ft (3.0–3.7 m) wide. This enclosed an area of 13 acres (5.3 ha), in which the foundations of at least 130 huts have been identified. It dates back to the Iron Age, but occupation probably extended over many centuries. Near Yeavering, in the valley of the Glen to the north of the hillfort, is the site of Ad Gefrin, the palace of the Anglo-Saxon Kings of Northumbria in the seventh century, although nothing can now be seen of it.

(4) *Memorial seat (75-975284)*

The seat is 'To the memory of Thomas Tindle (Tucker) Anderson 1894–1972 who loved this walk and these hills'. The grand stretch of drystone wall behind the seat was erected in 1988 by Arres and Son, dykers of Kelso, who were obviously sufficiently proud of it to put in a small inscribed stone to that effect. Drystone walls are referred to as 'dykes' in Scotland and the Border region, unlike eastern England where the word refers to ditches.

Route 22   Salter's Road

Most of the old ways which cross the Cheviot Hills into Scotland make superb walking routes. Salter's Road is no exception and few who follow it are likely to be disappointed. This walk follows Salter's Road from Alnham to Low Bleakhope in the Breamish valley, which is then followed to Alnhammoor near Linhope; the return route goes over Leafield Edge to rejoin Salter's Road for the final mile or so. With the exception of the Breamish valley, where a metalled road is used, the route is entirely upon good clear paths. The most exciting moment of the route is the exit from the wood at Ewartly Shank when a wonderful view opens up ahead.

Length: 12 miles (19 km).

View to the north-west from near Harehope Hill.

Ascent: 1650 ft (500 m).

Starting and finishing point: The T-junction at the centre of Alnham, about 7 miles (11 km) north-west of Rothbury (81-996109). There is no car-park at Alnham, but cars may be left at several points. (Make sure that they do not cause any obstruction for local people.)

Maps: Landranger 80 and 81; Pathfinder 487 (NT 81/91).

Route description (Maps 22A, 22B, 22C)
From the T-junction walk up the road signposted 'Alnham Church/Castle Hill/Ewartly Shank'. Soon pass the church on the R – see (1) Alnham Church – and then a large house – see (2) the Vicar's Pele. Where the road bends L towards a cattle-grid go R up a lane (PFS 'Shank House/Low Bleakhope'). Go through a gate and along a path by a wall, then up to the top L-hand corner of the field. Enter a lane to the L of a forest and continue up until the lane ends, then go half R up the moor to reach a moor road. Turn L.

   Where the moor road swings R through a gap in a fence, leave it to the L to a stile (painted white with a blue arrow). Take the grassy track beyond to cross a stream and then go up to a gate at the meeting-point of a wall and fence. This is a famous packhorse route – see (3) Salter's Road. Keep in the same direction to a stell. Go up the grassy slope half L from the stell and to the L of a broad shallow valley, to pick up a track. After 125 yards (115 m) go R at a fork, and about 75 yards (70 m) later L at another fork, then follow the track up to a gate in a fence at the top of the ridge. Continue over, soon descending on a holloway to the R-hand corner of a wood, then by the wood to a road.

   Turn R and walk up the road to the farm of Ewartly Shank. The way through the farm is marked by blue arrows. At the farm, bend L between the house and barns, and at the end R. Go over the stile on the R and alongside the fence to a gate leading into a wood. Take the path through the wood, leaving through a gate at the far side. (An extensive view opens up in front of you as you

MAP 22A

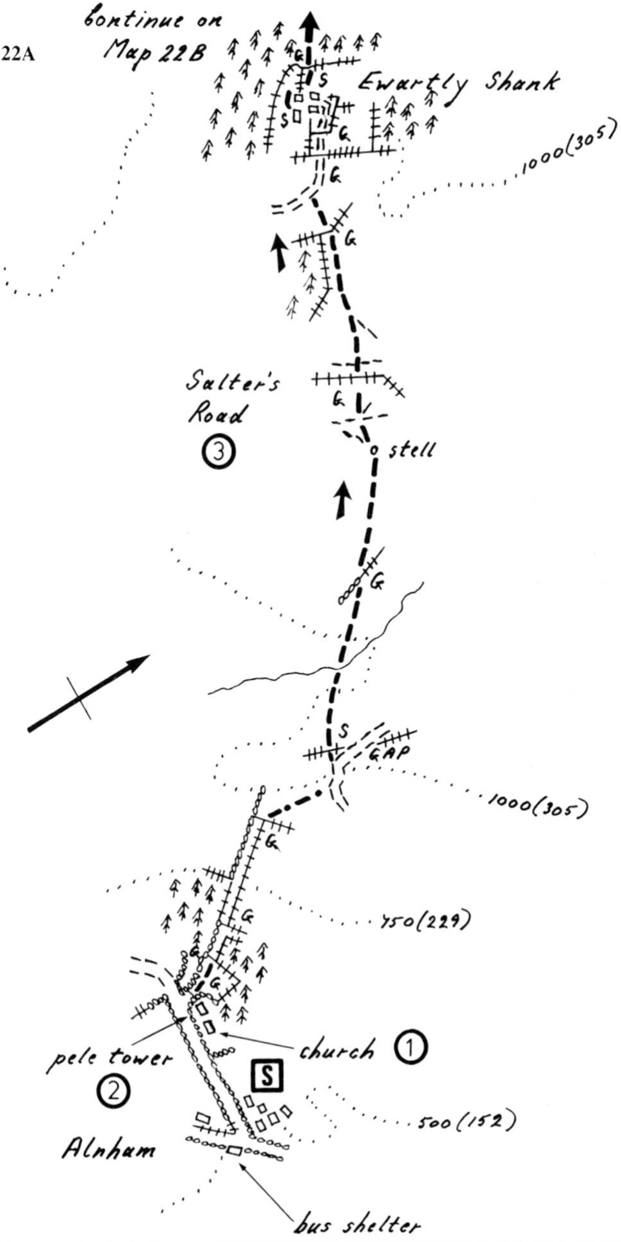

continue on Map 22B

Ewartly Shank

1000(305)

Salter's Road ③

stell

1000(305)

GAP

S

750(229)

pele tower ②

church ①

S

Alnham

500(152)

bus shelter

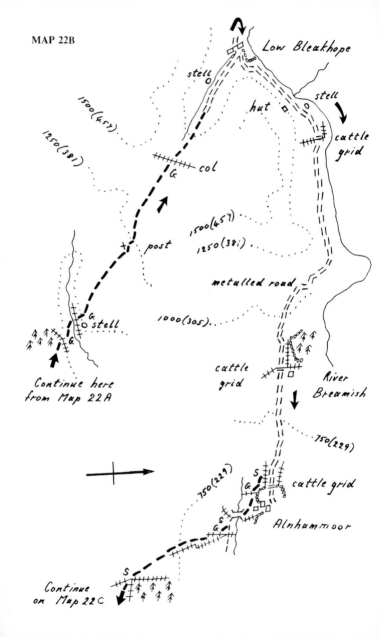

MAP 22B

Low Bleakhope

stell

1500(457)

1250(381)

stell

hut

cattle grid

col

G

1500(457)

1250(381)

post

metalled road

1000(305)

G stell

G

Continue here
from Map 22A

cattle grid

River Breamish

750(229)

750(229)

S

G

cattle grid

G

S

Alnhammoor

G

S

Continue
on Map 22C

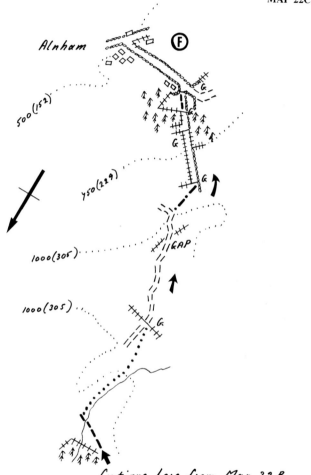

Alnham

Ⓕ

500(152)

750(229)

1000(305)

1000(305)

GAP

G

G

G

G

Continue here from Map 22B

leave the wood.) Take the track to the R which goes down to a
stream. Cross it, go through a gate and up the hillside through
zigzags. Follow the clear path as it climbs up to the top of a hill,
then down into a dip, and then up again, slanting to the L across
the hillside eventually to reach a gate on a col. On the other side
continue in the same direction, descending to the R of a stream.
As you descend, the path grows more distinct and wider.
Eventually after a long descent reach a road by the farm of Low
Bleakhope in the Breamish valley.

Turn R and walk along the road for 2½ miles (4 km). The road
is narrow, unfenced and normally quiet, for much of its way
accompanied by the Breamish, a lovely rocky river, the haunt of
dipper and of wagtail. Eventually approach a cattle-grid just
before the farm of Alnhammoor. Do not go up to the grid, but
over a stile in the fence on the R a short distance before it. Then
turn to the L and walk parallel with the road, towards the end
bending to the R alongside a wall to a gate. Go through it and
walk beside the wall, passing the farm to the R, then drop down to
a footbridge over a stream, the Shank Burn, where it joins the
Breamish.

Go over the footbridge and on to a stile by a gate. This leads to
a path which runs parallel with and to the R of the river. Just
before the next fence go up R to a gate. Go through it and up the
moor road. This leads at first by a fence, but later over the open
moor, to a gate and stile at the corner of a wood. Go over the stile
and walk along the path which runs along the top of the wood (i.e.
as indicated by the yellow arrow), soon crossing a stream.

Immediately after the stream turn R and walk up the L-hand
bank. After about ⅓ mile (500 m) start gradually to leave the stream
to the L, until you reach a moor road. Turn R along it, soon going
through a gate, then ½ mile (800 m) further go through a gap in a
fence. You are now on your outward path. Continue down the moor
road for about 300 yards (275 m), then leave it half R across the moor
to reach a lane at a corner. Go down the lane to its end at the far
corner of a wood, then down the field to a gate. Go through, by a
house and on to a road. Turn L and along the road, back to the T-
junction where you started earlier.

(1) *Alnham church (81-991110)*

The church of St Michael at Alnham was probably built about
1200, but after being ruinous for a long time was extensively
restored in 1870 and again in 1953, so that few of the original
features now remain. Even so, it is a charming building, reached
up a paved path from a lychgate set between tall trees. (As you
enter the churchyard, note the socket stones in the roots on each
side which probably held crosses in ancient times.) In overall plan
the church is a comparatively simple building, with no tower or
aisles, although three blocked-up arches on the north wall indicate
where a north aisle used to be. Of particular interest are an
octagonal font of 1664 and some old inscribed gravestones.

(2) *The Vicar's Pele (81-990110)*

Nothing testifies more impressively to the troubled state of the
Border in late medieval times than the ruins of the fortified tower-
houses and bastles which can be found throughout
Northumberland. Most of them were built by the lesser gentry of
the county, but some were the work of priests who had them built
near to their churches. A particularly good example of one of
these 'Parson's Peles' or 'Vicar's Peles' can be found at Alnham
near to the church. Originally it would have been three or four
stories high, with thick walls and small windows. The building at
Alnham was a youth hostel for a time, but is now a private house.
Other examples are at Corbridge, Whitton and Elsdon.

(3) *Salter's Road*

From earliest times the importance of salt as a preservative has
been widely recognized, particularly in the north where absence of
sufficient winter feed necessitated the killing of large numbers of
cattle each autumn. Supplies of salt were obtained from sites along
the coast where brine was evaporated or boiled down, or from
inland centres such as Droitwich in Worcestershire and Northwich
in Cheshire. The salt produced in this way was then carried by
packhorses into the towns where it was in demand. Saltways along
which the product was taken can be found along the entire east
coast of England from the Thames estuary to Northumberland,

and radiate out from the inland centres in the Midlands. One such saltway ran from the Northumbrian coast through Alnham to join with Clennell Street near Hexpethgate and then on into southern Scotland. To this day it is known as Salter's Road.

Route 23   Hadrian's Wall and the Whin Sill

When completed, Hadrian's Wall formed a continuous stone barrier, 15 ft (4.5 m) high and 6–9 ft (1.8–2.7 m) thick, with a total length of 73 miles (117 km), from Wallsend on the Tyne estuary to Bowness on the Solway Firth. In the course of the last 1½ millennia, however, most of what there was has disappeared, usually as a result of deliberate looting. Castle builders, Hanoverian road gangs, local farmers and enclosure workmen all found such a plentiful supply of ready stone too much to resist. For most of the way, therefore, only occasional remnants – mere scraps of what was there before – can now be found to indicate its original line. The great exception, however, is the central section where the Wall ran along the line of low hills which mark the emergence of the hard dolerite of the Whin Sill. Even without the Wall those hills would have given a walk sufficiently good to have been included here; with it they provide the best.

A large number of features of interest are passed on this walk; of these only the most important are described below. A great deal of additional information will be found, however, on the many information boards which have been placed along the Wall.

Length: 12 miles (19 km).

Ascent: 1800 ft (550 m).

Starting point: The B6318, ½ mile (800 m) from Greenhead towards Gilsland (86-657660).

Finishing point: The B6318, 7 miles (11 km) west of Low Brunton (86-822705).

Maps: Landranger 86; Pathfinder 546 (NY 66/76) and 547
(NY 86/96); OS Historical Map & Guide 'Hadrian's Wall'.

Route description (Maps 23A, 23B, 23C, 23D)
Before starting, read – if you have not already done so – the
general description of Hadrian's Wall given on page 33.

(a) *Greenhead to Walltown Quarry.*
From Greenhead, walk up the road towards Gilsland until you see
Pennine Way signs. There turn R through a gate by some cottages
and go along to a railway crossing. Cross the line – with care! It is
too early in the walk to be run over – and then a footbridge – see
(1) the Newcastle–Carlisle Line. Go up the path on the L bank of
the stream until you reach a farm road; there turn R to a
footbridge. The ruin on the hill nearby was largely built from
looted Wall material – see (2) Thirlwall Castle. Follow the farm
road up through a gate and then L and R bends. The farm road
peters out into a path which rises up the hill by a prominent ditch;
this was the fighting ditch of the Wall, although no trace of the
Wall itself is now left on this section. Keep by it until you reach a
road at the top.

Turn R and then L at a PW sign immediately after the car-park
entrance. A few yards down the road is the entrance to a Wall fort
– see (3) Carvoran – and the Roman Army Museum.

(b) *Walltown Quarry to Cawfields Quarry.*
Follow the path by a fence – see (4) Walltown Quarry – to a
further PW sign; there turn L and continue down to a road.
Immediately leave it again up a path on the L. Soon reach the
road again and go along it over a cattle-grid to a PFS 'Hadrian's
Wall/Walltown Crags'. Leave the road to the L and climb up to
the top of the ridge. The section of Wall along the top is one of the
finest.

Turn R and follow the Wall – see (5) Turret 45A Walltown
Crags – until it ends, and then the edge of a quarry until you can
drop down into a valley – this is the so-called 3rd Nick of
Thirlwall, see (6) the Nine Nicks of Thirlwall. Cross the ladder
stile in the valley and climb up on the far side. Pass a further turret
(44B) and go along the top until you can descend into a second

MAP 23A

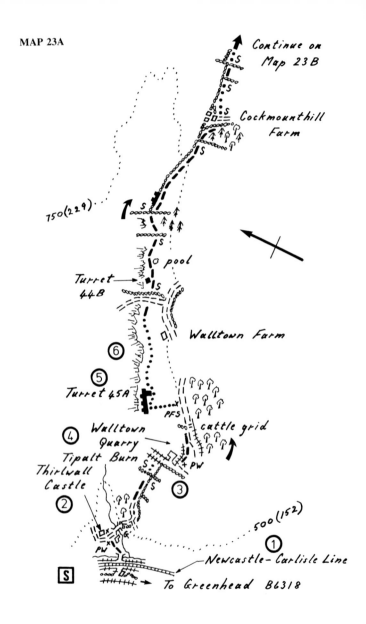

Continue on
Map 23B

─S
─S

─S Cockmounthill
Farm

─S

750(229)

─S

pool

─S

Turret
44B

Walltown Farm

⑥

⑤
Turret 45A

PFS

cattle grid

④
Walltown
Quarry
Tipalt Burn
Thirlwall
Castle

PW

─S
─S

③

②

500(152)

①

PW
S

Newcastle-Carlisle Line

To Greenhead B6318

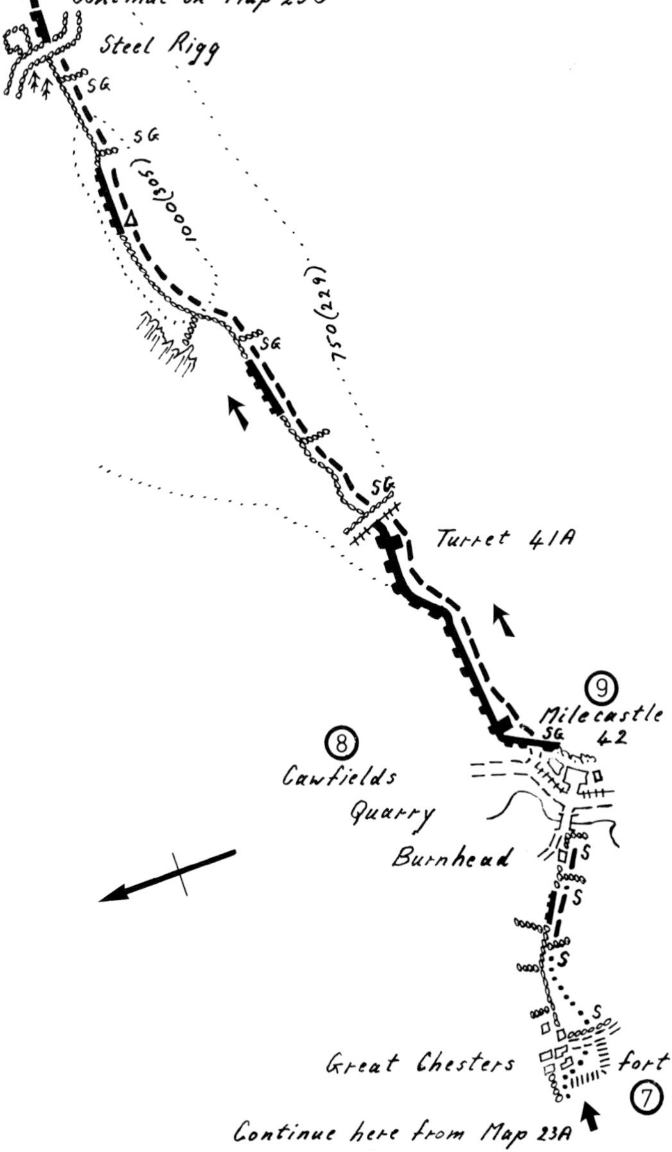

Continue on Map 23C

Steel Rigg

SG

SG

1000(305)

750(229)

SG

SG

Turret 41A

⑨

Milecastle
SG 42

⑧

Cawfields

Quarry

Burnhead

S

S

S

S

Great Chesters fort

⑦

Continue here from Map 23A

MAP 23C

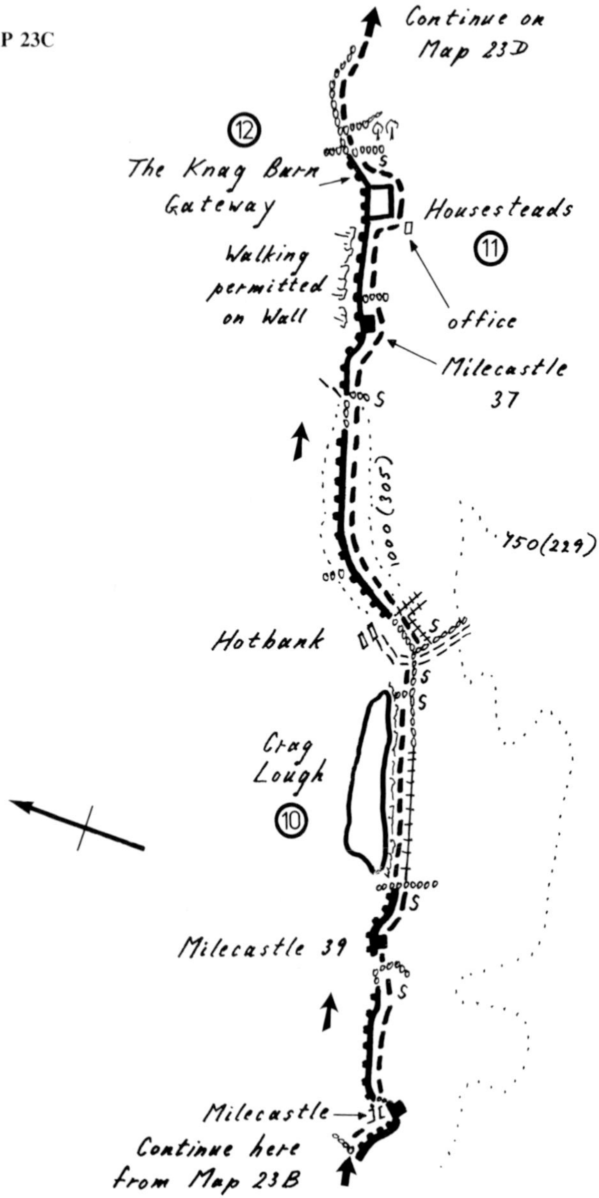

Continue on
Map 23D

⑫

The Knag Burn
Gateway

S

Housesteads

⑪

Walking
permitted
on Wall

office

Milecastle
37

S

1000 (305)

750 (229)

Hotbank

S

S

Crag
Lough

S

⑩

Crag Lough

S

Milecastle 39

S

Milecastle

Continue here
from Map 23B

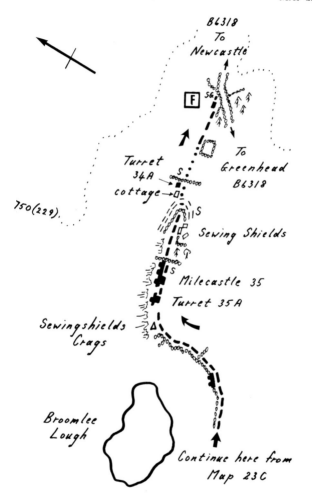

B6318
To
Newcastle

F S6

To
Greenhead
B6318

Turret
34A
cottage→

750(229)

S

Sewing Shields

S

Milecastle 35

Turret 35A

Sewingshields
Crags

△

Broomlee
Lough

Continue here from
Map 23C

valley (the 2nd Nick). Then over another top and down into a third valley (the 1st Nick). (It will be coming clear by now that if you are to enjoy Hadrian's Wall then you must be prepared to work for it! Be assured, there is more of the same to come.)

Rise up and along to a ladder stile which leads into a wood. Go through the wood, leaving on the far side at a further stile. Pass to the R of the buildings of Cockmounthill Farm, and continue in the same direction by a sturdy wall until you reach a second farm, Great Chesters. The ruins on the R are another fort – see (7) Great Chesters. Again pass the farm on the R, going over a ladder stile and continuing by the wall until you can cross it at a stile just after a cottage. Go R down to a road. Across is a car-park and lake – see (8) Cawfields Quarry.

(c) *Cawfields Quarry to Steel Rigg.*
Turn L and shortly, where the road bends L, go R up a track. Go through a gate and climb up L by the Wall to a milecastle – see (9) Milecastle 42. Continue beyond the milecastle by the Wall – there is a good view of the Vallum down to the R. Eventually reach the road near Shield on the Wall. Cross and continue, now with a drystone wall on the L, soon rising up to an Ordnance Survey obelisk. This is a superb viewpoint, particularly towards the loughs to the north of the Wall. Now continue, still by the wall, until you reach the road near Steel Rigg – Turret 39B was sited just before the road.

(d) *Steel Rigg to Housesteads.*
(The section of Wall ahead is in the care of the National Trust who are, at the time of writing, doing a considerable amount of work upon it. As a result of this there is a diversion of paths in this area which may change in the near future. In all cases follow any waymarks. One feature of this stretch is that walking is allowed on the top of the Wall.)

Go along the top of the Wall until you reach a fence where you should drop off to the L and down to a temporary bridge. Rise up to a ladder stile where you cross to the R-hand side of the Wall. Continue across three dips, one of which has a milecastle (39), to enter a wood with Crag Lough – see (10) the Northumbrian loughs – down to the L. Follow a delightful path through the wood to a

stile at the far end. Go along to a farm road and turn R over a
ladder stile, then immediately L over a second, to resume the
same line of walking. The path keeps to the R of the wall as it
bends L and rises up by Hotbank Farm, passing the site of a
milecastle (38). Continue by the Wall to another milecastle (37),
where you can again climb on to the Wall. Continue through the
wood to the corner of Housesteads fort.

Housesteads is undoubtedly one – if not the – most interesting
feature along this stretch of Wall. IT SHOULD NOT BE MISSED. Drop
down off the Wall at the corner and go by the wall of the fort to
the office/museum, where a ticket to enter may be obtained – see
(11) Housesteads.

(e) *Housesteads to B6318.*
After viewing, leave by the East Gate and turn L back to the Wall.
Continue to follow the Wall on its R-hand side, dropping down
into a small valley – see (12) the Knag Burn Gateway. From the
gateway rise up to a corner where you enter a wood over a ladder
stile. Go through the wood and along the Wall as before, bending
L after ½ mile (800 m) and rising up to the Ordnance Survey
obelisk on Sewingshields Crags. (The Wall ends just before the
obelisk at the edge of a cliff.)

Beyond the obelisk pass a turret (35A) and then a milecastle
(35), and continue until you pass to the L of some farm buildings.
Towards the end of the farm do not take the path down the steep
slope to the L, but keep on the top, going through a wood until
you can leave over a ladder stile at the far end. Keep in the same
direction to the R of a cottage to reach a stile in a wall by a turret
(34A). Further along, pass a small walled enclosure (a splendid
section of ditch begins on the L). Pass a final turret (33B), and go
on until you reach your finishing point on the B6318.

(1) *The Newcastle–Carlisle Line*
This line, which so usefully serves the villages of the Tyne Gap, is
the only cross-country railway link between the Forth-Clyde
isthmus and the Aire Gap, a distance of about 150 miles (240 km).
It was completed in 1839. It is claimed that the station at Wylam,
opened in 1835, is the oldest railway station in the world still in use

for passenger traffic. Appropriately, this was also the birthplace of George Stephenson in 1781 and it was at Wylam Colliery that Puffing Billy and Wylam Dilly, two early working steam-locomotives, were employed from 1813.

(2) *Thirlwall Castle (86-659661)*
The picturesque ruin on the low hill above the Tipalt Burn is called Thirlwall Castle, but this is rather a presumptuous title. It was actually a fortified tower-house built in 1346 when the Border troubles were at their height and Lowland landowners felt the need for some protection. It was L-shaped, four stories high, with thick walls built largely with stone looted from the Wall. The de Thirlwall family owned it until the eighteenth century, hence its name.

(3) *Carvoran (86-667658)*
Carvoran – its Roman name was Magnis – was an early pre-Wall fort built where the Maiden Way meets the Stanegate. It was certainly rebuilt in stone towards the end of Hadrian's reign, about AD 136–8, but otherwise at the moment almost nothing is known of its history. Probably of more interest is the nearby Roman Army Museum with its displays of life-sized figures of legionary and auxiliary soldiers. Information about opening times can be obtained from Roman Army Museum, Carvoran, Greenhead, via Carlisle, CA6 7JB; telephone: Gilsland (0697) 2485.

(4) *Walltown Quarry (86-669659)*
Whinstone – dolerite of the Whin Sill – was quarried here for use as roadstone until 1978. When work ceased, more than 40 acres (16 ha) of the ridge had been removed, along with a substantial section of the Wall. Fortunately Northumberland County Council purchased the site and, with the aid of a grant from the Department of the Environment, is now restoring it for the use of visitors as an historical and archaeological theme park.

(5) *Turret 45A Walltown Crags (86-673663)*
This was built around AD 120 as part of the Stanegate System before the construction of the Wall, probably as a free-standing

watchtower. Later, when the adjoining sections of the Wall were constructed, the tower was butted into them as a turret.

(6) *The Nine Nicks of Thirlwall*

The narrow steep-sided valleys which cut across the Whin Sill are one of the more interesting – and tiring – features of the walk along the Wall. Although certainly a result of ice-flow during the Ice Age, the exact mechanism by which they were formed is still uncertain; the most recent theory is that they were produced by high-pressure meltwater flow under the ice. Unfortunately, work at Walltown Quarry removed some of the Nicks so that the name 'Nine Nicks of Thirlwall' is more a comment on what once was than on what is now. Ice-flow towards the south also accounts for the prominence of the Whin Sill, which was much more resistant to erosion than neighbouring sedimentary rocks; a slight dip of the rock-beds to the south producing the steep scarp which faces north and the gentle slope to the south. Neighbouring parallel – but lower and more rounded – ridges of limestone and sandstone were produced in the same way by erosion of adjoining shales.

(7) *Great Chesters (86-704668)*

Along with Carrawburgh, this was the last fort to be added to the Wall, probably in AD 128. As yet it is unexcavated, so there is comparatively little to be seen, but the fort strong-room (in the centre within a protecting fence) is worth a brief pause. The Roman name of the fort was Aesica or Esica.

(8) *Cawfields Quarry (86-714666)*

Like Walltown Quarry, met earlier in the walk, this was another source of the dolerite used in roadmarking – also, as at Walltown, destroying a good stretch of the Wall in the process. Work finished here in the 1950s, and during 1972–74 the site was reclaimed by Northumberland County Council as a picnic site.

(9) *Milecastle 42*

One of the most photographed milecastles on the Wall, Number 42 narrowly escaped destruction, for the lip of the quarry is only a

short distance away. It was probably built by the Legion II
Augusta.

(10) *The Northumbrian loughs*

The lakes to the north of the Wall – Crag, Greenlee and Broomlee
Loughs – were formed when water collected in rock hollows left
between the ridges after the Ice Age. In the past there were others
in this area, e.g. Caw Lough, but these are now silted up. In the
winter and during periods of migration wildfowl, waders and swans
visit the loughs. The word 'lough' is special to Northumberland
and should be pronounced 'loff'.

(11) *Housesteads (86-790688)*

The layout of all Roman forts was along the same general lines
and this is seen to perfection at Housesteads (Roman name
Velurcion or Borcovocio). The fort was rectangular, with rounded
corners, and extended over an area of 5 acres (2 ha). The
surrounding wall was constructed of stone 4–5 ft (1.2–1.5 m) thick
and 12–14 ft (3.6–4.3 m) high, reinforced at the rear by an earth
embankment. A tower was placed at each corner and there were
others along the sides. The main gate was to the east, but there
were other gates on each of the sides; that to the north, which now
faces a steep drop, led to an incline. All were massive and secured
by guard-rooms. The most important building of the fort was the
Headquarters which was placed in the centre at the junction of the
two main roads of the fort, the Via Principalis and the Via
Praetoria. Immediately south of it was the commandant's house
and to the north the granaries. Barrack blocks were grouped on
three sides, with hospital and workshops, and latrines stood in the
south-east corner. The hillside below the fort was the site of an
extensive civilian settlement, but only one or two buildings are
uncovered.

  The fort and neighbouring museum are open all the year, except
for around Christmas and New Year's Day. There is a charge for
admission.

'. . . the best-preserved latrine in Roman Britain': Housesteads.

(12) *The Knag Burn Gateway (86-791689)*

The Wall was amply provided with gates at the forts and
milecastles. The gate by the Knag Burn, a short distance from the
north-east corner of Housesteads, is unusual as it went directly
through the Wall itself. It was probably constructed early in the
fourth century to allow easier access to and from the civilian
settlement which had grown up around Housesteads. The gateway
had a passage on the south side with gates at each end and flanking
guard turrets. This arrangement would allow travellers and their
animals to be examined before being allowed through. It is
intriguing to see that the Knag Burn still flows under the Wall and
through a culvert constructed more than eighteen centuries ago.

Route 24   The ascent of The Cheviot

As it is the highest point in the Cheviot Hills, the ascent of The
Cheviot itself is an essential expedition. The route taken by most
walkers, however – a fairly direct approach from Langlee over
Scald Hill, followed by a return down the same path – has little to
recommend it. Nor can very much be said for the summit itself, for
it is one of the boggiest areas to be found anywhere, so bad that
the final objective of the Ordnance Survey obelisk is sometimes
almost impossible except for the most determined. Even the
consolation of a decent view is lacking. The route described here,
however, which reaches Scald Hill by a more circuitous way over
Cold Law and Broadhope Hill – both magnificent viewpoints – and
then returns along the length of the valley of the Harthope Burn,
is a very different proposition, worthy to rank among the best in
the Cheviot Hills. Over most of the route little difficulty in route-
finding should be experienced, since fences, the burn or clear
paths are followed; the short descent from Scotsman's Cairn to the
Harthope Burn, across featureless fellside with some potential for
error, can be confusing in thick mist, however, and demands the

The Roman culvert which carries the Knag Burn under Hadrian's Wall
near Housesteads; constructed more than 1800 years ago, it was excavated
in 1856 and 1936.

carrying of map and compass. Some of the paths used on this route are concessionary.

Length: 11 miles (18 km).

Ascent: 2550 ft (780 m).

Starting and finishing point: The valley of the Harthope Burn, to the south-west of Wooler, a short distance beyond the farm of Langlee (75-959229). Drive up the road along the narrow road passing Langlee (on the opposite side of the stream to the L), until you reach notices marking the parking limit for cars; there park on the small area to the R by a stream.

Maps: Landranger 75 and 80; Pathfinder 475 (NT 82/92) and 487 (NT 81/91).

Route description (Maps 24A, 24B, 24C)
From the small parking area walk back along the road for about ¼ mile (400 m) until you reach a PFS 'Cold Law 1' on the L. (*Note*: This is the second PFS on the L.) There turn L up the hillside following a lovely green path up through bracken to the L of a small stream; in the higher reaches the way is marked by short wooden posts. Eventually, near to the top of the ridge, leave the path half R and follow the posts up the pathless fellside to the prominent rocky summit of Cold Law. On the edge where you reach the summit area there is a small stone shelter offering a resting place with magnificent views over to the Northumbrian coast.

Go over the top to the Ordnance Survey obelisk and beyond to a fence. Turn L. Follow the clear path to the L of the fence; soon this bends half R and rises up to a corner. Go through the small gate at the corner and up the moor (no path) towards the top of Broadhope Hill. Although comparatively featureless – and, therefore, hardly worth visiting on its own account – this top offers an even better viewpoint than Cold Law.

Return to the small gate and turn R (i.e. L to your original

MAP 24A

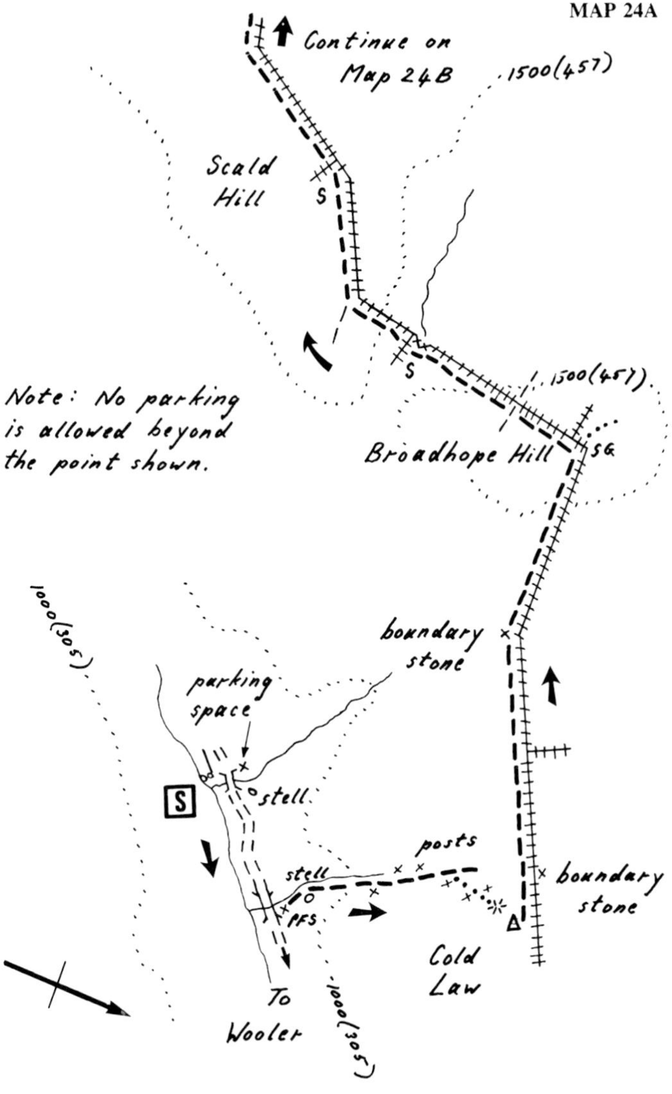
Continue on Map 24B
1500(457)
Scald Hill
S
S
1500(457)
Note: No parking is allowed beyond the point shown.
Broadhope Hill
SG
1000(305)
boundary stone
parking space
S
stell
posts
stell
PFS
boundary stone
Cold Law
To Wooler
1000(305)

MAP 24B

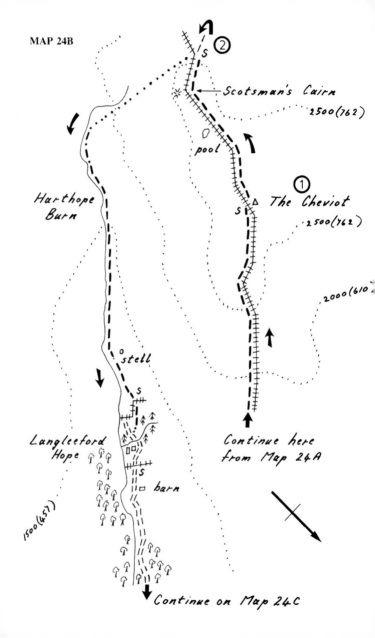

Scotsman's Cairn

2500(762)

Harthope
Burn

pool

① The Cheviot

s

2500(762)

2000(610)

stell

s

Langleeford
Hope

s

barn

1500(457)

Continue here
from Map 24A

Continue on Map 24C

parking space

F

notice

x

Langleeford

G

S

Continue here
from Map 24B

direction). Keep by the fence, soon crossing a shallow valley and then a stile. Where the fence turns to the R, turn with it, climbing to the summit of Scald Hill. (The prominent path joining here from the L is the main route up The Cheviot.) Go over the stile just after Scald Hill and then ascend, keeping by the fence until you reach the summit of The Cheviot. The Ordnance Survey obelisk is on the opposite side of the fence and can be reached over a stile: see (1) The last flight of 44-6504.

From the obelisk continue over the top, now to the R of the fence. This is the route of the Pennine Way – see (2). After just over ½ mile (800 m) of slow descent, pass a stone wall shelter on the opposite side of the fence (Scotsman's Cairn), and some 300 yards (270 m) later reach a corner where the fence bends to the L. (Here the obvious path of the Pennine Way continues ahead.) Go over a stile in the corner and head half L. (i.e. approximately ESE, or a bearing of 112°), passing to the L of a broken stone wall after a few yards. Your route will gradually take you away from the stone wall as it descends the moor. After about ½ mile (800 m) reach a stream. Turn L following the stream down on its L bank on an intermittent path heading roughly north-east.

Continue to follow the L bank of the stream until, after 1¾ miles (3 km), you approach a group of trees in front of the farm of Langleeford Hope. Before the trees, go up to a stile and gate at the corner of a fence and then along to the L of a fence. Where the fence bends R, keep in the same direction, passing some sheep pens. Go into the wood and down to the R to a broad green track, then L along it over a ford. Continue to the farm, which is passed on its L-hand side, to a farm road.

Go along this farm road for another 1¾ miles (3 km) back to the parking place.

(1) *The last flight of 44-6504*

The remains of the American B17 Flying Fortress 44-6504 have lain on the north-west slopes of The Cheviot near Braydon Crag since December 1944. The plane took off from Molesworth, near Cambridge, on a bombing mission to Ulm in Germany, but formation was broken over the Low Countries because of bad weather, and eventually the mission was aborted. After losing its way, the bomber crossed the Northumbrian coast near Seahouses and crashed on The Cheviot in thick cloud. The navigator and bombardier were killed but the other four members of the crew, some of whom were injured, managed to get away from the aircraft before the bomb load exploded, and were later found and rescued by local shepherds. One hero of the rescue was the collie Sheila who was awarded the Dickin Medal by the People's Dispensary for Sick Animals for her valiant efforts. It is thought that the aircraft's navigator may have been fed false bearings by German radio operators who picked up his distress signals.

(2) *The Pennine Way*

The Pennine Way, which runs along the main ridge of the Cheviot Hills from Byrness to Kirk Yetholm, makes a detour during its final miles to visit the summit of The Cheviot. Neither views nor good walking result from this, however, and many walkers, keeping a wary eye on the time and their growing weariness, give it a miss.

Route 25   The Northumbrian Coast: Alnmouth to Beadnell

The coastline of Northumberland is one of the finest in the British Isles: a magnificent stretch of superb sandy beaches, dunes and rocks; a birdwatcher's paradise; still comparatively unspoilt and free of undue commercial pressures. Arguably the outstanding section is from the mouth of the Aln to the harbour at Beadnell, and this is the route given here, but longer journeys are possible (see page 318). The mouth of the Aln, the ruins of Dunstanburgh Castle, seabird colonies, the fishing villages of Boulmer, Craster, Low Newton-by-the-Sea and Beadnell, and distant views of Coquet Island and the Farne group are the main features, but it is the solitude, and the sound of the wind and the sea and the calling of seabirds, that you are most likely to remember. *Note*: A short section of shoreline near Alnmouth is used on this route which may be impassable or inadvisable at high tide or in bad weather. In addition, further along there are several sections where the beach will give the better walking, although there are alternative ways. It is recommended, therefore, that you obtain information about the tides and weather before you start, and take these into consideration.

Length: 15 miles (24 km).

Ascent: This is impossible to estimate as it will depend on the actual route taken, but walkers can leave Alnmouth safe in the knowledge that there is very little ascent, for the route keeps either to the flat and level beach or to the coastal path, which is almost as flat and level.

Starting point: Alnmouth (81-246102).

Finishing point: The harbour at Beadnell (75-237285).

Maps: Landranger 75 and 81; Pathfinder 477 (NU 21/22).

Route description (Maps 25A, 25B, 25C, 25D)
  (a) *Alnmouth to Boulmer.*
(See Map 5, p. 109 for alternative start over the ridge.) Go down the main street in Alnmouth to reach the mouth of the river – for information about the village see (1). There go over the dunes to the beach and turn L. Walk along the lovely firm sands for 1¼ miles (2 km) until you see some caravans up on the L, followed soon afterwards by some large buildings. (The shore here is rocky in patches, but is not difficult to walk, using either strips of sand or flat rocky 'pavement' areas.) About 250 yards (230 m) after the buildings, at a notice 'Caution. Cliff top erosion. Please take care', and where a small stream comes down to the beach, there is a choice of routes – the beach or a path up on the L.

  If you take the path you should reach a rough road after 350 yards (320 m) with a PFS 'Foxton Hall/Alnmouth' at the front of some chalets. Cross and go to the R to a fence corner; there turn L

The starting point of Route 25: the beautiful estuary at Alnmouth.

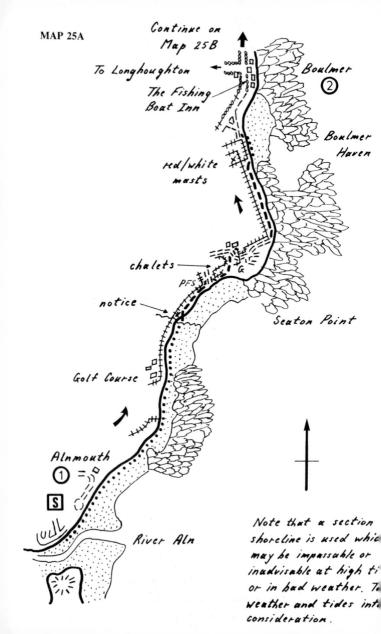

MAP 25A

Continue on
Map 25B

To Longhoughton

The Fishing
Boat Inn

Boulmer
②

Boulmer
Haven

red/white
masts

chalets

PFS

G

notice

Seaton Point

Golf Course

Alnmouth
①

S

River Aln

Note that a section
shoreline is used which
may be impassable or
inadvisable at high ti
or in bad weather. To
weather and tides int
consideration.

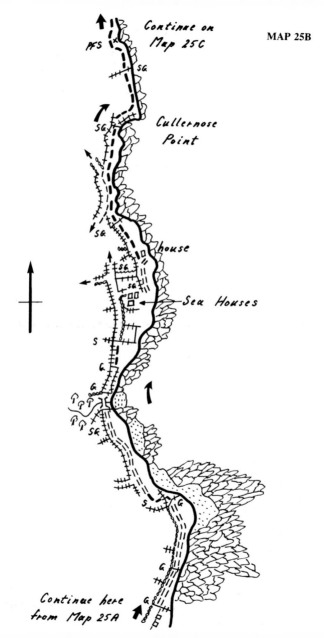

MAP 25B

Continue on
Map 25C

PFS

SG

Cullernose
Point

SG

SG

house

SG

SG

Sea Houses

S

G

G

P

P

SG

S

G

G

G

Continue here
from Map 25A

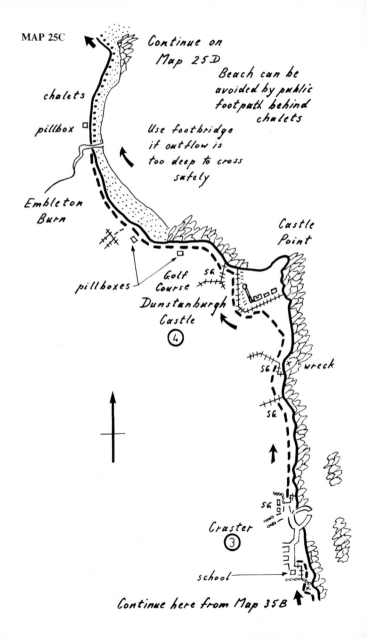

MAP 25C

Continue on
Map 25D

Beach can be
avoided by public
footpath behind
chalets

chalets

pillbox

Use footbridge
if outflow is
too deep to cross
safely

Embleton
Burn

Castle
Point

pillboxes

Golf
Course

SG

Dunstanburgh
Castle

④

SG   wreck

SG

SG

Craster
③

school

Continue here from Map 35B

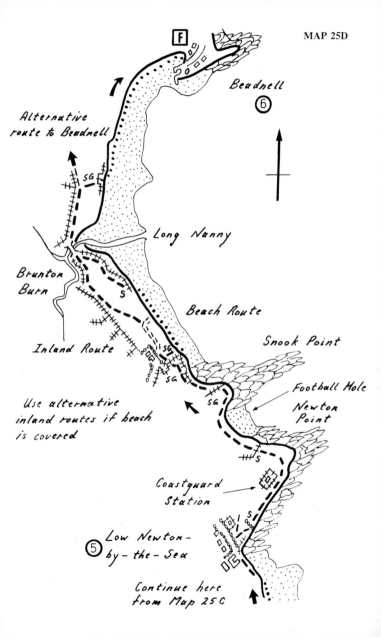

F

Beadnell

⑥

Alternative
route to Beadnell

SG

Long Nanny

Brunton
Burn

S

Beach Route

Inland Route

Snook Point

SG

SG

Football Hole
Newton
Point

SG

Use alternative
inland routes if beach
is covered

S

Coastguard
Station

⑤ Low Newton-
by-the-Sea

Continue here
from Map 25C

and walk along the edge of the cliff with the chalets on your L. After a few yards you reach a fence. Keep to the R of this until you reach a farm road; there turn R. Continue along it, passing the farm, until you reach the junction of three tracks at a fence corner. Take the one to the L which immediately bends R and runs parallel with a fence. This leads back to the shore.

Continue along the path keeping to the R of the fence, or along the sand of the beach, until you reach the road in Boulmer. Turn R into the village. The Fishing Boat Inn is on the R. See (2) for details about Boulmer.

(b) *Boulmer to Craster.*

Go along the road through the village, keeping straight ahead at a road junction. Soon go through a gate and along a rough road. This leads back to the beach at a gate. Keep on the rough road parallel with the beach and by a wall, until you reach another gate. Go through and half L over a footbridge to a ladder stile. Keep on the path beyond for over ¼ mile (400 m) until you reach the end of a road (to Longhoughton). Keep going in the same direction along the coast path to the R of a fence. Eventually reach a gate and a new concrete footbridge over a stream coming on to the beach.

Cross the footbridge and walk up the rough road ahead, soon going through a gate. At a PFS keep ahead, with a fence to the L. Continue in the same direction, keeping by the fence for ½ mile (800 m), until you reach a road just after a large farm (Sea Houses). Turn R through a small gate and go along a path to the sea. At the end go through another small gate and turn L.

Go up the path parallel with the shore (i.e. in the direction of Craster as indicated on the PFS), passing a house to the L. Soon the path meets the coast road; do not go into the road but keep on the path throughout. Eventually the path reaches a small gate with a prominent cliff over to the R (Cullernose Point). Go through and half R up the path above the cliff. At the end, the path swings L parallel with the shore. Follow the path for ⅓ mile (500 m) until you reach the old school at Craster. Go over the ladder stile to the

Craster.

R and along by the school fence to a small playing-field; there turn L to the road. Go R along the road to the harbour at Craster – for information on Craster and the harbour, see (3).

(c) *Craster to Low Newton-by-the-Sea.*
Go by the harbour, along the road ahead, and through a small gate which leads to the coast path. Follow this for 1 mile (1.6 km) to the gate which leads up to Dunstanburgh Castle – see (4). Pass the castle to the L, soon reaching the shore again, then L along the coast path away from the castle. Keep on this for ¾ mile (1.2 km), passing a golf-course, until you reach a crossing path (this is about 100 yards, 90 m after the second of two pillboxes). Continue in the same direction along the coast. A public right of way follows the dunes, passing to the L of some chalets, which will take you right to Low Newton-by-the-Sea – see (5). If the tide permits, however, it is far better to take to the beach where the firmness of tide-washed sand will enable you to maintain a good pace until you reach the village. Either way you will have to cross the outflow of Embleton Burn; if this is too deep to cross safely, then use a footbridge a short distance inland.

(d) *Low Newton-by-the-Sea to Beadnell harbour.*
Go up the road, turning R over a stile opposite St Mary's Cottages (PFS 'Beadnell'). Walk along the coast path around Newton Point, passing the coastguard station to the R. After the Point pass the firm sands of Football Hole and then the rocky promontory of Snook Point. Continue along the path (not on the dune slopes!) for 300 yards (270 m), then go half L to a small gate by a car-park. From here there are two possible ways, depending upon your inclination and the tide:
(1) *Beach route.* Turn R on to the beach and walk L along the beach for ⅔ mile (1.1 km) until you approach the estuary of Long Nanny (i.e. a wide gap in the dunes). There go L up a path over the dunes to a stile in the corner of a fence. Cross and follow the fence to a bridge over the burn (the area on the opposite side of the fence is a nature reserve and should not be entered).
(2) *Inland route.* From the small gate by the car-park go L to a gate. Do not go through, but turn R at a PFS 'Beadnell' to a small gate. Go through and on to a farm road. Keep in the same

direction, with a fence to the L and the dunes to the R. Eventually where the fence bends to the L keep in the same direction along the path to the bridge.

Cross the bridge and go half R on a path by a fence. This path continues into Beadnell, but is not particularly interesting. If the tide allows, it is far better to go along it until another fence joins from the L, then go R on a path which takes you back to the beach. Turn L and walk along the beach until you reach the harbour at Beadnell. See (6) Beadnell.

Note: Although the next stretch to Seahouses and Bamburgh can be walked and is not without interest, it is probably best to finish the walk at Beadnell harbour. After that the busy B1340 hugs the coast, and holidaymakers and the establishments that cater for them are more in evidence. The quality of the walking is also not what it was. Far better to finish here while memories of those miles of wonderfully quiet beaches, bays, rocky headlands and bird-haunted tidelines are still clearly etched in your mind.

(1) *Alnmouth* – see page 112

(2) *Boulmer (81-267143)*
Although Boulmer (pronounced Boomer) is a slightly spartan place, it offers a welcome mid-day resting point on the long walk up the coast. Of particular interest will be the Fishing Boat Inn which gives excellent hospitality. The inn has a painting by A. H. Marsh showing the women of the village dragging a lifeboat over the sands in preparation for a launch; there is also a collection of photographs of the men of Boulmer who fought in the Second World War. Boulmer was – and still remains – a fishing village, for Boulmer Haven just to the south offers a sheltered anchorage, well shielded from the force of the sea by two long arms of rock (the North and South Reins) which almost enclose it. The narrow gap between the Reins is marked by the tall red and white posts on the shore opposite. In the old days Boulmer was a centre for smuggling, particularly of gin. It was also the home from 1825 of a lifeboat maintained by the RNLI. When this was withdrawn in

1968, after sterling work, the people of Boulmer were sufficiently incensed to found their own life-saving service; the station of the Boulmer Volunteer Lifeboat Service can be seen to the left as you enter the village.

(3) *Craster and Craster Memorial Harbour* – see page 157

(4) *Dunstanburgh Castle* – see page 161

(5) *Low Newton-by-the-Sea (75-242246)*
Low Newton – also called Newton Seahouses – was a fishing village, for nearby St Mary's Haven, protected on the south by the Emblestone and on the north by Newton Point, provided a welcome sanctuary from the sea. The main feature is the lovely quadrangle, The Square, open to the sea on one side so that cobles could be drawn in on stormy days. The Ship Inn is among the cottages at the far end. Almost the entire village with some adjoining land was bought by the National Trust in 1980 and 1982, with funds from Enterprise Neptune and a donation from the Hunter Association of the Trust.

(6) *Beadnell (75-237286)*
The best things about Beadnell are the lovely little harbour and the old limekilns just behind them. They were the result of an agreement in 1798 between Richard Pringle, who built the first kiln, and John Wood, who built the harbour. The limestone and coal (in the proportion of two to one by volume), which were extracted on Wood's estate, were brought to the top of the kiln on a tramway and the lime produced taken away by ship. The enterprise was so successful that later John Wood built a second and then a third kiln on the site. The kilns, now used to store fishermen's pots and tackle, are in the care of the National Trust to whom they were given in 1935 by Miss A. Craster.

Route 26   The Confluence of the Allens

The West and East Allens rise at the most southerly point of Northumberland in an area of high summits and county boundaries, and flow for about 10 miles (16 km) in a northerly direction before joining together just to the south of Allen Banks. The upper reaches of both valleys and their meeting point are areas of considerable beauty. Lovely riverside paths, high hillside terraces, beautiful deciduous woodlands and finally a return over Dryburn Moor, with remains of the old lead-mining industry, make up this outstanding walk. Much of the early part of the route to Harlowbank is waymarked with yellow arrows.

Length: 14 miles (23 km).

Ascent: 1650 ft (500 m).

Starting and finishing point: Allendale Town (87-839559). Cars may be parked at the centre of the town.

Maps: Landranger 87; Pathfinder 559 (NY 65/75) and 560 (NY 85/95).

Route description (Maps 26A, 26B, 26C)
Go down the Whitfield/Haltwhistle road, which soon descends steeply and swings to the L. Immediately after the bend go back half R down a footpath (PFS 'Allenmill/Oakpool'), which leads to the river bank. Follow the footpath to the R of the river – notice the lined tunnel opening on the R just before crossing a footbridge; see (1) the Blackett Level Portal. After ¾ mile (1.2 km) reach a road. Turn L and cross the river over a bridge. On the far side go R (PFS 'Oakpool') back on to the river bank.
   Go along the path through a deciduous wood for ¼ mile (400 m), then half L away from the river up to a small gate. Keep by a wall for a few yards, then go half L again alongside a row of trees to cut the corner and rejoin the river further along. Keep by the river until you reach a wall, then turn half L to a farm road which leads to a farm. Go through the small gate at the corner of the farm area, pass in front of the house and then over the footbridge just beyond. Again keep by the river, soon entering a coniferous wood over a stile. At the far end leave the wood over a

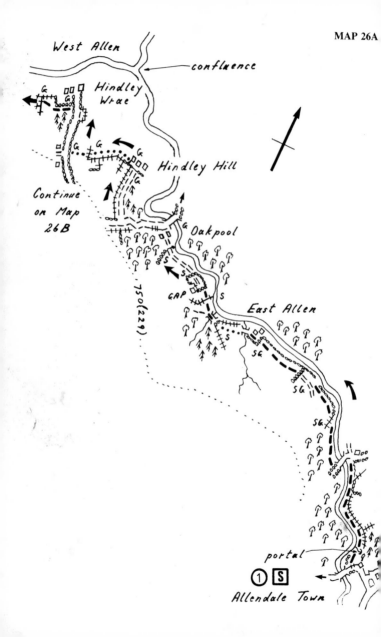

West Allen

confluence

Hindley
Wrae

Hindley Hill

Continue
on Map
26B

750(229)

Oakpool

GAP

East Allen

SG

SG

SG

portal

① Ⓢ

Allendale Town

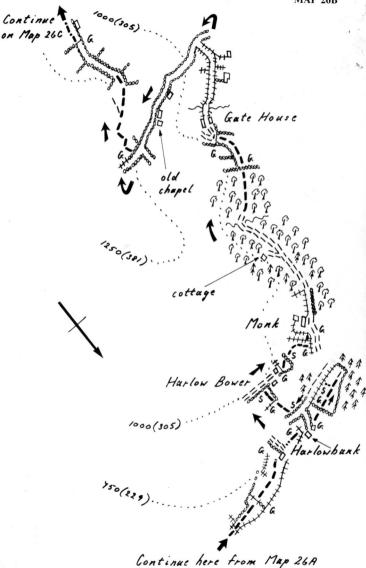

Continue
on Map 26C

1000(305)

Gate House

old
chapel

1250(381)

cottage

Monk

Harlow Bower

S

S

G

S

G

1000(305)

G

Harlowbank

750(229)

G

G

Continue here from Map 26A

MAP 26C

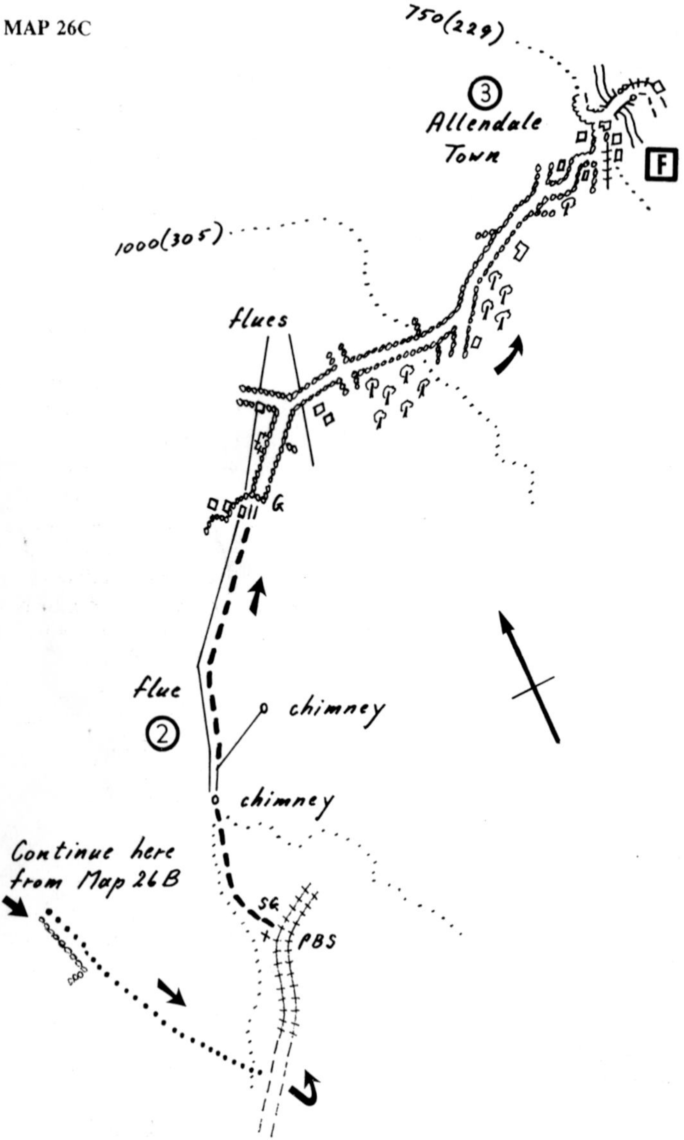

750(229)

③ Allendale Town

F

1000(305)

flues

G

flue
②

chimney

chimney

Continue here
from Map 26B

SG

PBS

ladder stile and continue in the same direction to pass a second farmhouse on its R. Just beyond, reach the farm road and follow this to a third farm; there go through the farmyard into a road.

Turn L and follow the road uphill through a delightful wood with good views down to the river on the L. Where the wood ends, go R down a side road (PFS 'Hindley Hill/Wide Earls'). At Hindley Hill enter the farmyard and turn L to the far gate, i.e. that to the L of a barn. Go through and up the L-hand edge of the field, aiming for another farm at the top of the hill. At the top go through a gate and then a second gate to enter a lane in front of the farm buildings. Turn R down the lane.

At the end of the wood on the L just before a farm, Hindley Wrae, go L through a gate and alongside a wall. Where the wall ends, go half R to a gate in the far corner. Follow the path beyond, keeping parallel with the fence on the L (later a wall), until you reach a farmhouse after ½ mile (800 m). Go through the gate to the L of the house and continue in the same direction (no path) to a gate to the L of the next farm, Harlowbank. Turn R and then L in front of the house and pass through a gate immediately after a small barn. The path is obvious, leading across the field. In the middle of the second field go up to the L to a ladder stile and into a road. Turn L.

About 30 yards (27 m) after the end of the farm road to Harlowbank turn R over a stile and head up a steep field, keeping parallel with a wood over to the R. At the top of the field go through a gate and continue climbing to the L of a wall, to reach a ladder stile which leads into a farm road. Turn R along it, soon passing a farm (Harlow Bower) to the L. Go through a gate to the R of a barn (yellow arrow) and straight ahead to a small gate beside a wall. Now follow the field down to a step stile; from here Monk Farm, which is your immediate destination, can be seen in the near distance, slightly L. A line of telegraph poles goes across the field ahead; follow these until you reach the fifth pole where a waymarking arrow points to the R to a field corner. There go through a small gate and follow a further arrow to the L. Finally go along by a fence to a field gate near Monk Farm; there bear R, and then L, along a farm road.

At a fork, immediately before a cottage, go R. The way grows gradually less distinct, but remains clear as it goes through a lovely deciduous wood with good views down to the R. At the end of the wood leave through a gate and continue in the same direction to the R of a wall, to eventually reach a gate in a corner. Go through and down to a farm, Gate House, and a road.

Go along the road until you reach a T-junction after ½ mile (800 m). There turn L steeply uphill. After ¾ mile (1.2 km), where a road joins from the L, go R through a gate (PFS 'Dryburn Moor'). Follow the clear path which later curves to the L and into a walled lane. At the far end of the lane go through a gate and alongside a wall. Where the wall bends to the R keep in the same direction, heading up the moor (no path) for ½ mile (800 m) until you reach a road – the regular black and white snow poles will probably be seen first. Turn L.

Where the road bends to the R, go through the small gate on the L (PBS 'Carriers Way/Fell House') and follow the clear path which heads towards two prominent chimneys. Reach the L-hand chimney (short and squat) and continue alongside the obvious flues beyond. Where the flues separate, take the L-hand one keeping to its R. Eventually pass a farm and enter a walled lane. The chimneys and flues were connected to smelt-mills lower down – see (2) below.

The way back to Allendale Town is now along a road. At a T-junction go R and then straight across at a crossroads. At a further T-junction turn L. After ⅓ mile (500 m) walk down a minor road to the R, which soon bends downhill to a further T-junction. Go L. At a main road go R over a bridge and up to the centre of Allendale Town where you started the walk.

(Apart from one or two tea-rooms, there is little in Allendale to make you linger, although it is not an unattractive place. It does, however, have its moments – see (3) Guizers and kits, for one of them.)

(1) *The Blackett Level Portal (86-838560)*
The masonry arch from which a small stream emerges is the entrance to a drainage level which takes water from several mines

in the East Allendale ore-field. Work on it began in 1854 with the intention of eventually driving it for 7½ miles (12 km), but it had only reached 4½ miles (7 km) when work was abandoned in 1903, owing to the collapse of the local mining industry.

(2) *The moor chimneys and flues*

Lead-mining took place in both West and East Allendales and near Blanchland; there were also other important mines just over the Border to the south, e.g. on Alston Moor. The ore extracted was usually galena (lead sulphide) which had then to be smelted to release its lead content. To do this the ore was first dressed, i.e. broken up into small pieces and sorted to remove as much rubbish as possible, and then heated with wood or coal to oxidize and reduce the ore to the metal. As can be imagined, the fumes from this heating process were very damaging to health and the environment, partly because of the nature of the gases produced and partly because of the low temperature at which lead volatilizes, and they were removed from the vicinity of the smelting-mill by a flue. It was discovered around the middle of the nineteenth century, however, that valuable lead, hitherto lost by volatilization, could be condensed out from the gases by the use of very long flues, and these were built at some of the larger smelting-mills. The flues were usually wide stone-lined tunnels built up a moorland hillside; a chimney was provided at the end to give a draught through the system. These flues were later cleaned out, thus increasing the quantity of lead produced from the smelting; they also had the advantage of saving the mill owner from expensive litigation for any damage done to the surrounding area.

The two chimneys and flues seen along this walk were built between 1845 and 1850 under the direction of Thomas Sopwith, chief mining agent of the Beaumont family who owned several mines, to serve a smelting-mill near the East Allen. The total length of the flues was about 5 miles (8 km). Long lengths are now in a collapsed state, but other sections are remarkably intact.

(3) *Guizers and kits*

Fire festivals of one sort or another were once fairly common in Britain. Nowadays, however, few of them survive, with the great exception, of course, of 5 November celebrations which are still held throughout the length and breadth of the land. (Although even these, with the present sensible emphasis on safety, are not what they were once upon a day!) Allendale Town is one of the few places which still holds one, along with Hatherleigh in the West Country and Biggar over the Border.

In Allendale the real action begins just before midnight on New Year's Eve. A number of tar barrels, known as 'kits' and filled with combustible materials, are lit and paraded in a line around the town, accompanied by the local band. The kits are carried on the heads of local men, brightly dressed for the occasion, known as 'guizers'. The parade finishes at an enormous fire in the square. Although the event itself is over fairly quickly, as can be imagined the actual festivities are rather more prolonged and the local inns do a roaring trade. As usual with these things, the origin of the custom is now obscure.

Route 27   The Usway Burn and Clennell Street

This is a glorious route which follows the Usway Burn from Alwinton almost as far as the Border ridge and then returns down Clennell Street, an old packhorse and droving way. Despite its length, the small amount of climbing and the easy going underfoot – along lovely grassy paths and rough forest roads – should bring it within the reach of even moderate walkers. Its finest moments are on the descent into the Coquet valley towards Shillmoor, where a superb path slants down across the hillside, and then later at its northern extremity where Clennell Street is joined – but every yard of the way should be highly enjoyable.

Length: 14 miles (23 km).

One of the moor chimneys which served a smelting mill near the East Allen; the rubble interior had an outer shell of dressed stone.

Ascent: 1900 ft (580 m).

Starting and finishing point: The National Park car-park in Alwinton (80-920063).

Maps: Landranger 80; Pathfinder 487 (NT 81/91) and 499 (NT 80/90).

Route description (Maps 27A, 27B, 27C)
Go into the road from the car-park and turn R. After 1 mile (1.6 km) go through a small gate in the fence on the R. (If you miss this, note that it is a short distance *before* a small hut on the R.) Follow a lovely grassy path up the hillside to a stile in a fence. As you climb, note the bare slope on the far side of the Coquet: this is Barrow Scar and is the best place to see a sequence of the Cementstone Group described on page 26. Soon cross a further stile and go on to a moor road. Turn R. After 100 yards (90 m), go L at a junction, aiming for a post on the top of a hill. (This post – and others following – contains a blue arrow.) Keep in the same direction to another post and to the edge of the hill, with a lovely view ahead down to the farm of Shillmoor at the confluence of the Usway Burn and the Coquet.

Go straight ahead down a holloway – this is an ancient way known as Pass Peth – to a delightful grassy path which slants to the R down and across the hillside. Eventually go through a small gate in a fence and continue on to cross a stream. Go up half L from the stream and along a path to a post on a moor road. Go straight across and along the path opposite to the R of the Coquet until you reach a stile in a fence soon after crossing another small stream (Wholehope Burn). Beyond, continue to the R of a wall until you reach a farm road. Go L along this, over a bridge and to the L of the buildings at Shillmoor.

Turn R between barns and the house and walk up to a gate. This leads to a rough military road which goes up the valley of the Usway Burn. Follow this for 1¾ miles (3 km) until you reach a gate in a fence. Soon after, reach a second gate in a wall leading to the farm of Batailshiel Haugh.

MAP 27A

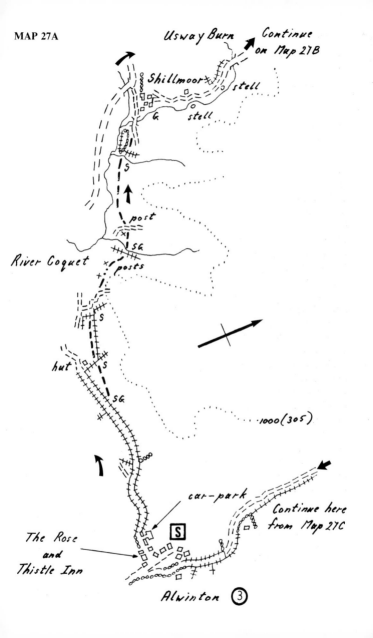

Usway Burn

Continue on Map 27B

Shillmoor

stell

stell

G

stell

S

post

x

SG

River Coquet

x

posts

S

hut

S

SG

1000 (305)

car-park

Continue here from Map 27C

The Rose and Thistle Inn

S

Alwinton ③

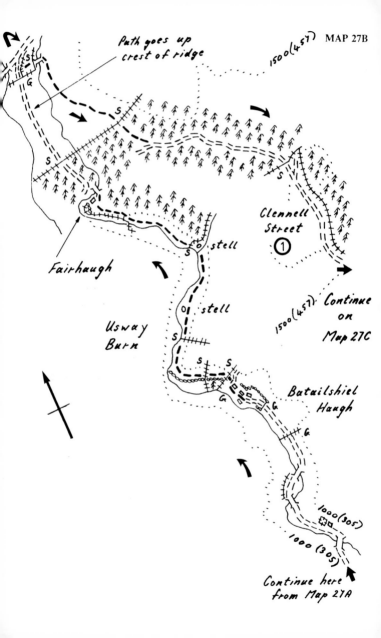

Path goes up
crest of ridge

1500(457)   MAP 27B

Clennell
Street

①

Fairhaugh

stell

stell

Usway
Burn

1500(457) Continue
on
Map 27C

Batailshiel
Haugh

1000(305)

1000 (305)

Continue here
from Map 27A

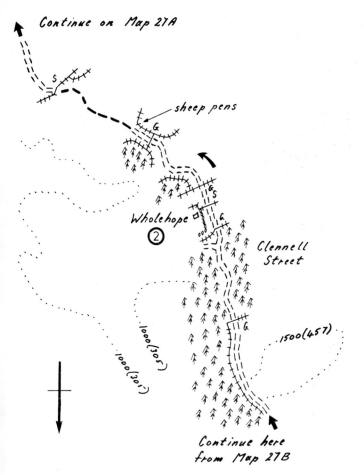

Continue on Map 27A

sheep pens

S

G

Wholehope
②

G
S

G

Clennell
Street

1000(305)

1000(305)

1500(457)

G

Continue here
from Map 27B

The public right of way is waymarked and goes along the farm road, passes the bungalow and barns, and goes through a gate at the end of the barns; from there the path rises to a stile in a fence to the right of a small group of conifers. From the stile, continue to the R of a wall, gradually dropping down until you reach the Usway Burn beyond the sheep pens.

Keep by the burn for 1 mile (1.6 km) until you reach a stell at the corner of a forest and at the confluence of two streams. Pass the stell on the L, going over a stile in a fence shortly afterwards. Follow the clear path just inside the forest, keeping near the L-hand stream for ¾ mile (1.2 km). At the end, the path leaves the stream and goes alongside a wall, passing the farmhouse of Fairhaugh to a footbridge. Go over the bridge and up to a forest road; there turn R. The forest road goes up, over the top of the hill and down to a stile and gate. Beyond follow the grand path which rises up the crest of a ridge with steep slopes dropping away on each flank. At the top go through a gate and up by a fence.

After about 75 yards (70 m) go R over a stile and down the hillside to a footbridge. Take the path which rises to the R on the opposite side to enter a forest after ⅔ mile (1.1 km). This is the line of an old way – see (1) Clennell Street. Follow the narrow path ahead, soon joining with a forest road running in the same direction. Now keep on this forest road as it goes through the forest for about ¾ mile (1.1. km); then in the open (but with the forest close by on the L) for 1 mile (1.6 km); and finally through a second stretch of forest for ⅔ mile (1.1. km). At the end of this second stretch, where the forest road bends L, go ahead down a path to a gate.

Leave the forest and continue on the obvious track to the R of a wall. At the end of the wall go over a stile by a hut and ruin – see (2) Wholehope youth hostel – and then continue down the field to a gate to the R of the forest. Continue along the moor road until you reach a fence, then go along with the fence on your R. Where the fence ends by some sheep pens, continue in the same direction, curving to the R. Go over the moor and down to a

Batailshiel Haugh on the Usway Burn.

fence, there bending to the L to a gate and stile. Go over the stile and up the moor road. Soon this goes by a fence, then a wall, to the entrance to a lane. This will take you back to Alwinton – see (3).

(1) *Clennell Street*
The old road of Clennell Street runs from Alwinton in Upper Coquetdale to Cocklawfoot in the valley of the Bowmont Water on the Scottish side of the Border. It is certainly an ancient route, going back to medieval times and possibly even to prehistoric, and walkers who use it nowadays are following in the footsteps of a host of fellow-travellers – monks, Scottish drovers, tough packmen, mosstroopers, and probably a smuggler or two – who went that way. It takes its name from Clennell near Alwinton.

(2) *Wholehope youth hostel (80-902093)*
The small ruin on the left just after leaving Kidland Forest was originally a shepherd's cottage, but is better known for its time as a simple and unmanned youth hostel. This closed about 1960. Pronounced 'Woolup'.

(3) *Alwinton (80-921064)*
Alwinton is a small but delightful village, the highest in Coquetdale, situated at the junction of two ancient roads, The Street and Clennell Street. Man has been here for a long time, for there are Iron Age hillforts on Gallow Law and on Clennell Hill, with cultivation terraces on Lord's Seat, all only a short distance away. The Church of St Michael and All Angels, about ½ mile (800 m) from the village on the Harbottle road, was built on a steep hillside overlooking the junction of the Coquet and the Alwin, so that a steep flight of ten steps has to be negotiated in going from the nave to the chancel. Beneath the latter there is a crypt, constructed towards the end of the thirteenth century and last used in 1868, which contains the remains of members of the Selby family who lived at Biddlestone Hall, thought to be the

Approaching Fairhaugh in Kidland Forest.

model for Osbaldistone Hall in Sir Walter Scott's *Rob Roy*. It is said that one vicar of Alwinton had the misfortune to be evicted by a parishioner who turned his dwelling into an ale-house; wherever that was, it has now gone, along with the Red Lion, but the village can still boast one delightful pub, the Rose and Thistle. A good time to visit Alwinton is the second Saturday in October when the Alwinton Border Shepherds' Sheep Show is held.

Route 28   Housesteads to Bellingham

This route follows the path of the Pennine Way from the Wall to Bellingham, except for the first mile or so where the Way's start from Twice Brewed is replaced by one more to the east. This change has the advantage of bringing the walker by Housesteads – without doubt the finest fort along the Wall – and along the superb section over Cuddy's crags. North of the Wall, the way is over low-lying moorland followed by forest, until the final miles when it crosses farmland. Although the route lacks spectacular features, it should nevertheless give a highly enjoyable day of walking on which you are likely to meet few others. There are youth hostels at or near both ends of the route (Once Brewed and Bellingham), also guest-houses and hotels.

Length: 15 miles (24 km).

Ascent: 1350 ft (410 m).

Starting point: The Housesteads car-park on the Military Road, B6318 (87-794684).

Finishing point: Bellingham (80-839834).

Maps: Landranger 80 and 87; Pathfinder 522 (NY 88/98), 534 (NY 87/97), 533 (NY 67/77) and 546 (NY 66/76).

Route description (Maps 28A, 28B, 28C, 28D)
Leave the car-park at the far end by the Museum and refreshment

bar and walk up the broad path towards the fort – see (1)
Housesteads. Do not enter the fort, but go up the L-hand side to
the Wall at the top of the ridge. (If you have not been here before
then you *must* pay a visit to the fort – the office for your entrance
fee is at the south-west corner. But keep a wary eye on the time!)
Climb the ladder stile on to the Wall and turn L. Walk along the
Wall top until you reach Milecastle 37 – see (2) – then descend on
the L-hand side. Continue along by the Wall until you reach a
crossing wall in the second dip (Rapishaw Gap).

Cross a ladder stile to the R and follow the path which goes half
R (PFS 'Pennine Way') away from the Wall. This crosses an area
of flat moor to a ladder stile in a wall. Go over and continue in the
same direction on a farm road, i.e. roughly parallel with the wall
on the L. Soon cross a further ladder stile on a ridge top and
follow the path on the opposite side, which descends to the L over
a small stream, Jenkins Burn, and then swing R. At a PFS go L to
a stile in a wall. Greenlee Lough is on the L and Broomlee Lough
on the R – see (3) for an account of their formation. Descend the
steep slope ahead and go over a footbridge. Beyond the footbridge
at a PW sign turn R, and 150 yards (140 m) later turn half L. At a
junction of three walls go over a further ladder stile and then a
footbridge, then round a wall corner to still another stile which
leads into a farm road.

Turn R along the farm road, which immediately enters a forest,
and continue along it for ¾ mile (1.2 km). At an open area on the
L leave the forest road at a white PW acorn, continuing in the
same direction on a footpath. Follow the footpath for a further
¾ mile (1.2 km) to the end of the forest. Leave over a stile,
continuing on a clear path in approximately the same direction
across an open area of moor; dark walls of conifers press in on
three sides and the long swell of Hawk Side blocks the fourth. On
the opposite side re-enter the forest and begin a long, gradual
descent on a wide path. (A short distance along the fence to the R
where the path enters the forest is Comyn's Cross – see (4).) Soon
reach a forest road and turn R along it, leaving to the L (i.e.
keeping in the same direction where the road bends) after a few
yards. Follow the PW signs across two further forest roads, to

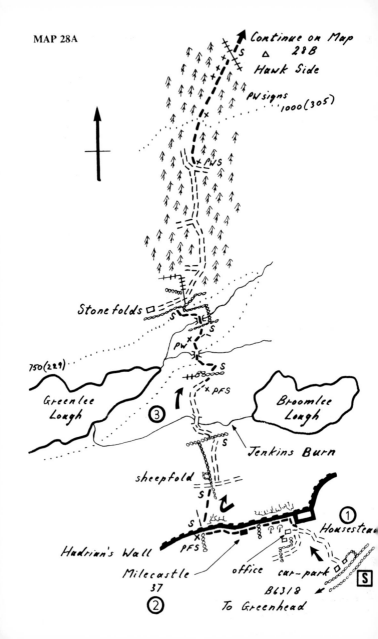

Continue on Map 28B
Hawk Side
PW signs
1000 (305)

PWS

Stone folds
S
S
PW ×
S
750 (229)
++
Greenlee Lough
× PFS
③
Broomlee Lough
S
Jenkins Burn
sheepfold
S
S
Hadrian's Wall
PFS ×
Milecastle
37
②
① Housesteads
office
car-park
B6318
To Greenhead
S

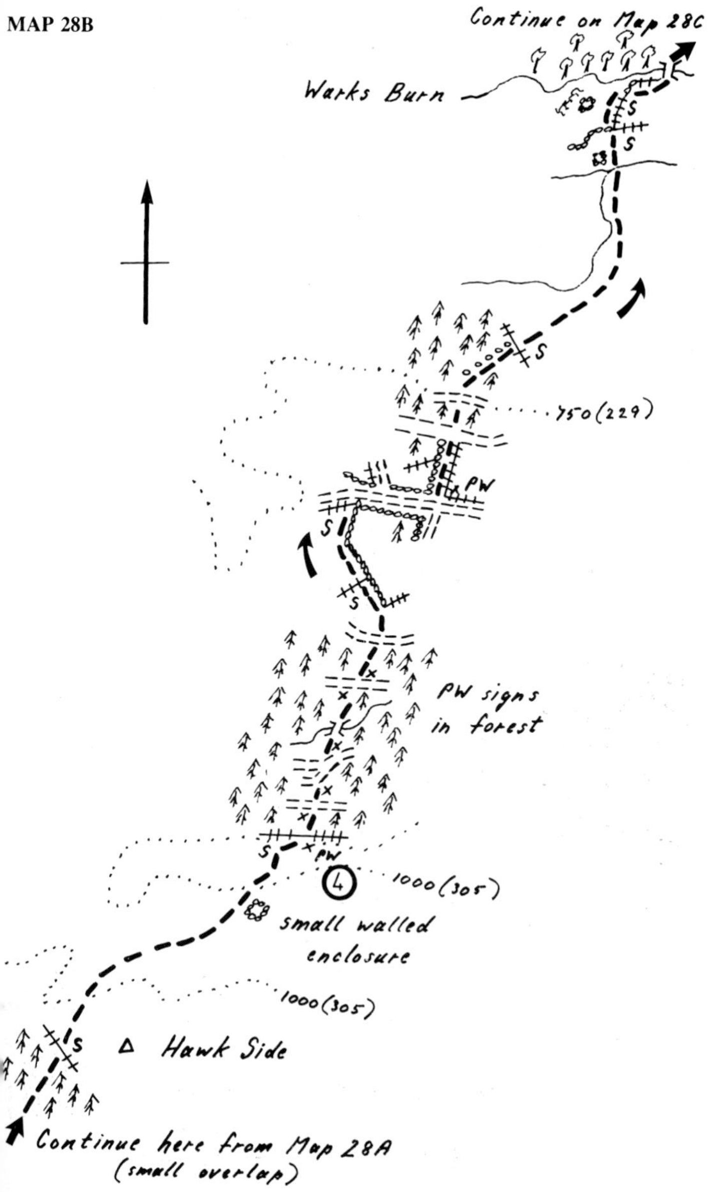

Continue on Map 28C

Warks Burn

750(229)

PW

S

S

S

PW signs
in forest

S PW

④ 1000(305)

small walled
enclosure

1000(305)

△ Hawk Side

S

Continue here from Map 28A
(small overlap)

MAP 28C

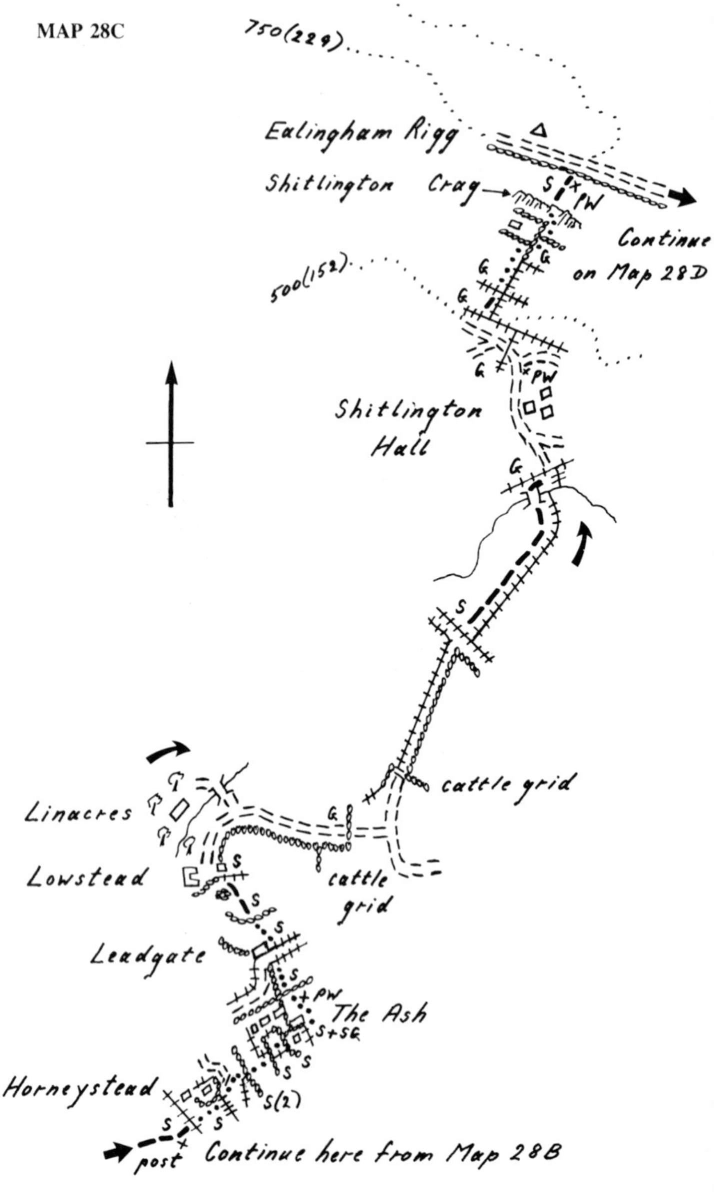
750(229)
Ealingham Rigg
Shitlington Crag
S
PW
Continue on Map 28D
G
500(152)
G
G
G
PW
Shitlington Hall
G
S
cattle grid
Linacres
G
Lowstead
S
cattle grid
S
S
Leadgate
S
PW
The Ash
S+SG
S
S
Horneystead
S(2)
S
S
post
Continue here from Map 28B

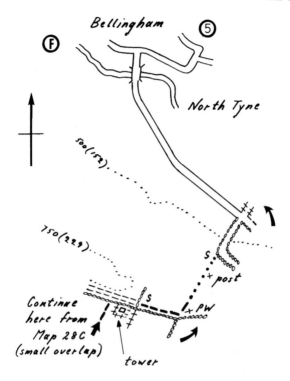

Bellingham

(5)

(F)

North Tyne

500(152)

750(229)

S

x post

S

x PW

Continue here from Map 28C (small overlap)

tower

eventually reach a corner formed by a wall and a fence. Go ahead
alongside the wall until you reach a road. There turn R.

After 150 yards (140 m) turn L (PW sign). Soon cross a road
and continue on the path to the end of the forest. Keep in the
same direction, gradually moving L to reach a small stream which
is followed down – there are good views ahead of moorland and
farmland. Eventually descend to a stream, cross it, and rise up to a
wall corner. Keep to the R of a wall until you can cross at a ladder
stile, then keep by a fence, and later a wall, until you reach a
stream, Warks Burn. Go to the R over a wall, and continue until
you can cross over a footbridge.

Rise up from the footbridge, soon bending half R to the top of a
wood, then at a post turn half L to a stile in a fence. Continue to a
stile in front of a farmhouse (Horneystead). (At the present time,
refreshments can be obtained here.) Go round the farm to the R
to a corner formed by a fence and wall. Cross two stiles here, and
then head directly for the next farm, crossing two fields to a ladder
stile to the L of a large barn. Go between a wall and the barn to a
small gate, then a stile. Turn L to pass the farm on the R, to a stile
in a wall. Go up the field to R of wall to reach a road by a third
farm, Leadgate. Go over the stile opposite and down the field to a
ladder stile, then up half R, aiming to the R of a further farm
which soon becomes visible. Go through a stile at the farm
(Lowstead) and into the farmyard by a gate, then turn R between
barns to a farm road.

Walk along the road until you reach a T-junction; there go L.
After ½ mile (800 m) reach a second T-junction and cross to a
stile opposite. (As you approach this second junction, note the
pronounced ridge-and-furrow (locally rigg-and-furrow) pattern in
the fields on each side of the road; this was produced by the old
method of cultivation where the fields were ploughed in narrow
strips with the tilth turned into the centre.) Go up to the L of
fence, then down to an obvious footbridge. Turn R, and walk on
to a second footbridge. Cross it, and then immediately turn L
through a gate. Follow a farm road by a stream, passing sheepfolds
and then a farm, to a fork (PW sign). Go L, through a gate, and
walk on for 150 yards (140 m), then go R through the first gate on

the R. Go up the field to the L of a fence to a gate at the top, then walk directly up towards the prominent crag, which is climbed up a stony groove slanting to the L. At the top head directly up the moor to reach a ladder stile which leads into a moor road. Turn R.

Go along the moor road, soon crossing a ladder stile. 350 yards (320 m) later, where the wall bends at a PW sign, head L over the moor, aiming for a tall post in the distance. Reach a road at a bend and turn L, descending to a T-junction. Go L. After 1 mile (1.6 km) cross a bridge over the North Tyne and turn R into Bellingham.

(You will, no doubt, be tired after your long day and wish for nothing more than a hot bath and a good meal and an evening spent in convivial company. If, however, you have the time for it, there are a few interesting things to see around Bellingham (pronounced 'Bellinjum') – see (5) below for the location of information about them.)

(1) *Housesteads*: see page 246.

(2) *Milecastle 37*: see page 169.

(3) *The Northumbrian loughs*: see page 246.

(4) *Comyn's Cross (86-800736)*
There is a story that this marks the spot where the sons of King Arthur slew a local chieftain named Comyn or Cumming. King Arthur is, however, one of the most shadowy figures around, and if you believe this then you will probably believe anything. Nowadays, there is very little cross there, and the remains do not justify the detour, unless you are very determined to obtain your money's worth.

(5) *See pages* 87–92. If you are of masochistic tendencies and staying overnight in Bellingham, then there may also be time to visit Hareshaw Linn – see Route 2.

Route 29   The ascent of The Schil

Walkers and climbers in the British Isles have traditionally
accepted 2,000 ft (610 m) as the point where mountains begin and
mere hills end. Whilst this may well be a convenient yardstick for
those who enjoy compiling lists of heights and those who take
pleasure in ticking them off, it would be a mistake to regard it as
anything more than an artificial device to bring a little order into
an unruly world. No peak illustrates this better than The Schil,
which fails by a mere 15 ft (5 m) to reach the magic figure, yet
which is a peak *par excellence*, far better than some twice its
height, affording one of the finest views in the whole of
Northumberland.

The route described here would in any case have been worth
doing, even without The Schil, for it combines a superb stretch of
largely unspoilt ridge with a magnificent walk down the valley of
the College Burn. Any walkers met with during the ridge walk are
probably not doing the same route as you, but are Pennine
Wayfarers on their final miles to the end at Kirk Yetholm. Their
air of superiority should be unmistakable.

Although some of the road through the College valley is
metalled, the way is quiet and pleasant and walkers should not find
that this detracts from their pleasure. Those considering the use of
a pick-up car somewhere along the valley, however, should note
that for most of the year only twelve cars per day are allowed
beyond Hethpool, and then only by permit; during the lambing
season (approximately 12 April to 12 May) no cars whatsoever are
allowed. In any event, no vehicles may be taken beyond the point
where the metalled road ends near Mounthooly. Permits – which
are free – may be obtained from Sale and Partners, Estate Agents,
18 Glendale Road, Wooler, Northumberland; telephone: Wooler
(0668) 81611.

There is a mountain refuge hut on the main ridge near Red
Cribs (74-880201).

Length: 14 miles (23 km).

Ascent: 2400 ft (730 m).

Starting and finishing point: Hethpool (74-895283), about 1.5 miles (2.5 km) down the College valley from Westnewton, which is on the B6351 road west of Wooler. Cars may be parked on the grass verge just outside the village, but ensure that they do not obstruct local traffic.

Maps: Landranger 74; Pathfinder 475 (NT 82/92).

Route description (Maps 29A, 29B, 29C)
From Hethpool walk back along the road for about 300 yards (275 m) to the sharp bend; there go through the gate on the L. Follow the narrow road beyond for 1½ miles (2.5 km), going R at a junction after 1 mile (1.6 km), until you reach the farm of Elsdonburn. Follow the road up into the farm area and go through a gate on the R immediately after the house.

Keep on the farm road beyond, soon going through a gate. After the gate go R at a junction and continue to follow the farm road down and over a stream to a gate on the opposite side. In the field beyond, head half L to reach a gate at the extreme R-hand edge of the coniferous wood on the opposite side. Go through and round the corner to the L. Follow the path which runs between the wood and the stream until you reach the far end of the wood.

From the wood keep in the same direction for 200 yards (180 m); here the stream that you are following bends to the L just beyond a meeting with another small stream. There turn R, drop down and cross the stream at some convenient point. Rise up slightly L until you reach the top of the ridge (there are numerous crossing paths, but the way up to the ridge is over grass and through bracken). As you near the top make a short detour to the cairn on the top of the small hill to the R for a superb view. Away from the ridge on the far side notice the prominent hill-top with two concentric rings of fortifications, this is Green Humbleton.

From the ridge top go half L to a small gate in a wall. (This is the England-Scotland Border, which is marked for most of its distance – although not here – by a fence, usually called the

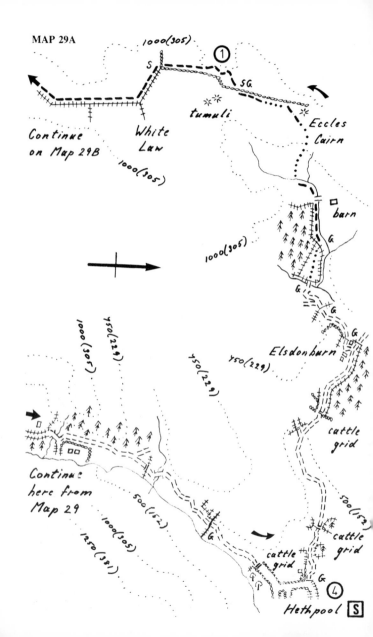

MAP 29A

1000(305)

①

S

SG

tumuli

Eccles
Cairn

Continue
on Map 29B

White
Law

1000(305)

barn

G

1000(305)

G

G

G

Elsdonburn

G

750(229)

750(229)

cattle
grid

1000(305)

750(229)

Continue
here from
Map 29

500(152)

cattle
grid

1000(305)

G

cattle
grid

500(152)

1250(381)

G

cattle
grid

④

Hethpool [S]

Continue
on Map
29C

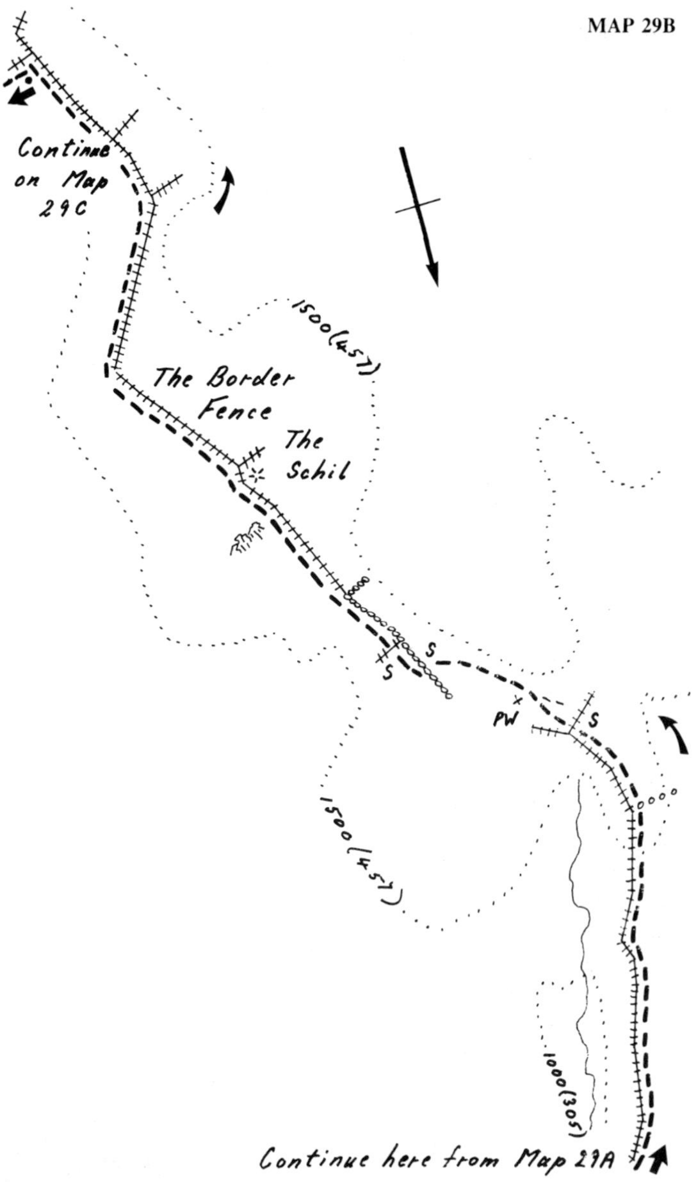

The Border
Fence

The
Schil

1500(457)

S

S

S

PW

1500(457)

1000(305)

Continue here from Map 29A

MAP 29C

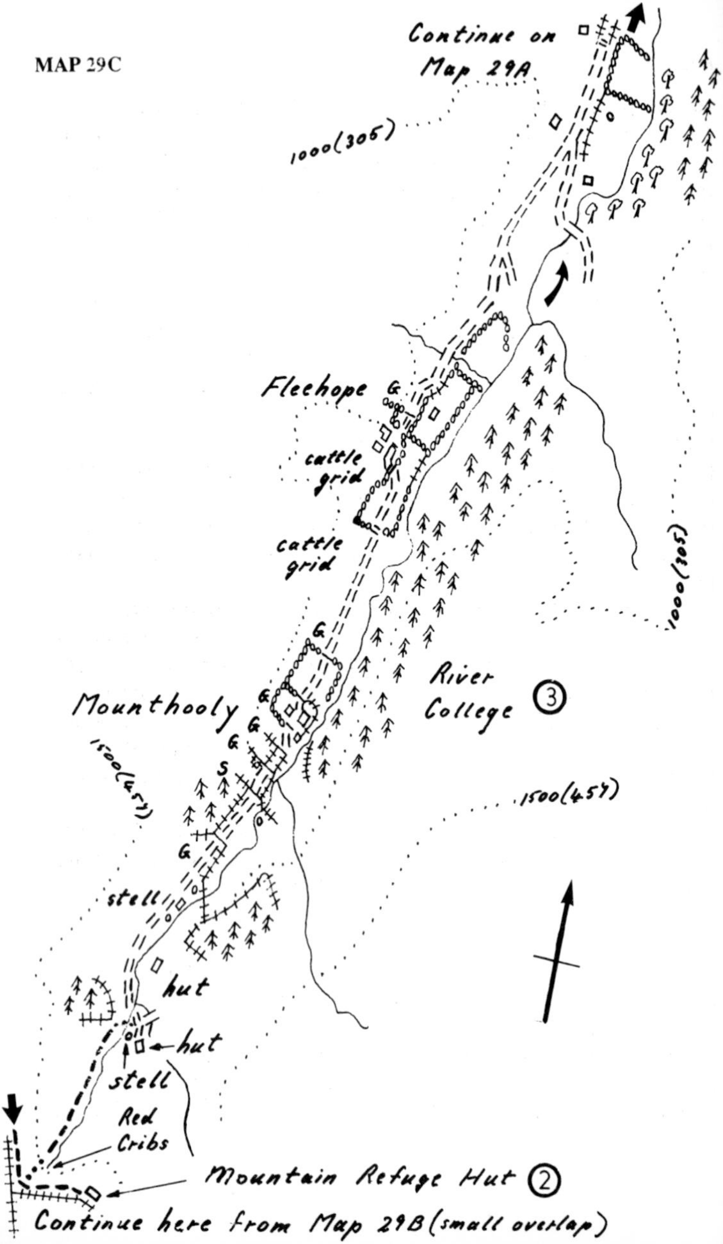

Continue on
Map 29A

1000(305)

Flechope G

cattle
grid

cattle
grid

G

G
Mounthooly G
G

River
College ③

1500(457)

S

G

1500(457)

stell

hut

hut

stell

Red
Cribs

Mountain Refuge Hut ②

Continue here from Map 29B (small overlap)

Border Fence.) Turn L and follow the wall to the next gate – see
(1) The Pennine Way. Go through and turn L, following the path
on the opposite side by the wall. Follow the wall as it descends,
then rises up to a ladder stile on the ridge top. The Border Fence
starts here. Turn L and follow the path to the R of the Fence along
the ridge to the summit of White Law (marked by a sharp turn of
the Fence at a junction).

Keep by the fence for a further 1½ miles (2.5 km) until you
reach a fence junction. There go over a stile and take the path
which descends ahead, away from the fences, to a prominent
signpost. At the signpost go L, soon reaching a ladder stile over a
drystone wall. Cross and turn R. Follow the path to the L of the
wall – later the Fence – as it rises up to the summit of The Schil.
(The highest point is on the splintered rocks on the opposite side
of the Fence – go there for one of the most magnificent views in
the Cheviot Hills.) Continue by the Fence, now descending. The
Fence bends to the L just after a wood and goes across to a small
mountain refuge hut – see (2).

Return from the hut for ⅓ mile (500 m) to the bend in the
Fence before the wood; there turn R and go over to the far side of
the ridge. Locate a path to the L of prominent bare red slopes at
the head of a small valley (Red Cribs). Follow this path down,
keeping to the left of the valley. Soon reach the corner of a wood
with a small hut and a stell over to the R. Go over to the R to
locate a moor road coming from the hut; turn L along it to pass
the stell on its R-hand side.

Follow this moor road – later metalled – for 4¾ miles (7.5 km)
through the College Valley until you reach Hethpool – see (3) the
College Valley and (4) the Collingwood Oaks.

(1) *The Pennine Way*
Having travelled as far as the gate in the Border wall in
comparative solitude, walkers may be surprised by the sudden
appearance of small parties of heavily ladened figures coming
along the ridge in the opposite direction. These are Pennine Way
travellers on the final miles of their journey. It is unlikely that
attempts at conversation will prove fruitful, as they will by then be

in a state of ecstasy and will have no time for inferior beings – such as you – who are not on the same journey as themselves. The ridge walk over White Law is an alternative to the older and more popular route which descends from near Black Hag into the valley of the Halter Burn.

(2) *The mountain refuge hut near Auchope Cairn (74-880201)*
Originally a railway wagon stood on this site – although actually on the Scottish side of the Border Fence – placed there by the Border Rescue Team for Roxburgh County Council in 1971. It was brought up using a tractor and trailer from the Sourhope Farm Research Station. As this was falling into a dilapidated condition, it was replaced by the present hut in 1988. The hut was first erected at Brandon in the Breamish valley and then air-lifted by helicopter from Mounthooly in the College valley.
Northumberland National Park Wardens, Voluntary Wardens and the Fell Rescue Team, assisted by 202 Squadron, RAF Boulmer, were involved. The hut is dedicated to Stuart Lancaster – who also has a memorial on Windy Gyle – and is under the jurisdiction of the Northumberland National Park Authority. Walkers are welcome to use the shelter, but should leave it in a clean and tidy condition.

(3) *The College Valley*
The great Ice Age of the Pleistocene period ended about 10,000 years ago, i.e. in geological terms comparatively recently. Altogether it lasted some 2 million years, although it was by no means a continuous period of intense cold but actually consisted of a number of separate glaciations broken by intermediate interglacials of relatively warmer weather. During the worst periods a huge ice-sheet, which had developed over Scandinavia, covered the North Sea where it joined with a British ice-sheet which had developed separately. Ireland, Scotland and Wales were entirely covered by ice, and the sheet extended as far south as the line of the Severn and Thames estuaries. The ice moving down

The mountain refuge hut near Auchope Cairn.

from Scotland covered all but the highest ground in the Cheviot Hills, although it appears likely that small separate ice-caps developed there also.

The moving ice had a profound effect on the landscape of the Cheviot Hills, signs of which are still clearly discernible today. The rounded shape of the hills is the result of ice-moulding; the meandering, braided course of the College and its tributary, Lambden Burn, over flat valley floors suggests the action of valley glaciers; and the characteristic 'cirque' shape of the Bizzle and The Hen Hole shows that they were probably once occupied by small glaciers. The long straight line of the College as far as Hethpool is owing to a fault which developed in the Hercynian Orogeny (see page 26), whilst the deviation lower down was probably due to a blockage by glacial deposits which forced it on to another path.

(4) *The Collingwood Oaks (74-898289)*

The oaks on The Bell above Hethpool were planted by Admiral Cuthbert Collingwood, who lived at Lilburn Tower, near Wooler, with the intention of providing timber for naval ships. Unfortunately – or perhaps, fortunately – they did not thrive well enough for this purpose. Collingwood, one of the most outstanding officers at the time of the Napoleonic Wars, commanded the lee line at Trafalgar and assumed command after Nelson's death.

Very strenuous routes

Route 30   The Border Ridge

The Cheviot Hills run in a great arc from the valley of the South Tyne north of Gilsland to near Wooler, much of it along the centre section of the English-Scottish Border. Although the character of the southern part has been considerably altered by extensive afforestation, that to the north of Redesdale remains comparatively unchanged and is a walking area *par excellence*. Of all the routes in this region, the full traverse of the central ridge, along the main watershed, is without equal. Its length, the amount of climbing involved and the roughness of the ground taken together, however, make it a route for the very few.

There are two mountain refuge huts along the route – see below.

Length: 27½ miles (44 km) – including The Cheviot.

Ascent: 4900 ft (1500 m) – including The Cheviot.

Starting point: The small church at Byrness on the A68 (80-771023).

Finishing point: Kirk Yetholm (74-827282) – just over the Scottish Border.

Maps: Landranger 74 and 80; Pathfinder 475 (NT 82/92), 486 (NT 61/71), 487 (NT 81/91) and 498 (NT 60/70).

Accommodation: As this is a long and strenuous route which requires an early start and/or a late finish, many walkers will wish to use accommodation at the start and end of the route. There are youth hostels, hotels and guest-houses at both Byrness and Kirk Yetholm.

Route description (Maps 30A, 30B, 30C, 30D, 30E, 30F, 30G)

   (a) *Byrness to Chew Green.*

From the church – see (1) Byrness and Northumberland's smallest church – cross the road and turn L for a few yards, then go R up a path in front of a cottage. Immediately after the entrance to Byrness Cottage, go R through a small gate (PW sign) and by a fence. At the end go through a small gate into a forest. Cross a forest road and take the path opposite. This goes up and then down, to cross another forest road in a dip. Beyond, climb again, crossing two further forest roads, to eventually reach a small gate at the top edge of the forest. Go through it and climb up by a small crag to the top of Byrness Hill. The concrete slab there was originally the base of a small fire watchtower.

   Turn half L along the top of the ridge between two blocks of coniferous forest. Continue along this ridge for 3 miles (5 km), keeping roughly parallel with the forest on the L; at the end of the forest, where three fences meet, cut across to a stile. Along this section the red notices to the R mark the boundary of a military training area – see (2) the Otterburn Training Area.

   (b) *Chew Green to Yearning Saddle.*

Continue in the same direction, keeping to the R of a fence until this bends half L at a PW sign. Here turn R and follow a path across the moor. Do not be tempted to follow the path up to the L towards the ridge, but instead drop down half R to a small gate by the stream and at the corner of prominent earthworks – see (3) the Chew Green camp. Go through the gate and down a sunken track along the bottom edge of the earthworks, parallel with the stream. At the far side turn L and go up by the earthworks to the north-east corner. Now go R over a ford and follow a clear path which rises up the hillside – this is the line of an important Roman road, see (4) Dere Street. Soon this goes through a gate and then up to a fence corner.

   Once this point is reached all route-finding difficulties are behind you, for this fence follows the crest of the ridge throughout the entire route until the final miles after The Schil. (The ascent of The Cheviot has also a short fenceless section, if the detour from the main route is undertaken.) As it follows the English–Scottish

MAP 30A

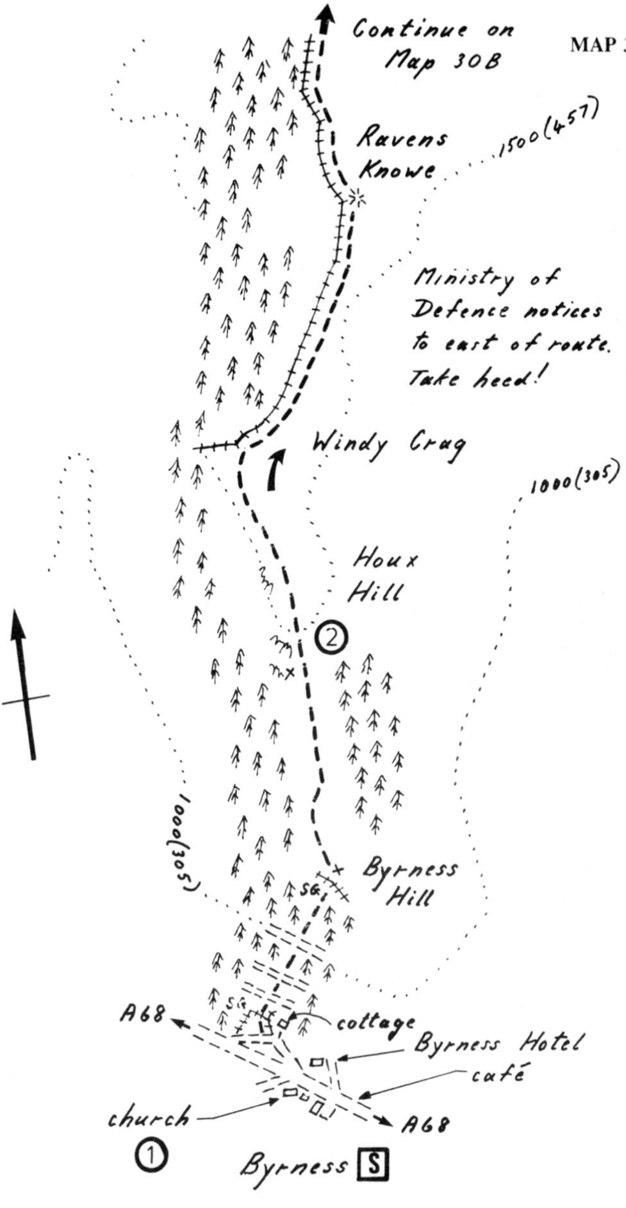

Continue on
Map 30B

Ravens
Knowe

1500 (457)

Ministry of
Defence notices
to east of route.
Take heed!

Windy Crag

1000 (305)

Houx
Hill

②

1000 (305)

Byrness
Hill

SG

A68

cottage

Byrness Hotel
café

church

A68

① Byrness S

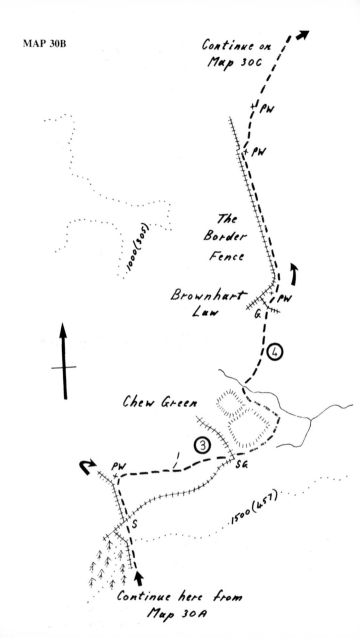

Continue on
Map 30C

PW

PW

*The
Border
Fence*

*Brownhart
Law*

PW

G.

④

Chew Green

PW

③

SG

1000(305)

1500(457)

S

Continue here from
Map 30A

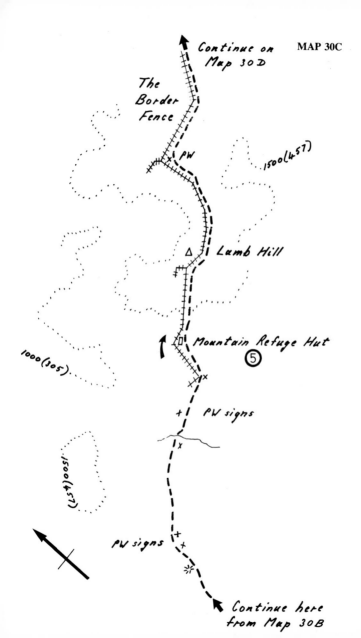

MAP 30C

Continue on
Map 30D

The
Border
Fence

PW

1500(457)

△ Lamb Hill

Mountain Refuge Hut
⑤

1000(305)

PW signs

1500(457)

PW signs

Continue here
from Map 30B

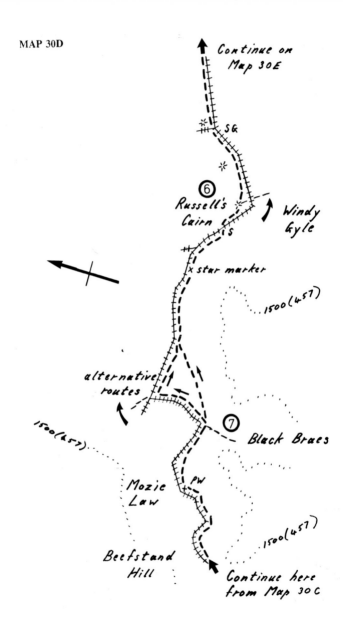

Continue on
Map 30E

SG

⑥
Russell's
Cairn

Windy
Gyle

IS

x star marker

1500 (457)

alternative
routes

⑦
Black Braes

Mozie
Law

PW

1500 (457)

1500 (457)

Beefstand
Hill

Continue here
from Map 30C

Continue on Map 30F

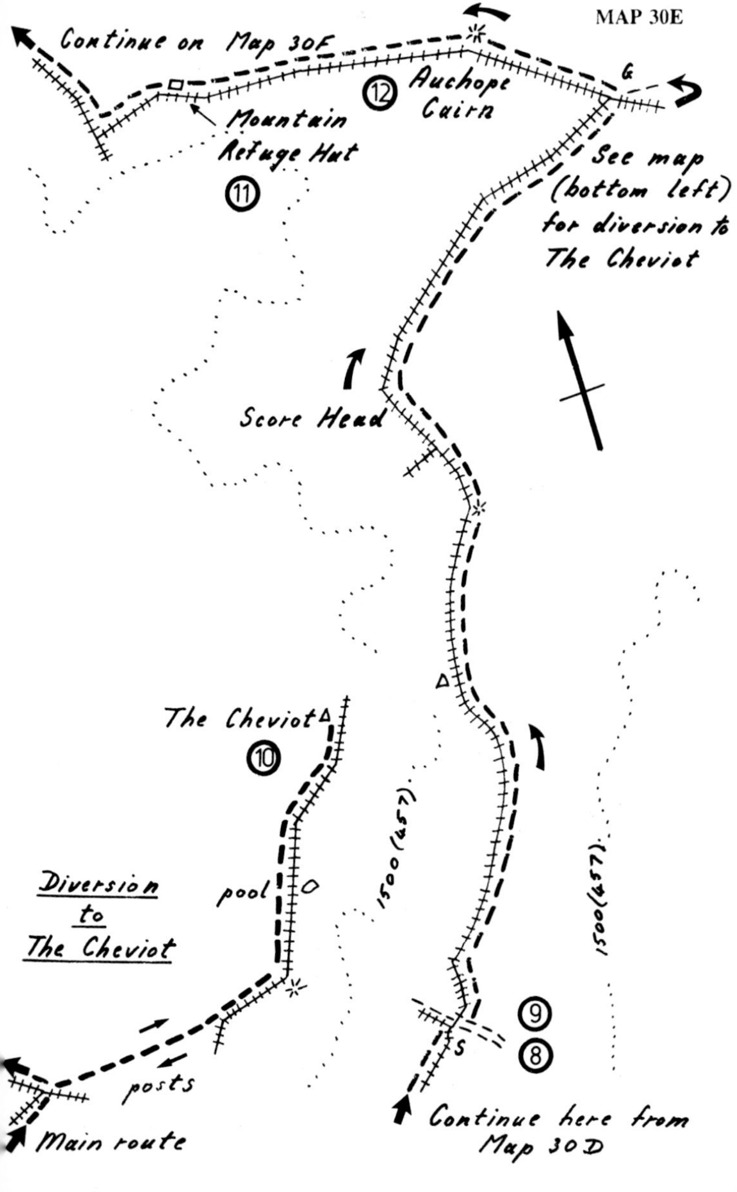

Mountain
Refuge Hut

⑪

⑫ Auchope
Cairn

G

See map
(bottom left)
for diversion to
The Cheviot

Score Head

The Cheviot △
⑩

Diversion
to
The Cheviot

pool

1500 (457)

1500 (457)

⑨
⑧

S

posts

Main route

Continue here from
Map 30D

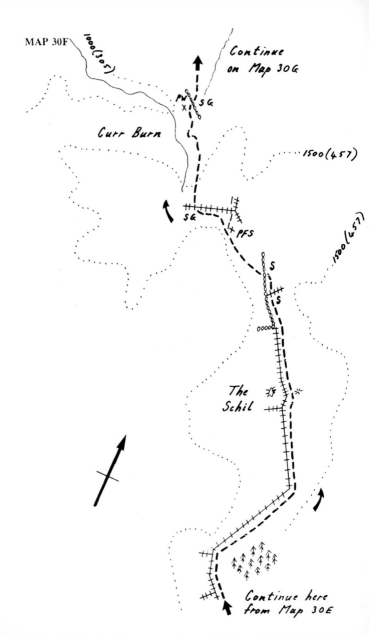

MAP 30F

1000(305)

Continue
on Map 30G

Curr Burn

PW   SG
X

1500(457)

SG

PFS

1500(457)

S

S

The
Schil

Continue here
from Map 30E

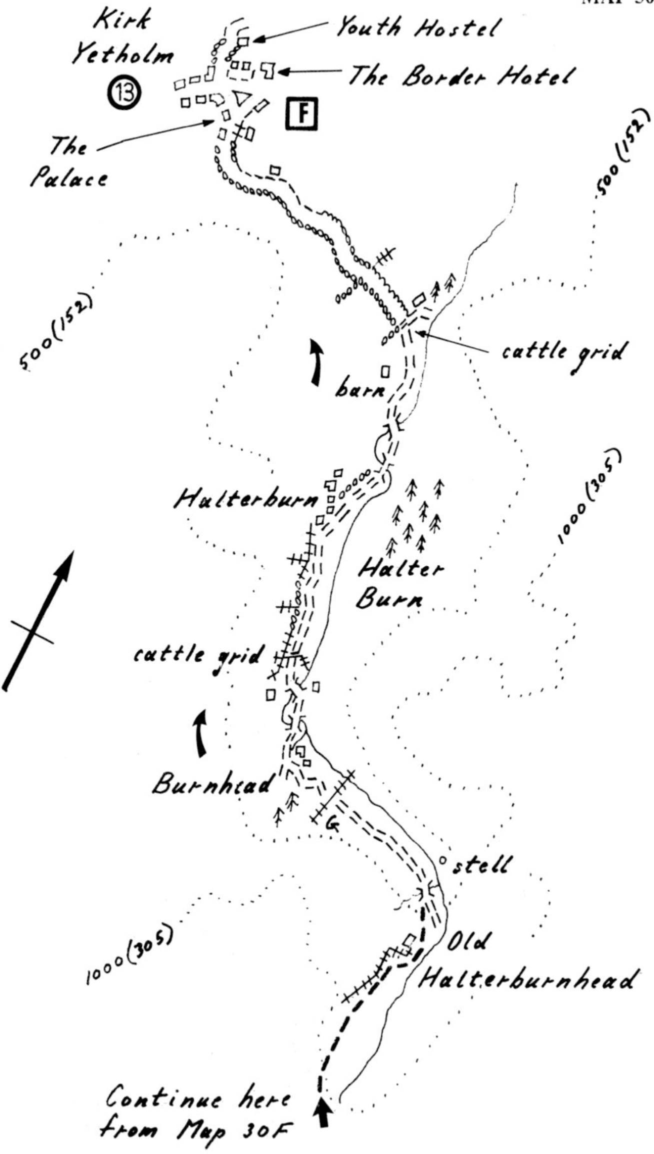

Kirk
Yetholm
⑬

Youth Hostel

The Border Hotel

The
Palace

F

500 (152)

500 (152)

cattle grid

barn

Halterburn

Halter
Burn

1000 (305)

cattle grid

Burnhead

stell

1000 (305)

Old
Halterburnhead

Continue here
from Map 30F

Border it is generally known as the Border Fence (hereafter called the Fence).

Go up by the Fence, leaving it after about ⅔ mile (1.1 km) at a PW sign. The path (marked by further signs) crosses the open moor until it meets the Fence again much further along; duckboards have been placed along the way over one particularly boggy area. Keep by the Fence, eventually reaching another corner; there go with it to drop down to a small hut – see (5) the mountain refuge hut, Yearning Saddle.

(c) *Yearning Saddle to The Corner.*

Now continue to follow the Fence for 8 miles (13 km), keeping around the top of the ridge, until the Border Fence turns sharply to the L with another fence coming in from the R. Throughout, the path keeps to the R of the Border Fence, except in the vicinity of Windy Gyle where it crosses over to the opposite side to visit the summit cairns, returning to the R side about 1¼ miles (2 km) later. In general, the path keeps close to the Fence, although in one or two places walkers have cut corners and a clear alternative path has developed.

Along the way the route goes over a whole series of tops, from which wonderful all-round views can be obtained. At about the half-way point of this section you reach the summit of Windy Gyle, which gives the finest views of all – see (6) Russell's Cairn.

In days gone by, several packhorse trails and drove roads crossed the ridge. Their way is still clear and used by walkers – see (7) The Street, (8) Clennell Street, and (9) Salter's Road.

(d) *The Corner to The Cheviot.*

At the Corner cross over the fence ahead, i.e. that coming in from the R, and head half R at a bearing of 92°, following a line of posts. Soon reach a fence corner. Climb with the fence, keeping on its L-hand side, until you reach the Ordnance Survey obelisk which marks the summit of The Cheviot. Return by the same route. (The way up to the top is rough and, frankly, there is nothing that is particularly exciting when you do get there. The only justification, therefore, for climbing The Cheviot – and hence for deviating from the route – is that it is the highest top in the Cheviot Hills: a 'must' for peak-baggers and others of similar

masochistic tendencies. There is, however, one inhabitant of wild
and lonely places that quite likes The Cheviot – see (10.)

(e) *The Corner to Kirk Yetholm.*

At the junction of the fences continue along the Border Fence, i.e.
to the L of your original direction, soon reaching the top of
Auchope Cairn. Beyond, descend steeply to a col on which there
is a second hut – see (11) the mountain refuge hut near Auchope
Cairn. The prominent valley to the R during the descent is the
upper reach of the College Burn – see (12) The Hen Hole.

From the hut follow the Fence up to the summit of The Schil
(the actual summit is an upthrust of rock on the Scottish side),
which is a superb summit with an incredible view. On a good day,
it is the place for that last afternoon rest.

Drop down by the Fence to a col where a wall starts on the L.
Continue by the wall, soon going over a stile. About 250 yds
(225 m) later, cross a ladder stile to the L and follow a path away
from the wall. At a junction (PFS) take the L-hand path, soon
coming to a small gate. Follow a wide path down to the R of a
stream; at a col (PW sign) go R to a small gate in a wall. The path
beyond curves across the hillside, eventually reaching a fence and
passing to the R of a ruin (rookery in trees). Just beyond, reach a
farm road and follow it down to the farm of Burnhead where it
joins a metalled road. Follow the road for 2½ miles (4 km) to Kirk
Yetholm – see (13) Kirk Yetholm and the Faa gypsies.

(1) *Byrness and Northumberland's smallest church (80-770023)*
The church by the roadside at Byrness, which measures a mere 29
× 18 ft (8.8 × 5.5 m), is said to be the smallest in
Northumberland. Of particular interest is the stained-glass window
in memory of the workmen who lost their lives in the construction
of the Catcleugh Reservoir only a short distance away. It is
claimed that nearby Cottonshopeburnfoot and
Blakehopeburnhaugh have the longest place-names in England,
but controversy rages as to whether these should be taken as single
words or split into two or more constituent parts. The main
community at Byrness is the forestry village, one of three built in
the 1950s (see page 40).

(2) *The Otterburn Training Area*: see page 49.

(3) *The Chew Green camp (80-788085)*

This is a complex area of earthworks which marks several camps or forts established in Roman times. The first to be constructed was a large marching camp, probably built by the Ninth Legion on its journey northwards during Agricola's campaign into Scotland in AD 80. This was a temporary camp set up for protection when the legion stopped for the night, and consisted of an earth rampart with a timber palisade, inside which tents would be arranged in a regular order. Later a small permanent convoy post was set up for traffic along Dere Street, which runs by the fort. The next major phase of activity belongs to the middle of the following century, when the Antonine Wall on the Forth-Clyde isthmus was in use and when traffic along Dere Street was again at a high level. Presumably the post was found insufficient, for it was replaced by a small permanent fort with two external enclosures used to house wagons and animals. As the fort was in a valley, a signal station was positioned on the ridge to the north. It is likely that this fort continued in use long after the Antonine Wall was finally abandoned, since outpost forts were still retained and had to be supplied. Eventually, however, with the fading of Roman aspirations north of the Wall the fort at Chew Green was abandoned.

(4) *Dere Street*

Dere Street was the name given in Saxon times to the great Roman road, probably built during Agricola's advance into Scotland in AD 79–80, which ran from the legionary fortress of Eburacum (York), where it met Ermine Street, to a fort at Inveresk on the Firth of Forth. The exceptionally large number of marching camps, signal stations and forts along its length testify to its importance as a highway, particularly during Agricola's campaign, when the Antonine Wall was in use, and later to supply outpost forts north of the Wall.

(5) *The mountain refuge hut, Yearning Saddle (80-804129)*

The small hut on the Border Fence at Yearning Saddle is a mountain refuge hut which replaced a railway van that once stood there. There is little enough of it either outside or in, but it is a welcome sight to those seeking a little shelter from the elements, or for any walkers benighted in these inhospitable hills. A visitors' book records those who passed this way. If you use this hut, then please leave it afterwards in a clean and tidy condition.

(6) *Russell's Cairn*: see page 219.

(7) *The Street*: see page 219.

(8) *Clennell Street*: see page 283.

(9) *Salter's Road*: see page 235.

(10) *Wild goats*

No truly wild goats live anywhere in the British Isles, but feral herds, i.e. domestic stock that have become wild, exist in many areas, such as around the Ogwen valley and the Rhinogydd in North Wales, in the Hebrides, and in parts of the Scottish Highlands. Small numbers also exist in the Cheviot Hills, but summer visitors are unlikely to see them, for they are shy, timid creatures who remain on the higher, isolated slopes. In the winter months they come lower and even into the valleys themselves if the food supply is sufficiently desperate. Goats are gregarious animals who live in small herds controlled by one master male (billy), although the females (nannies) become solitary for the birth of their young (kids). The rut takes place in October and the young are born the following March or April, normally one or two kids to each nanny.

(11) *The mountain refuge hut near Auchope Cairn (74-880201)*:
see page 298.

(12) *The Hen Hole (74-885203)*
The impressive ravine which runs down the western flank of The
Cheviot, roughly parallel with the line of descent from Auchope
Cairn, is The Hen Hole. Cut into the edge of the granite which
forms the Cheviot massif, it shows some of the features of
glaciation and probably held a small glacier some time at the end
of the Ice Age. Local legend had it that fairies dwelt there and
there are tales of hunting parties that went into The Hen Hole and
never returned. Even in these more enlightened times it is a place
that can still grip the imagination. The Scottish Mountaineering
Club journal for 1907 mentions climbing on the crags in The Hen
Hole, but interest was not really aroused until after the Second
World War. Today there are about 30–40 climbs, mostly on the
north side of the burn.

(13) *Kirk Yetholm and the Faa Gypsies (74-826281)*
Gypsies began to arrive in western Europe in significant numbers
during the early part of the fifteenth century – although they had
probably appeared for the first time much earlier than that – and
reached England and Scotland about a hundred years or so later.
Their place of origin is unknown, but it is thought that their move
westwards was the result of Turkish incursions into parts of eastern
Europe. (The name 'gypsy' is a corruption of 'Egyptian', but it is
doubtful if they really came from that country: north-west India is
a more likely possibility.) The gypsy families tended to allocate
themselves certain areas or circuits, and the Borders became the
home of the Faa or Faw family who mainly came from England,
with a capital at the 'gate town' of Kirk Yetholm. (Their name is
said to have been derived from Johnnie Faw, 'Lord and Earl of
Little Egypt', a gypsy tribal leader who entered into a treaty with
James IV of Scotland in 1540.) By the eighteenth and nineteenth
centuries a large gypsy community owned land there – with right
of pasture on the local commons – and engaged in trade, both
legal and illegal, throughout the Border region. At one time

10,000 people used to gather at Kirk Yetholm for the 'coronation' of the gypsy King, but the custom died out around the end of the nineteenth century. A cottage 'palace' can, however, still be found near the green.

Appendix

1 Other recommended routes

Long-distance routes

The Coquetdale River Walk
A route of 14 miles (22 km) from Rothbury (81-058016) to Felton (81-18503), which follows the Coquet downstream, is described in *Walks in Coquetdale*, a Northumberland County Council, National Park and Countryside Department publication.

Hadrian's Wall
Although the centre section of Hadrian's Wall, where it runs along the crest of the Whin Sill, is undoubtedly its finest, a traverse of the full length of 73 miles (117 km) from the Tyne to the Solway can be made, though the exact line of the Wall cannot always be followed. The Wall starts at Wallsend in Tyne and Wear, crosses Northumberland, and finishes at Bowness-on-Solway in Cumbria. The Wall can also, of course, be walked in the opposite direction, although an east-to-west route is perhaps more natural, since the features have been numbered in that direction.

   Guides and books are: *A Guide to Walking Hadrian's Wall*, Graham Mizon, Hendon Publishing Company; *A Walk along the Wall*, Hunter Davies, Quartet Books.

The Northumbrian Coast
The coastline of Northumberland is still largely unspoilt and is noted for its considerable interest and beauty, a fact which has been recognized by the designation of the section between Amble and Berwick-upon-Tweed as an Area of Outstanding Natural Beauty. Apart from Route 25 in this book, which explores the coast from Alnmouth to Beadnell, two other publications describe long-distance routes along it. These are: *Northumbrian Coastline*, Ian Smith, Sandhill Press, which describes the full length of the coast (from Berwick-upon-Tweed to North Shields) from a walker's point of view; and *Walks on the Northumberland Coast*, a Northumberland County Council, National Park and Countryside

Department publication, which details The Northumberland Coast
Walk, 25 miles (40 km) long.

The Pennine Way
This was the first long-distance route (now known as National
Trails) to be created by the Countryside Commission (or its
predecessor, the National Parks Commission). The Pennine Way
was the brainchild of Tom Stephenson, the first full-time secretary
of the Ramblers' Association, in 1935, but was not officially
opened until 24 April 1965. It runs for a nominal distance of 250
miles (402 km) from Edale in Derbyshire to Kirk Yetholm in
Borders, Scotland. It is a glorious route with a great deal of
variety, although predominantly it crosses mountain and moorland
areas. Twenty-five years after its creation it still remains the
longest, the hardest and the best known of all the National Trails.

It enters Northumberland on the Gilderdale Burn (87-699479),
between Alston and Slaggyford, and leaves it again at the northern
end of the Cheviot Hills, either north of White Law (74-854269) or
to the south of Black Hag (74-864233), depending upon the final
route taken.

A number of books have been published about the Way, some
of which are: *A Guide to the Pennine Way*, C. J. Wright,
Constable; *A Pennine Way Companion*, A. Wainwright,
Westmorland Gazette; *Pennine Way North* and *Pennine Way
South*, Tony Hopkins, Aurum Press/Countryside Commission/The
Ordnance Survey: *Great Walks: The Pennine Way*, Frank
Duerden, Ward Lock.

Facilities for disabled people
A pamphlet *A Disabled Visitor's Guide*, published by the
Northumberland County Council, National Park and Countryside
Department, describes the facilities available for disabled people
within the National Park and in the Country Parks.

2 Addresses of useful organizations

British Trust for Conservation Volunteers, 36 St Mary's Street, Wallingford, Oxfordshire, OX10 0EU. Telephone: Wallingford (0491) 39766. (Springwell Conservation Centre, Springwell Road, Wrekenton, Gateshead, Tyne & Wear, NE9 7AD. Telephone: Tyneside (091) 482 0111.)

Camping and Caravanning Club Ltd, 11 Lower Grosvenor Place, London, SW1W 0EY. Telephone: 071-828 1012/7.

Council for National Parks, 45 Shelton Street, London, WC2H 9HJ. Telephone: 071-240 3603.

Council for the Protection of Rural England, 25 Buckingham Palace Road, Warwick House, London, SW1W 0PP. Telephone: 071-235 9481.

Countryside Commission, John Dower House, Crescent Place, Cheltenham, Gloucestershire, GL50 3RA. Telephone: Cheltenham (0242) 521381.

English Heritage, Membership Department, Keysign House, 429 Oxford Street, London, W1R 2HD. Telephone: 071-973 3400. (Northern Area Office, Arnham Block, The Castle, Carlisle, Cumbria, CA3 8UR. Telephone: Carlisle (0228) 31777.)

English Tourist Board, Thames Tower, Blacks Road, Hammersmith, London, W6 9EL (Postal enquiries only).

The Forestry Commission, Public Information Division, 231 Corstorphine Road, Edinburgh, EH12 7AT. Telephone: 031-334 0303. (Conservancy Office for Northern England, 1A Grosvenor Terrace, York, YO3 7BD. Telephone: York (0904) 620221.)

The Long Distance Walkers Association, Membership Secretary, 7 Ford Drive, Yarnfield, Stone, Staffordshire, ST15 0RP. Telephone: Stone (0785) 760684.

The National Trust, 36 Queen Anne's Gate, London, SW1H 9AS. Telephone: 071-222 9251. (Northumbria Regional Office, Scots' Gap, Morpeth, Northumberland, NE61 4EG. Telephone: Scots' Gap (067 074) 691.)

Nature Conservancy Council, Northminster House, Peterborough, Cambridgeshire, PE1 1UA. Telephone: Peterborough (0733) 40345. (North-east England Regional Office, Archbold House,

Archbold Terrace, Newcastle upon Tyne, NE2 1EG. Telephone: Tyneside (091) 2816316/7.)

Northumberland and Newcastle Society, 6 Higham Place, Newcastle upon Tyne, NE1 8AF. Telephone: Tyneside (091) 261 4384.

Northumberland County Council, National Park and Countryside Department, Eastburn, South Park, Hexham, Northumberland, NE46 1BS. Telephone: Hexham (0434) 605555.

Northumberland County Council, The Planning Department, County Hall, Morpeth, Northumberland, NE61 2EF. Telephone: Morpeth (0670) 514343.

Northumberland Wildlife Trust, The Hancock Museum, Barras Bridge, Newcastle upon Tyne, NE2 4PT. Telephone: Tyneside (091) 232 0038.

Northumbria Tourist Board, Aykley Heads, Durham, DH1 5UX. Telephone: Durham (091) 384 6905. (There are Tourist Information Centres at Alnwick, Amble, Belford, Bellingham, Berwick-upon-Tweed, Corbridge, Haltwhistle, Hexham, Kielder Water, Morpeth, Once Brewed, Rothbury, Seahouses and Wooler.)

Ordnance Survey, Romsey Road, Maybush, Southampton, SO9 4DH. Telephone: Southampton (0703) 792000.

Otterburn Training Area, Otterburn, Newcastle upon Tyne, NE19 1NX. Telephone: Tyneside (091) 2611046.

The Ramblers' Association, 1/5 Wandsworth Road, London, SW8 2XX. Telephone: 071-582 6878. The RA has a number of local Groups around the area of the Park; the addresses of Group Secretaries change frequently but an up-to-date list can be obtained from the Head Office.

Youth Hostels Association (England and Wales), Trevelyan House, 8 St Stephen's Hill, St Albans, Hertfordshire, AL1 2DY. Telephone: St Albans (0727) 55215. (Area Office, Bowey House, William Street, Newcastle upon Tyne, NE3 1SA. Telephone: Tyneside (091) 284 7473.)

3   Glossary

Bastle: a fortified farmhouse, usually of two stories, built in some parts of the Border region from the middle of the sixteenth century for protection against small raiding parties.

Burn: a stream.

Buttress: a prominent rock face standing out from a hillside.

Byre: a cowshed.

Cairn: a heap of stones marking a mountain summit or a hill-top or part of a route.

Cleugh: a valley cut into moorland by a stream. (Clough in the lower Pennines.) Pronounced 'cluff'.

Col: a dip in a ridge between two hills, sometimes offering an easy way from one valley to the next.

Crag: a cliff.

Dale: a valley.

Dyke or dike: a drystone wall.

Ewe: a female sheep after first shearing or lamb.

Fell: an area of high moorland, used both generally, e.g. fell-walker, and in specific place-names, e.g. Girdle Fell, Comb Fell.

Glidders: scree.

Grough: a channel cut into the soft top surface of peat moors by running water. Pronounced 'gruff'.

Gully: a wide and steep cleft down a rock face.

Hag: an isolated grassy-topped mound with walls of bare peat. A common feature on moors.

Haugh: an area of relatively flat ground near to a stream. Pronounced 'harf'.

Heft: a group of sheep which normally grazes together and remains within a particular area. Also applied to the area of ground itself.

Hope: a strip of good land in a narrow valley.

Hirsel: a flock of sheep looked after by one shepherd, or the entire stock belonging to one farm.

In-bye: improved and enclosed fields around a hill farm.

Knowe: a small hill, e.g. Saddlers Knowe. Pronounced 'now'.

Law: a hill, e.g. Yarnspath Law.

Lough: a lake, e.g. Broomlee Lough. Pronounced 'loff'.

Moss: a particularly marshy area on a moorland, e.g. Bloody Moss.

Out-bye: rough grazing land away from a hill farm.

Pass: a relatively easy passage across a ridge with high ground on each side.

Pele-tower: a small fortified tower-house, sometimes surrounded by a palisade or wall, built by a wealthy landowner for protection during the Border troubles.

Ridge: used in several slightly different ways. A narrow buttress of rock, a spur of a mountain, or a long and substantially horizontal fell-top, sometimes with several summits and cols.

Rigg: an outlying spur of a hill.

Scramble: a climb up fairly broken rock requiring the use of hands for balance purposes, but not difficult enough to justify the use of a rope even for a fairly inexperienced party.

Scree slope: a slope covered with a layer of small rock fragments, produced by the weathering of higher cliffs (see glidders).

Sike: a small stream.

Steading: a farm area of house and surrounding barns.

Stell: a circular enclosure surrounded by a drystone wall used during the gathering of sheep.

Traverse: a movement across a rock face or fell-side without any loss of, or gain in, height.

Tup: an uncastrated male sheep (also ram).

Watershed: a ridge separating river basins so that the streams on opposite sides – even though they rise very near to each other – flow in different directions.

Index

Illustrations are indicated by *italics*. With a few important exceptions place-names have only been included if they are on or near to the routes described.